FROM
CAXTON TO CARLYLE

T0382296

FROM
CAXTON TO CARLYLE

A Study of the Development of Language,
Composition & Style in English Prose

BY

J. H. FRANCIS, M.A.

Author of
A Course of English Poetry

CAMBRIDGE
AT THE UNIVERSITY PRESS
1937

CAMBRIDGE
UNIVERSITY PRESS

University Printing House, Cambridge CB2 8BS, United Kingdom

Cambridge University Press is part of the University of Cambridge.

It furthers the University's mission by disseminating knowledge in the pursuit of education, learning and research at the highest international levels of excellence.

www.cambridge.org
Information on this title: www.cambridge.org/9781107536784

© Cambridge University Press 1937

First published 1937
First paperback edition 2015

A catalogue record for this publication is available from the British Library

ISBN 978-1-107-53678-4 Paperback

Preface

This book consists of a selection of passages representative of English prose from the fourteenth to the middle of the nineteenth century, a point beyond which the subject could not be pursued without exceeding the compass of a single volume, or without abridging passages that are now long enough to achieve self-contained interest.

In the chronological arrangement of passages and in the commentary appended to each chapter I have attempted to trace the gradual development of language and composition as instruments of style, to show the relation between the passages and their period, and to furnish such details of literary history and biography as may lead to easier appreciation.

My grateful acknowledgments are due to Professor W. D. Thomas, of University College, Swansea, and Mr David Williams, of University College, Cardiff, for their careful reading of the manuscript, and for their valuable suggestions and helpful criticism.

J. H. F.

October 1937

Contents

Introduction

The student of prose literature would be well advised to begin his approach by directing his attention more closely than is usual to the principles underlying the elements of vocabulary, grammar and composition; and to postpone, until these fundamentals are fully understood, his concern with those niceties of idiom and felicities of phrase and rhythm that belong to the realm of style. To approach along these lines is to follow, step by step, the processes by which nature herself develops the power of expression both in the individual and in a nation as a whole—processes which it will be instructive to attempt to analyse.

The evolutionary force in the development of language is a constant striving towards the perfect fusion of thought and word. Primitive races are virtually inarticulate, and the first need of advancing civilisation is to learn or invent words. Man easily finds names for material objects, but a new conception, a variation of normal emotional experience, is imprisoned in his own consciousness until a word or group of words gives it a local habitation and a name. The terms thus invented become in turn the starting-point of fresh advances in thought, with the result that one cannot always decide whether ideas beget words or words ideas. To what extent thought can exist and be exercised in the mind if there are no words to formulate it is a problem for the psychologist to determine, but there can be no doubt that the interchange of ideas, the influence of one personality on another, is dependent on the invention of words, without which the ground captured by one generation would have to be conquered afresh by each succeeding generation.

Next comes a phase in the development of language when man's attention is directed less to the building-up of vocabulary than to the means of showing the connection of ideas by a corresponding relation of words. It is a need of which he will have felt conscious from the first, but gradually the practice and experiment of generations will crystallise into a system of grammar, and what we call accidence and syntax will come into being. There will come a time, too, when man becomes dissatisfied with the limitations of the spoken word; he will devise characters and symbols with which to exchange messages with those in distant parts and to leave records that will survive the brief life of his own generation. Once the art of writing is mastered, the development of a language is rapid. The meaning and sound of words become more stable, grammar becomes more systematic and more widely adopted. The uniformity thus acquired checks the tendency of the spoken language to split into those local dialects, which, without a centralising authority, form the nucleus of distinct new languages. Records in writing are the storehouse of the myths and legends of tribes of common origin whom the battle of life has dispersed over a wide region. Mountains, rivers and seas may set a limit to their wanderings, but it is their common heritage of tradition rather than geographical situation that welds them into a nation. Racial tradition, preserved and fostered by the art of writing, is the parent of literature.

We now approach the third and final stage when the adult language, by virtue of an adequate vocabulary and a system of grammar of proved efficiency, is properly equipped to record the mental and spiritual development of the nation. From this point onwards attention is directed less to fashioning the instrument than to experiments in the ideal way of using it. The quest of beautiful and appropriate phraseology, aiming at the perfect union of sense and sound, introduces into language a new element, that of style.

Such in broad general terms is the normal course of development of a language, with vocabulary, grammar, composition and style coming each into successive prominence, but with none at any time completely excluding the others. All these successive stages are discernible in English, though the story of the progress of our language is complicated by the Norman Conquest, which had consequences without parallel elsewhere. We shall find that English was already in possession of a fair vocabulary, a sound grammatical system, an ancient poetical tradition and a prose literature in the making, when the influence of French threw it back into the melting-pot, and introduced problems of remoulding which protracted the early stages of development up to about the middle of the fourteenth century; that for the succeeding hundred years or so, emphasis was on composition; and that from then onwards, and especially during the Elizabethan era, there was a preoccupation with style, which resulted about the time of the Restoration in the tradition still obtaining in modern English prose.

In tracing the history of origins and development, in noting the difficulties that our ancestors surmounted, we cannot fail to develop our own faculties of perception and appreciation. Our advance is over firm ground, for the method brings us into contact only with the literature that has survived the test of time, the most relentless and infallible of critics. It is true that good books may sink into oblivion, but bad books are forgotten at once. Those that have come down to us owe their survival to some distinctive and enduring quality: they retain the imprint of a master mind. But if we are to get full value out of the classics we must cultivate the historical sense, taking into account the spirit of the time, the object of the writer, and his perhaps limited resources of technique. It would be absurd, for example, to adopt an attitude of superiority towards King Alfred as a writer because his prefaces lack the subtlety of those of Bernard Shaw. To appreciate masterpieces of a technique less developed than that of our own times we need not only imaginative sympathy but the special knowledge that is acquired by the study of origins and development.

Since the subject of our study is that particular branch of literature known as prose, it would be well at the outset to ask ourselves what prose is. Prose requires no definition to be recognised, but an attempt to define it will perhaps reveal principles of which many who make daily use of their pens seem to be in ignorance.

Prose, in the etymological sense, is that form of speaking or writing which results from the arrangement of words in straightforward fashion. Subject to certain qualifications, this conception still holds good, for to this day the structure of prose is determined mainly, though not entirely, by the meaning. There can, of course, be no intelligible form of composition in which meaning has ceased to be an important factor, but that meaning is not the only principle of word arrangement is proved by the existence of verse. In verse words are so disposed that there emerges some regular and preconceived pattern of sound, which we call metre. In English verse the feature of which patterns in sound are made is stress. Let us take as an illustration two verse lines:

(1) The Lotus blooms below the barren peak.
(2) They love not poison that do poison need.

In both these lines there are two distinct elements, meaning and rhythm. The rhythm is metrical, and is the same in both lines, the stress falling on the even syllables. In (1) the order of words is logical; it so happens that the logical arrangement complies with the pattern of stress. In (2) the logical order has been changed to comply with that pattern. If then there should be conflict between the claims of rhythm and those of logic, it is the latter that must be sacrificed, the meaning being made slightly less clear in order that the prescribed rhythm may be maintained.

To understand under what conditions the structure of verse will be preferred to that of prose we must consider briefly the nature of rhythm. Rhythm, as we have seen, is an effect of sound, and as such appeals to the senses rather than to the mind. It is a means of communicating emotion quite independent of any other aid such as the meaning of words. The beating of a drum, for example, or the gallop of horses is exciting. Hence verse, because its structure is dictated more by rhythm than meaning, should be primarily the medium of an appeal to the senses; it will be used most appropriately in poetry, the intention of which is not logical but emotive.

The distinction between prose and verse is one of form; between prose and poetry the opposition is of a different nature, for verse and poetry are not synonymous terms, and it is a mistake to assume that poetry necessarily expresses itself in verse. Neither does the difference lie in the subject, but rather in the way in which the writer reacts to it. Poetry is the outcome of emotional exaltation, under the influence of which language falls spontaneously into rhythm, so that even thought becomes lyrical, appealing to the understanding through the emotions, as in Wordsworth's

> "Nor less I deem that there are Powers
> Which of themselves our minds impress;
> That we can feed this mind of ours
> In a wise passiveness."

This suggests some of the limitations of prose; its foundations are so firmly imbedded in logic that there are aspects of experience which it lacks the subtlety or delicacy to express. Such are those intuitions and fancies too insubstantial for the light of pure reason, which take shape only when rhythm adds a touch of magic to the words. The effect of Shakespeare's

> "We are such stuff as dreams are made on,
> And our little life is rounded with a sleep"

owes much to the rhythm.

But—to revert to our definition—though meaning is the main factor in the structure of prose, it would be wrong to suppose it is the only factor. In olden days, when few people could read, the most usual form of prose was oratory, which had to please the ear as well as convince the understanding. The word "prose", as now used, evokes the image of written or printed characters, which transmit thought through the eye alone. We are apt to forget that these are merely symbols, the visual equivalent of what is audible or sub-audible. The nature and arrangement of the sounds, whether heard in a physical sense, as when a passage is read aloud, or heard only in the mind, as when one reads to one's self, are still essential considerations, and to some extent modify the purely logical order of words. Among the elements of prose that contribute towards beauty of sound and satisfaction of the ear is rhythm.[1] The potentialities of rhythm are exploited to the full, as we have seen, in verse, where the rhythm, being quite independent of logic, may result in a grouping of syllables that cuts the words, as in

The Lót-|us bloóms | belów | the bár-|ren péak |

In prose, however, the logical element is always uppermost, and the only grouping possible, with one exception, is that of entire words, each group being separated naturally, as in speech. Even so, it will be found that prose often shows recurrence of stress regular enough to give it a character which, though not metrical, is definitely rhythmical. The chief forms of such recurrence are:

1. *Gradation*, that is to say, "a gradual increase or decrease in the number of syllables in successive feet".

2. *Balance*, the poising of the stresses in one sentence or part of a sentence against the stresses in another sentence or part.

3. *Cadence*, a disposition of stressed syllables, occurring in emphatic places (that is, generally before a pause) of so marked a rhythmical character as to cut across words as metre does.

---

[1] The student is referred to *The Rhythm of English Prose* by N. R. Tempest, Cambridge University Press.

With this brief mention, these and other features of the rhythm of prose must be left for more detailed treatment as occasion arises.

There are two points of view from which it is customary to regard prose: *composition*, which is concerned with the material and its form; and *rhetoric*, which deals with intention. Composition comprises the choice and grouping of words; the disposition of words into clauses, sentences, paragraphs, etc., according to the accepted rules and practices of syntax, and to considerations of usage, idiom and euphony. It embraces devices of diction, figures of speech, and the rhythm resulting from the arrangement of words. The chief virtue of prose, if composition were its only aspect, would be the frigid perfection attained by breaking no rule. But composition is merely the instrument, and its study is an arid pursuit except in relation to rhetoric.

From the point of view of rhetoric, prose may be classified, roughly and somewhat arbitrarily, according to the intention that is uppermost. The classification most generally adopted results in three main types: Descriptive, Explanatory (or Expository) and Persuasive. Description may be defined as the art of making the reader visualise things or people, actual or invented. If pure, it would be the most objective of all forms of writing. When there is added to description a sequence of actions, resulting in an impression of movement, we get Narrative. Exposition comprises science, the most impersonal variety of writing, and criticism. Persuasion is the art of making the reader think as the writer thinks, or feel as he feels. Of course, none of these types is exclusive of the others, and there are many kinds of prose in which they are combined. Description and narrative, for example, are generally coloured by the feelings of the writer, who, in describing objects or narrating actions, may be persuading us to like or dislike them. Criticism seeks not only to expound but also to persuade. History is more than plain narrative.

The novel, the most composite of prose forms, is primarily descriptive and narrative; but it is also persuasive, for the author often has some social theory or philosophy of life to inculcate, and he makes us share the joys and sorrows of the people he creates.

Each category of prose has its own peculiar and appropriate qualities of style. Thus successful narrative calls for simplicity, persuasion for eloquence, and so on. But there is one quality common to all categories, and that is clarity. It pertains to the whole and to its parts; it will have its origin in a lucid conception of the main theme, unifying the whole, and it will be evidenced in an orderly marshalling of facts and ideas. But clear thinking is not a guarantee of lucid expression. There must be, also, not only mastery of the technique of composition but a strict adherence to its underlying principles. For prose, as we have said, is a logical form determined by the meaning; and it is when some other principle takes command of the structure that composition, even of a practised technique, exposes itself to criticism. This is why Elizabethan prose literature, with its poetical constructions, is no longer a model for the stylist: clarity was not its first aim. The true test of a writer is not "Is he eloquent?" but "Is his meaning clear?"

Clarity in composition will depend on

    (*a*) the order of words,
    (*b*) the choice of words.

(*a*) There is no abstract principle of logic governing the order of words in a sentence. In older languages of a synthetic character like Latin, Greek and Anglo-Saxon, the relation of the various parts was indicated by inflection, and the order of words was governed largely by considerations of emphasis:

Noctu ambulabat in publico Themistocles, quod somnum capere non posset. CICERO.

Most modern languages, including English, have evolved the

analytic construction, the relation of words being indicated by prepositions and auxiliaries, which have made inflections redundant. Since a noun has the same form whether subject or object, the clue to its function is its position in the sentence or clause. The result is a conventional order of words. But this order is not the same in all analytic languages: the German language, for instance, has retained in relative clauses the old Germanic order of subject, object, verb. The principle that the various adjuncts should be in proximity to the related parts is universally accepted, but in English the adjective normally precedes the noun, in Romance languages it comes after it. Moreover, the logical position of words can be modified by idiom: thus, although the preposition normally precedes the noun, it is more idiomatic, and therefore more correct to say, "What are you looking for?" than "For what are you looking?" It is evident then that the order of words is established by usage, and is logical in the sense that it is the conventional means of making the meaning clear.

This conventional order is the basis of well-written prose, and should always be preferred to any other, unless there is some specific and justifiable reason for changing it. That is to say, *every variation of the natural order should be significant*, and *no variation should be tolerated which tends to the slightest ambiguity or obscurity*. Within these limits, however, variations are numerous, some being designed for emphasis, some for rhythm or general beauty of sound. In the following passage the changes from the natural order are due partly to motives of rhythm and partly to maintain the smooth flow of description by moving groups of words into a connective position:

Frequent, too, *are the village churches* standing by the roadsides, each in its own little garden of Gethsemane. *In the parish register* great events are doubtless recorded. Some old king was christened or buried in that church; and a little sexton, with a rusty key, shows you the baptismal font, or the coffin. *In the churchyard are a few flowers and much green grass....And over this scene* the village pastor looks from his window in the stillness of midnight, and says in his heart, "How quietly *they rest, all the departed*!"

In the following sentence the effect sought by Carlyle is emphasis. By bringing a displaced part into unusual prominence at the beginning and by withholding the subject, the key to the meaning, till the end, he exacts our close attention:

On all sides are we not driven to the conclusion that *of the things man can do or make here below by far the most momentous, wonderful and worthy, are the things we call books?*

(*b*) Choice of words. Since words are not, like mathematical signs, mere symbols of a concept, but have a history and associations inseparable from it; since, moreover, they have qualities apart from meaning, qualities of sound and stress that make music and rhythm, the problem of diction is to reconcile clarity and precision with propriety and beauty.

There is a tradition in criticism that English prose divides itself, from the point of view of style, into two kinds, the plain and the ornate. The term "plain" is applied to that style, literal, direct and concrete, which favours the short and simple word, generally of Anglo-Saxon origin. The ornate style, allusive, figurative or abstract, tends to a diction in which polysyllabic words derived from the learned languages are in high proportion. It is doubtful whether this rather artificial distinction can be applied to the work of our greatest writers, since their greatness is largely due to the ease with which they adapt their diction and style to the occasion. But the norm in diction is the short and simple word. The reason for its preference will be more apparent as our study proceeds; let us say briefly in passing that prose in which short words predominate has a more distinctive rhythm, a better musical tone and a higher emotional value than prose that is over-burdened with polysyllables. But the various forms of ornateness have their legitimate place in composition: in a work of an imaginative or poetical character language becomes

figurative; in philosophy abstractions are proper and inevitable; in criticism there is a need for the specialised terminology
that turns the concrete "books" into "literature". But any
departure from the norm of directness, resulting in what
might be called oblique diction, must be able to justify itself
in rhetoric. In fine, the guiding principle in the choice of
words is appropriateness. Neglect or ignorance of this
principle, apparently so self-evident, is all too common in
English prose. To decorate an uninspired passage with
archaic or pseudo-poetical phrases and elegant devices, to
dress commonplace thought in grandiose terms, are temptations to which the foibles of human nature expose writers in
all languages; but in our own there are more pitfalls for the
pretentious than in any other. The reasons are to be found in
the history of our literature. The English showed a genius
for poetry before they learned how to write prose, the secret
of which was not discovered until the seventeenth century,
by which time the passion for fine writing had become a
national vice. Then again, although learned words are to be
found in all modern languages in which the Latin of the
Renaissance was a formative influence, they were nowhere so
avidly accepted as in English. The acquisition of these words,
but for their too frequent abuse, would have been an un-
disputed gain to the language, which has unrivalled resources
of alternative or synonymous expression that could have been
derived from no single civilisation. The choice is not con-
fined to individual words. At an early stage in our literature
there is an intertwining of two distinct strands of expression
and rhythm: "Let me know whither you are bound", writes
Shakespeare, in plain Saxon; and the answer, bristling with
Latinisms, is: "My determinate voyage is mere extrava-
gancy."[1] It was the translators of the Bible who first appreciated the qualities peculiar to each element: the vividness,
vigour and homeliness of the Saxon; the stateliness, the
sonorousness and the more purely intellectual appeal of the

[1] *Twelfth Night*, I. 2.

Latin; and it was they who began to exercise that discrimination ever since found in the best English prose. The Latin element, however, had an unfortunate fascination for the learned as late as the time of Dr Johnson, and to this day grandiloquence persists as a cloak for poverty of thought and flagging inspiration.

THE FOUNDATIONS OF ENGLISH PROSE

The recorded history of the English people begins in the fifth century. The various tribes, conventionally classed as Angles, Saxons and Jutes, were closely related: they had the same traditions in legend and poetry, and, apart from dialect variations, they spoke the same language. That language belonged to the Germanic, or Teutonic, branch of Aryan, a linguistic family which included Latin, Greek and Celtic. Germanic had long since divided into two branches, High German, from which modern German is descended, and Low German, the ancestor of our own tongue. The invaders of Britain spoke pure Low German. Their vocabulary was comparatively limited, but it was adequate to express the simple needs of a race that had turned sea-rovers, whose business was fighting, who cared little for agriculture, commerce, politics or the fine arts, and who, under the influence of a harsh climate, were more given to action than to thought. There is no record that they had any prose, but there is evidence of a curiously developed poetic literature. Poetry with its stirring rhythms and vivid word-pictures was the natural medium of a culture based on heroic tradition.

The earliest extant example of old English prose dates from about the middle of the eighth century, and it was about that time also that the *Anglo-Saxon Chronicle*, possibly under the influence of King Alfred, began its unique record of national history, a record which was to continue without interruption down to the middle of the twelfth century. But it was the conversion of England to Christianity that had made prose a cultural and social necessity. In 597 Augustine landed in Kent, and in less than a century the new faith had penetrated to the remotest regions. At first Christianity gave a fresh stimulus to the old poetical forms, and some fine poems, such as *The Dream of the Rood*, were thus inspired. But to render into the vernacular the conceptions and philosophy of a remote and alien civilisation required a form of expression more closely resembling Latin, the source from which the doctrines of the new faith were derived. There was need also of an immensely expanded vocabulary. Among those who devoted themselves to evolving a native prose and to increasing the resources of the language was King Alfred. Many new words like *mass* and *priest* were of necessity borrowed or anglicised, but in respect of abstract terms the practice was to manufacture equivalents from native roots. The following may be quoted as examples: ge-cirredness (cirran, *to turn*), *conversion*; ā-liesednes (līesan, *to loosen*), *redemption*; hālgung (hālig, *holy*), *consecration*. The success that attended these efforts had results of far-reaching importance. It revealed the inherent adaptability of the language. It saved it from becoming latinised, or from being supplanted by a vulgar form of Latin, as the dialect of Gaul had been supplanted by what we now call French; and it gave to Anglo-Saxon a prestige which later enabled it to hold its own against the language of the Norman conquerors.

The following passage taken from Alfred's preface to his translation of *Bœthius* is given as an example of the kind of prose written at that time, and it will serve also to illustrate the old synthetic method of construction referred to in the introduction. We give an interlinear literal translation:

Ælfred cyning wæs wealstod þisse bec, and hie of
Alfred (the) king was translator of this book, and it from
boclǣdene on Englisc wende, swa heo nu is gedon. Hwilum
book-Latin into English turned, as it now is done. At times

he sette word be worde, hwilum andgiet of andgiete, swa-swa
he set word for word, at times meaning for meaning, just as
he hit þa sweotolost and andgietfullost gereccean meahte, for
he it most clearly and intelligibly relate could, considering
þæm mislicum and manigfealdum woruldbisgum, þe hine oft
the various and manifold world(ly) cares, that him often
ægþer ge on mode ge on lichaman bisgedon. Ða bisgu us
both in mind and in body busied. The cares to us
sind swiþe earforþrime þe on his dagum on þa ricu becomon
are very hard to count that in his days in the kingdoms befell
þe he underfangen hæfde.
that he undertaken had.

To the reader who is not a student of Anglo-Saxon the
above presents the appearance of a foreign language, and this
for four reasons. Firstly, spelling and lettering have changed;
secondly, the diction is wholly Germanic, whereas more than
half our words are of Romance origin (that is, they are
derived from Latin, or from Latin through French); thirdly,
the relations of words are indicated by inflections; and
fourthly, the order of words is in the old Germanic fashion.
Even in Alfred's time the grammatical system was showing
signs of disintegration, and the process was accelerated by
intermingling with the Danes, who spoke a language that
resembled that of the English closely enough to lead to confusion in the matter of inflections. Then came the Norman
Conquest, a seeming disaster that would have overwhelmed
the language of a people less tenacious than the English.
But, though during the next two hundred years nothing but
French was heard at court, castle and school, the bulk of the
population clung to their own manner of speech; and, with
the birth of a new national spirit uniting Norman and Saxon,
the discredited language of the conquered began to gain

ground. During its adversity it had followed the course of which we have noted the beginnings, continuing to simplify its grammar by eliminating redundant forms and by reducing inflections. If we refer to the extract from Alfred's preface we shall observe that the inflections of nouns, and of the adjectives, which agreed with them in number, gender and case, had clearly pronounced vowels, *þisse*, mislic*um*, woruld-bisg*um*, licham*an*, ric*u*. By about 1200 all such vowel terminations had been reduced to -*e*; which was still pronounced as a separate syllable. By Chaucer's time the pronunciation of final -*e* was becoming optional, and soon after it ceased to have any syllabic value. Earlier still, the old Germanic order of words in a subordinate clause, viz. subject, object, verb and auxiliary (e.g. as he it most clearly relate could), had been superseded by the Romance order of words that we now use.

In the matter of diction there was at first a sullen effort to preserve the integrity of the language. But English had long been out of touch with the Germanic tradition that had inspired her earlier poetic literature. Christianity had sapped its vitality, and the Church was dominated by Norman influence. France, in short, had become the chief fountain of progress and culture, and the reluctance to use Norman words gradually disappeared. By the time of Chaucer English had assumed a definitely modern form, as may be judged from the following extract from *The Tale of Melibeus*:

Thanne *Dame* Prudence, whan she saugh the gode wil of her housbonde, *delibered* and took *avys* in hir-self, thinkinge how she mighte bringe this nede unto a good *conclusion* and to a good ende. And whan she saugh hir tyme, she sente for thise *adversaries* to come un-to hir in-to a *privee place*, and shewed wysly un-to hem the grete goodes that comen of *pees*, and the grete harmes and *perils* that been in *werre*; and seyde to hem in a goodly *manere*, how that hem oughte have greet *repentaunce* of the *injurie* and wrong that they hadden doon to Melibee hir lord, and to hir, and to hir doghter.

The diction of Chaucer is hybrid; he uses the first convenient word that comes to his tongue, without giving a thought to its ancestry. In this passage of 110 words, thirteen of them (in italics), excluding proper names, are of French origin.

From the diction of this passage one might conclude that modern prose has not been built up on a foreign foundation; and though, later in its history, English was to borrow freely from Latin, it remained an essentially Teutonic language. In the immense vocabulary of to-day (which, on the authority of the Oxford English Dictionary, comprises some 400,000 words) foreign derivatives outnumber the native stock by about twenty to one; but the latter class, numerically so inferior, contains a core of short simple words that we cannot live without: they are those words that come unsought to our lips to express the needs, feelings and thoughts of everyday life.

The grammar of the passage would point to a similar conclusion: many important features of the old inflectional system have been retained. To this day what formal grammar we have is a simplification or corruption of that of Anglo-Saxon. Almost all the constructional parts of a sentence are of native origin, including elements so indispensable to composition as the verb *to be*; the auxiliaries; the inflections of the verb; the comparative forms of adjectives and adverbs; the pronouns; most of the prepositions; the essential conjunctions; a large number of affixes; and the articles. "If we endeavour", says Dr Morris, "to speak or write without making use of the native element (grammar or vocabulary), we shall find that such a thing is impossible."

Chapter I

The Fifteenth Century

1. THE PASTON LETTERS

To my right worshipful husband, John Paston, dwelling in the Inner Temple at London, in haste.

Right worshipful husband, I recommend me to you, desiring heartily to hear of your welfare, thanking God of your amending of the great disease that ye have had; and I thank you for the letter that ye sent me, for by my troth my mother and I were nought in hearts' ease from the time that we wist of your sickness, till we wist verily of your amending.

My mother behested another image of wax of the weight of you to our Lady of Walsingham, and she sent four nobles to the four orders of friars at Norwich to pray for you, and I have behested to go on pilgrimage to Walsingham and to St Leonard's for you. By my troth I had never so heavy a season as I had from the time I wist of your sickness till I wist of your amending, and yet my heart is in no great ease, nor nought shall be, till I weet ye be very whole.

Your father and mine was this day sev'night at Beccles, for a matter of the Prior of Bromholm, and he lay at Gerlyston that night, and was there till it was nine of the clock and the other[1] day. And I sent thither for a gown, and my mother said that I should none have than till I had been there anon, and so they could none get.

My father Garneys sent me word that he should have been here the next week and my emme[2] also, and play them here with their hawks, and they should have me home with them; and so God help me, I shall excuse me of my going thither if I may, for I suppose that I shall readilier have tidings from you here than I should have there....

---

[1] *other*, second, next.   [2] *emme*, uncle (cf. Oom Paul).

I pray you heartily that ye will vouchsafe to send me a letter as hastily as ye may, and that ye will vouchsafe to send me word how your sore do. *If I might have had my will, I should have seen you ere this time. I would ye were at home, if it were your ease, and your sore might be as well looked to here as it is there ye be now,* liever than a gown though it were of scarlet. I pray you if your sore be whole, and so that ye may endure to ride, when my father come to London, that ye will ask leave and come home when the horse should be sent home again, for I hope ye should be kept as tenderly here as ye be at London. I may none leisure have to do write half a quarter so much as I should say to you if I might speak with you. I shall send you another letter as hastily as I may. I thank you that ye would vouchsafe to re-member my girdle, and that ye would write to me at the time, for I suppose that writing was none ease to you. Almighty God have you in his keeping, and send you health.

Written at Oxnead, in right great haste, on *St Michael's even*[1] [1443].

Yours, M. PASTON.

To my well-beloved son, John Paston, be this delivered in haste.

Son, I greet you well, and let you weet that forasmuch as your brother Clement letteth me weet that ye desire faith-fully my blessing; that blessing that I prayed your father to give you the last day that ever he spake, and the blessing of all saints under heaven, and mine mote[2] come to you all days and times; and think verily none other but that ye have it, and shall have it, with that[3] that I find you kind and willing to the weal of your father's soul, and to the welfare of your brethren.

By my counsel, dispose yourself as much as ye may to have less to do in the world: your father said, "In little business lyeth much rest." This world is but a thoroughfare, and full of woe; and when we depart therefrom, right nought bear with us but our good deeds and ill; and there

---

[1] *St Michael's even*, 28 Sept.
[2] *mote*, may.
[3] *with that*, provided.

knoweth no man how soon God will clepe[1] him; and therefore it is good for every creature to be ready. Whom God
visiteth, him he loveth.

And as for your brethren they will I know certainly
labour all that in them lieth for you. Our Lord have you in
his blessed keeping, body and soul. Written at Norwich,
the 29th day of October [1444]. By your mother,

AGNES PASTON.

[1] *clepe*, call.

2. PREFACE (1485) TO MALORY'S *MORTE D'ARTHUR*: WILLIAM CAXTON

After that I had accomplished and finished divers histories, as well of contemplation as of other historical and worldly acts of great conquerors and princes, and also certain books of ensamples and doctrine, many noble and divers gentlemen of this royaume of England camen and demanded me, many and ofttimes, wherefore that I have not do made and imprinted the noble history of the Saint Greal, and of the most renowned Christian king, first and chief of the three best Christian and worthy, King Arthur, which ought most to be remembered among us English men tofore all other Christian kings. For it is notoriously known through the universal world that there ben nine worthy and the best that ever were. That is to wit three Paynims, three Jews, and three Christian men. As for the Paynims they were tofore the Incarnation of Christ, which were named, the first, Hector of Troy, of whom the history is common, both in ballad and in prose; the second, Alexander the Great; and the third, Julius Caesar, Emperor of Rome, of which the histories ben well-known and had. And as for the three Jews, which also were tofore the Incarnation of our Lord, of whom the first was Duke Joshua, which brought the children of Israel into the land of behest; the second David, King of Jerusalem; and the third Judas Maccabæus: of these three the Bible rehearseth all their noble histories and acts. And sith the said Incarnation have been three noble Christian men stalled and admitted through the universal world into the number of the nine best and worthy, of whom was first the noble Arthur, whose noble acts I purpose to write in this present book here following. The second was Charlemagne or Charles the Great, of whom the history is had in many places both in French and English; and the third and last was Godfrey of Bouillon,[1] of whose acts and life I made a book unto the excellent prince and king of noble memory, King Edward the Fourth. The said noble gentleman instantly re-

---

[1] *Godfrey of Bouillon*, leader of the First Crusade.

quired me to imprint the history of the said noble king and conqueror, King Arthur, and of his knights, with the history of the Saint Greal, and of the death and ending of the said Arthur; affirming that I ought rather to imprint his acts and noble feats, than of Godfrey of Bouillon, or any the other eight, considering that he was a man born within this realm, and king and emperor of the same; and that there be in French divers and many noble volumes of his acts, and also of his knights. To whom I answered, that divers men hold opinion that there was no such Arthur, and that all such books as ben made of him ben feigned and fables, bycause that some chroniclers make of him no mention, ne remember him no thing, ne of his knights. Whereto they answered and one in special said, that in him that should say or think that there was never such a king called Arthur, might well be aretted[1] great folly and blindness; for he said there were many evidences of the contrary. . . . I could not well deny but that there was such a noble king named Arthur, and reputed one of the nine worthy, and first and chief of the Christian men; and many noble volumes be made of him and of his noble knights in French, which I have seen and read beyond the sea, which ben not had in our maternal tongue, but in Welsh ben many and also in French, and some in English, but no where nigh all. Wherefore, such as have late been drawn out briefly into English I have after the simple conning that God hath sent to me, under the favour and correction of all noble lords and gentlemen, emprised to imprint a book of the noble histories of the said King Arthur, and of certain of his knights, after a copy unto me delivered, which copy Sir Thomas Malory did take out of certain books of French, and reduced it into English. And I, according to my copy, have done set it in imprint, to the intent that noble men may see and learn the noble acts of chivalry, the gentle and virtuous deeds that some knights used in those days, by which they came to honour; and how they that were vicious were punished and oft put to shame and rebuke; humbly beseeching all noble lords and ladies, with all other estates, of what estate or degree they been of that shall see and read in this said book and work, that they take the good and

[1] *aretted*, credited.

honest acts in their remembrance, and to follow the same. Wherein they shall find many joyous and pleasant histories, and noble and renowned acts of humanity, gentleness, and chivalries. For herein may be seen noble chivalry, courtesy, humanity, friendliness, hardiness, love, friendship, cowardice, murder, hate, virtue, and sin. Do after the good and leave the evil, and it shall bring you unto good fame and renown. And for to pass the time this book shall be pleasant to read in; but for to give faith and belief that all is true that is contained herein, ye be at your liberty; but all is written for our doctrine, and for to beware that we fall not to vice nor sin; but to exercise and follow virtue; by which we may come and attain to good fame and renown in this life, and after this short and transitory life, to come unto everlasting bliss in heaven, the which He grant us that reigneth in heaven, the blessed Trinity. Amen.

3. BALIN AND BALAN

From *Morte d'Arthur* (*c.* 1469): Thomas Malory

[*Balin and Balan set forth in quest of adventures, whereby they are at length parted. Balin wins great renown as Sir Balin le Savage, the knight of the two swords.*]

[*And upon a time Balin*] came by a cross, and thereon were letters of gold written, that said: "It is not for no knight alone to ride towards this castle." Then saw he an old hoary gentleman coming toward him that said: "Balin le Savage, thou passest thy bounds to come this way; therefore turn again, and it will avail thee." And he vanished away anon, and so he heard an horn blow, as it had been the death of a beast. "That blast", said Balin, "is blown for me; for I am the prize, and yet I am not dead." Anon withal he saw an hundred ladies and many knights that welcomed him with fair semblance, and made him passing good cheer unto his sight, and led him into the castle, and there was dancing and minstrelsy, and all manner of joy. Then the chief lady of the castle said, "Knight with the two swords, ye must have ado and joust with a knight hereby that keepeth an island; for there may no man pass this way, but he must joust ere he pass." "That is an unhappy custom", said Balin, "that a knight may not pass this way, but if he joust." "Ye shall not have ado but with one knight", said the lady. "Well," said Balin, "since I shall thereto, I am ready; but travelling men are often weary, and their horses too: but though my horse be weary, my heart is not weary; I would fain be there my death should be." "Sir," said a knight to Balin, "me thinketh your shield is not good, I will lend you a bigger; thereof, I pray you." And so he took the shield that was unknown, and left his own and so rode unto the island, and put him and his horse in a great boat. And when he came on the other side he met with a damoisel, and she said, "O knight, Balin, why have you left your own shield? Alas, ye have put your-self in great danger: for by your shield you should have been known. It is great pity of you as ever was of knight, for of thy prowess and hardiness thou hast no fellow living." "Me repenteth", said Balin, "that ever I came within this country;

but I may not turn now again for shame, and what adventure shall fall to me, be it life or death, I will take the adventure that shall come to me." ...

Then afore him he saw come riding out of a castle, a knight, and his horse trapped all red, and himself in the same colour. When this knight in the red beheld Balin, him thought that it should be his brother Balan, because of his two swords; but because he knew not his shield, he deemed it was not he. And so they aventured their spears, and came marvellously fast together, and they smote other in the shields; but their spears and their course were so big that it bare down horse and man, that they lay both in a swoon; but Balin was bruised sore with the fall of his horse, for he was weary of travel. And Balan was the first that rose on foot, and drew his sword, and went toward Balin, and he arose and went against him, but Balan smote Balin first, and he put up his shield, and smote him through the shield, and tamed his helm; then Balin smote him again with that un-happy sword, and well nigh had felled his brother Balan: and so they fought there together till their breaths failed. Then Balin looked up to the castle, and saw the towers stand full of ladies. So they went unto battle again, and wounded each other dolefully; and then they breathed ofttimes, and so went unto battle: that all the place there as they fought was blood red. And at that time there was none of them both but they had either smitten other seven great wounds; so that the least of them might have been the death of the mightiest giant in this world. Then they went to battle again so marvellously that doubt it was to hear of that battle for the great blood-shedding. And their hauberks unnailed, that naked they were on every side. At the last Balan, the younger brother, withdrew him a little, and laid him down. Then said Balin le Savage: "What knight are thou? for ere now I found never no knight that matched me." "My name is", said he, "Balan, brother unto the good knight Balin." "Alas!" said Balin, "that ever I should see this day." And therewith he fell backward in a swoon. Then Balan yede[1] on all four, feet and hands, and put off the helm of his brother, and might not know him by the visage, it was so full hewn and

---

[1] *yede*, went.

blooded; but when he awoke, he said, "O Balan, my brother, thou hast slain me, and I thee, wherefore all the wide world shall speak of us both." "Alas!" said Balan, "that ever I saw this day, that through mishap I might not know you: for I espied well your two swords, but because ye had another shield, I deemed ye had been another knight." "Alas!" said Balin, "all that made an unhappy knight in the castle, for he caused me to leave mine own shield to our both's destruction; and if I might live I would destroy that castle for the ill customs." "That were well done," said Balan, "for I had never grace to depart from them, since that I came hither, for here it happed me to slay a knight that kept this island, and since might I never depart; and no more should ye, brother, and ye might have slain me as ye have, and escaped yourself with the life."

Right so came the lady of the tower with four knights and six ladies and six yeomen unto them, and there she heard how they made mourn either to other, and said, "We came both out of one womb, and so shall we lie both in one pit." So Balan prayed the lady of her gentleness, for his true service, that she would bury them both in that same place there the battle was done; and she granted them with weeping it should be done richly in the best manner. "Now will ye send for a priest that we may receive our sacrament and receive the blessed body of our lord Jesus Christ?" "Yea," said the lady, "it shall be done." And so she sent for a priest, and gave them their rites. "Now," said Balin, "when we are buried in one tomb, and the mention made over us how two brethren slew each other, there will never good knight nor good man see our tomb but they will pray for our souls." And so all the ladies and gentlewomen wept for pity. Then anon Balan died, but Balin died not till the midnight after, and so were buried both....Soon after this was done Merlin came to King Arthur, and told him how Balin and Balan fought together the marvailest battle that ever was heard of, and how they were buried both in one tomb. "Alas!" said King Arthur, "this is the greatest pity that ever I heard tell of two knights; for in the world I know not such two knights." Thus endeth the tale of Balin and of Balan, two brethren born in Northumberland, good knights.

COMMENTARY

From the twelfth century onwards the English language, by
expanding its vocabulary and modifying its grammatical
structure, was gradually adapting itself to express the ideas
and ideals of continental culture introduced by the French.
These ideals, the spiritual strength of the Middle Ages,
sprang from two main sources, religion and chivalry. Religion,
as may be judged from the Paston Letters, was no mere
matter of outward observances, but the profound devotion
which had created the glories of Gothic architecture, inspired
crusades and pilgrimages, and led men's steps to the cloister
and the hermit's cell. Closely allied was the ideal embodied
in that code of conduct for Christian knighthood known as
chivalry. Of such material is great literature made; it
flourished in England and culminated in the poetry of Chaucer.
But already in Chaucer's *Prologue* there are allusions to greed
and self-seeking in the Church, and even before the Wars of
the Roses the canker had spread from the clergy to the
knighthood. In Sir Thomas Malory's *Morte d'Arthur*,
finished in 1470, and printed in 1485, the flame of chivalry
shoots up with the brightness that precedes extinction. The
story of King Arthur, which had occupied the attention of
writers in Latin, French, English and Welsh from the ninth
century onwards, had become an inextricable tangle of history
and legend. The surmise of historians is that the real Arthur
was a general appointed by the Romans as protector of
Britain when they withdrew their forces. That his duties took
him into Brittany is a theory supported by the Breton origin
of the older romances. Malory's material, on the authority
of Caxton, is a compilation from certain books of French; so
that Arthur, though British in name and associations, is an
ideal of knighthood French in conception.

For the preservation of the *Morte d'Arthur* we are indebted
to William Caxton, who, having learnt the new art of printing
in the Low Countries, set up his press at Westminster in

1477. Before his death in 1491 he had published more books in English than had appeared in the two centuries preceding. Hitherto there had been two ways of circulating literature, both of which gave verse an advantage over prose: those who plied the laborious trade of copying manuscript favoured verse for its higher artistic value and greater promise of permanence; those who retailed stories as a profession found that verse is more easily memorised than prose. It was the invention of printing that gave prose an equal opportunity.

The Paston Letters, though modernised in spelling and punctuation, have not required translation; and, as they stand, are a fair sample of the kind of English in ordinary use among the cultured classes of those times. A study of the diction will show that the fusion of the English and the French elements is complete. Words of native origin preponderate, and those that entered through Norman channels are thoroughly domesticated. *Hastily* and *heartily*, with the native suffix *-ly*, look equally English, though *haste* is French.

A conspicuous feature of the language is its monosyllabic character, due to the disappearance of the old system of inflections and the substitution of prepositions and auxiliaries. (Cf. the passage *...*.) This fondness for words of one syllable was perhaps, also, a reflection of the genius of a people that has never been expansive in speech. The influence of Latin during the Renaissance set up a counter tradition, but there has never been a time when a style in which short, simple words outnumber those of learned length has not found favour with some of our best writers.

It is evident that the elder of the two Pastons had a sense of style, but it would be hardly fair to form an opinion on the composition of the period from letters written "in right great haste". No allowance need be made for the *Morte d'Arthur*, which can be studied as a specimen of deliberate writing. From the point of view of composition the prose of Malory and his contemporaries gives the reader something of the impression of immaturity associated with the "essays" of

children. It is composed mostly of simple sentences joined
by conjunctions such as *and, but, so, then*. The mechanism of
the complex sentence had not been perfected; subordinate
clauses are introduced by *when* or *that*, and are used only with
reluctance: e.g. "he met with a damoisel, *and she* said...".
There is consequently a certain monotony of effect which
would be more noticeable but for the quaintness of the diction.
The method of composition, which was practically un-
checked by punctuation, was merely to tack sentence on to
sentence without reference to the principle of unity. Thus
sentences might be joined which we should divide, and
others separated which we should combine. The passage
beginning *Then afore him... it was not* shows that the complex
sentence was occasionally well managed. A few lines lower
down—*And Balan was the first*—the construction is more
typical of the fifteenth century, and illustrates what was for a
long time a fault common in English prose, the ambiguity
that arises from the unskilful use of pronouns (*and he arose
and went against him...*).

But as a work of art the *Morte d'Arthur* is a noteworthy
achievement. Malory is a master of narrative. Nothing
could be more simple than the diction, more direct and
economical than the manner of narration; there is no "fine
writing", none of that figurative language that tends to check
the speed of events and to blur the clear outline of the actual.
He has an eye for nothing but the object and the event. There
is no personal comment: his characters come to life and speak
for themselves. His masterly interweaving of dialogue and
narrative is far in advance of anything achieved by his predecessors. Not only does it give vividness to the story, but
it modulates the rhythm of a language that had not yet
evolved variety of sentence construction. There is deep
feeling, but Malory's sympathies are implied, not expressed.
The sense of impending doom conveyed in the words *That
blast is blown for me* is an example of the powerful emotional
effects of which Malory is a master, and they are fully revealed

in the scene of the dying brothers, the pathos of which cannot often have been surpassed.

Another respect in which Malory contributed to the development of the art of prose is suggested by a passage in Caxton's preface: *And for to pass the time this book shall be pleasant to read in; but for to give faith and belief that all is true that is contained herein, ye be at your liberty.* "These words", it has been remarked, "are memorable as marking the beginning of prose fiction; history and fable, so long inextricably entangled, are here drawing apart from one another; literature is proclaiming itself an art, and declaring a purpose beyond the scope of the humble chronicle."[1]

In the decade or two that separates Caxton from Malory the craftsmanship of prose made great advances. There is more to Caxton's credit than the establishment of printing in England. In his search for material he translated copiously from foreign literatures, and by many critical remarks in his prefaces and elsewhere, he proved himself a man of letters fully alive to the shortcomings of his own language; he applied himself assiduously to raising the standard of style in English. It will be noticed that Malory's reluctance to form complex sentences has disappeared, and that there is consequently a greater variety in movement and rhythm. The very first sentence of the excerpt is, however, a warning sign of a fault that became prevalent in Elizabethan prose, that is, a tendency to put more meaning into one period than could be borne without strain.

[1] Sir Walter Raleigh, *The English Novel.*

Chapter II

The Renaissance

1. IN PRAISE OF THE BOW

From *Toxophilus*[1] (1545): Roger Ascham

Tox. Divers countries and times have used always divers bows, and of divers fashions. Horn bows are used in some places now, and were used also in Homer's days, for Pandarus' *Iliad, 4* bow, the best shooter among all the Trojans, was made of two goat horns joined together, the length whereof saith Homer, was sixteen handbreadths, not far differing from the length of our bows.

Scripture maketh mention of brass bows. Iron bows, and steel bows, have been of long time, and also now are used *Psalm, 17* among the Turks, but they must needs be unprofitable. For if brass, iron or steel, have their own strength and pith in them, they be far above man's strength: if they be made meet for man's strength, their pith is nothing worth to shoot any shoot with all.

The Ethiopians had bows of palm tree, which seemed to *Hero. in pol.* be very strong, but we have none experience of them. The length of them was four cubits. The men of Inde had their bows made of a reed, which was of a great strength. And no marvel though bow and shafts were made thereof, for the *in Thalia* reeds be so great in Inde, as Herodotus saith, that of every joint of a reed, a man may make a fisher's boat. These bows, *Arrianus, 8* sayeth Arrianus in Alexander's life, gave so great a stroke, that no harness or buckler though it were never so strong, *in Polym* could withstand it. The length of such a bow, was even with the length of him, that used it. The Lycians used bows made of a tree, called in Latin Cornus, (as concerning the name of it in English, I can sooner prove that other men call it false,

---

[1] *A dialogue between Toxophilus, Lover of the Bow, and Philologus, Lover of the Book.*

than I can tell the right name of it my self) this wood is as
hard as horn and very fit for shafts, as shall be told after.

As for brasell,[1] Elm, Wych, and Ash, experience doth
prove them to be but mean for bows, and so to conclude Yew
of all things, is that, whereof perfect shooting would have a
bow made.

This wood as it is now general and common amongst
English men, so hath it continued from long time and had in
most price for bows, amongst the Romans, as doth appear in
this half verse of Virgil. *Taxi torquentur in arcus.* Yew fit   Virgilius
for a bow to be made on.   *Georg.* 2

Now as I say, a bow of Yew must be had for perfect shooting at the prickes, which mark, because it is certain, and
most certain rules may be given of it, shall serve for our
communication, at this time. A good bow is known, much
what as good counsel is known, by the end and proof of it,
and yet both a bow and good counsel, may be made both
better and worse, by well or ill handling of them: as often
chanceth. And as a man both must and will take counsel, of
a wise and honest man, though he see not the end of it, so
must a shooter of necessity, trust an honest and good bowyer
for a bow, afore he know the proof of it. And as a wise man
will take plenty of counsel afore hand what soever need, so a
shooter should have always three or four bows, in store,
what so ever chance.

Phi. But if I trust bowyers always, sometime I am like
to be deceived.

Tox. Therefore shall I tell you some tokens in a bow, that
you shall be the seldomer deceived. If you come into a shop,
and find a bow that is small,[2] long, heavy and strong, lying
straight, not winding, not marred with knot gall,[3] windshake,
wem,[4] freat[5] or pinch, buy that bow of my warrant. The best
colour of a bow that I find, is when the back and the belly in
working, be much what after one manner, for such oftentimes
in wearing, do prove like virgin wax or gold, having a long
fine grain, even from the one end of the bow, to the other:
the short grain although such prove well sometime, are for

---

[1] *brasell*, brazilwood, redwood.   [2] *small*, slender.
[3] *gall*, fault.   [4] *wem*, blemish.
[5] *freat*, weak place.

the most part, very brittle. Of the making of the bow, I will
not greatly meddle, lest I should seem to enter into an other
man's occupation, which I can[1] no skill of. Yet I would
desire all bowyers to season their staves well, to work them
and sink them well, to give them heats convenient, and
tillerings[2] plenty. For thereby they should both get themselves a good name, (And a good name increaseth a man's
profit much) and also do great commodity to the whole
Realm. If any men do offend in this point I am afraid they
be those journeymen which labour more speedily to make
many bows for their own money sake, than they work
diligently to make good bows, for the common wealth sake,
not laying before their eyes, this wise proverb:

Soon enough, if well enough.

Wherewith every honest handicraftsman should measure, as
it were with a rule, his work withal. He that is a journeyman,
and rideth upon another man's horse, if he ride an honest pace,
no man will disallow him: But if he make Post haste, both he
that oweth[3] the horse, and he peradventure also that afterward
shall buy the horse, may chance to curse him.

[1] *can*, know.
[2] *tillerings*; tillering, testing on a tiller, an instrument of wood in which
a bow is placed to try how it bends.
[3] *oweth*, owneth.

2. A FAREWELL TO LOVE

From *Euphues*,[1] *the Anatomy of Wit* (1578): John Lyly

Euphues having thus given her his last farewell, yet being solitary began afresh to recount his sorrow on this manner.

Ah Euphues into what a quandary art thou brought? in what sudden misfortune art thou wrapped? it is like to fare with thee as with the Eagle, which dieth neither for age, nor with sickness, but with famine, for although thy stomach hunger yet thy heart will not suffer thee to eat. And why shouldest thou torment thyself for one in whom is neither faith nor fervency? O the counterfeit love of women. Oh inconstant sex. I have lost Philautus, I have lost Lucilla, I have lost that which I shall hardly find again, a faithful friend. Ah foolish Euphues, why diddest thou leave Athens the nurse of wisdom, to inhabit Naples the nourisher of wantonness? Had it not been better for thee to have eaten salt with the Philosophers in Greece than sugar with the courtiers of Italy? But behold the course of youth, which always inclineth to pleasure, I forsook mine old companions to search for new friends, I rejected the grave and fatherly counsel of Eubulus,[2] to follow the brainsick humour of mine own will. I addicted myself wholly to the service of women to spend my life in the laps of ladies, my lands in maintenance of bravery, my wit in the vanities of idle sonnets. I had thought that women had been as we men, that is true, faithful, zealous, constant, but I perceive they be rather woe unto men, by their falsehood, jealousy, inconstancy. I was half persuaded that they were made of the perfection of men, and would be comforters, but now I see they have tasted of the infection of the Serpent, and will be corrosives. The

[1] Euphues, a witty and wealthy young gallant of Athens, goes to Naples, and becomes a friend of Philautus, by whom he is introduced to Lucilla. Lucilla, though betrothed to Philautus, becomes enamoured of Euphues, and the two friends are estranged. But when Lucilla finds a third lover, Euphues regains the friendship of Philautus, and returns to Athens to resume the study of philosophy.

[2] *Eubulus*, an elderly gentleman who offers much sage advice to Euphues on his arrival at Naples.

physician saith it is dangerous to minister physic unto the
patient that hath a cold stomach and a hot liver, lest in giving
warmth to the one he inflame the other, so verily it is hard to
deal with a woman whose words seem fervent, whose heart
is congealed into hard ice, lest trusting their outward talk, he
be betrayed with their inward treachery. I will to Athens
there to toss my books, no more in Naples to live with fair
looks. I will so frame myself as all youth hereafter shall
rejoice to see mine amendment than be animated to follow
my former life. Philosophy, physic, divinity, shall be my
study. O the hidden secrets of Nature, the express image of
moral virtues, how they begin to delight me. The Axioms of
Aristotle, the Maxims of Justinian, the Aphorisms of Galen,
have suddenly made such a breach into my mind that I seem
only to desire them which did only erst detest them. If wit
be employed in the honest study of learning what thing so
precious as wit? if in the idle trade of love what thing more
pestilent than wit? The proof of late hath been verified in
me, whom nature hath endued with a little wit, which I have
abused with an obstinate will, most true it is that the thing
the better it is the greater is the abuse, and that there is nothing
but through the malice of man may be abused.

Doth not the fire (an element so necessary that without it
man cannot live) as well burn the house as burn in the house
if it be abused? Doth not treacle as well poison as help if it
be taken out of time? Doth not wine if it be immoderately
taken kill the stomach, enflame the liver, murder the drunken?
Doth not physic destroy if it be not well tempered? Doth not
law accuse if it be not rightly interpreted? Doth not divinity
condemn if it be not faithfully construed? Is not poison
taken out of the honeysuckle by the spider, venom out of
the rose by the canker, dung out of the maple tree by the
scorpion? Even so the greatest wickedness is drawn out of
the greatest wit, if it be abused by will, or entangled with the
world, or inveigled with women.

But seeing I see mine own impiety, I will endeavour myself
to amend all that is past, and to be a mirror of godliness
hereafter. The rose though a little it be eaten with the canker
yet being distilled yieldeth sweet water, the iron though
fretted with the rust yet being burnt in the fire shineth

brighter, and wit although it hath been eaten with the canker of his own conceit, and fretted with the rust of vain love, yet being purified in the still of wisdom, and tried in the fire of zeal will shine bright and smell sweet in the nostrils of all young novices.

As therefore I gave a farewell to Lucilla, a farewell to Naples, a farewell to women, so now do I give a farewell to the world, meaning rather to macerate[1] myself with melancholy than pine in folly, rather choosing to die in my study amidst my books, than to court it in Italy, in the company of ladies.

[1] *macerate*, to soften by steeping: to mortify.

3. A DEDICATORY EPISTLE[1]

Being the preface to the *English Voyages* of Richard Hakluyt (1589)

To the Right Honorable Sir Francis Walsingham Knight,
Right Honorable, I do remember that being a youth, and
one of her Majesties scholars at Westminster that fruitfull
nurserie, it was my happe to visit the chamber of M.
Richard Hakluyt my cosin, a Gentleman of the Middle Temple,
well knowen unto you, at a time when I found lying open
upon his boord certeine bookes of Cosmographie, with an
universall Mappe: he seeing me somewhat curious in the
view thereof, began to instruct my ignorance, by shewing me
the division of the earth into three parts after the olde
account, and then according to the latter, and better distribution, into more: he pointed with his wand to all the
knowen Seas, Gulfs, Bayes, Straights, Capes, Rivers, Empires,
Kingdomes, Dukedomes and Territories of ech part, with
declaration also of their special commodities, & particular
wants, which by the benefit of traffike, & entercourse of
merchants, are plentifully supplied. From the Mappe he
brought me to the Bible, and turning to the 107 Psalme,
directed mee to the 23 & 24 verses, where I read, that they
which go downe to the sea in ships, and occupy by the great
waters, they see the works of the Lord, and his woonders in
the deepe, &c. Which words of the Prophet together with
my cousins discourse (things of high and rare delight to my
yong nature) tooke in me so deepe an impression, that I constantly resolved, if ever I were preferred to the University,
where better time, and more convenient place might be
ministred for these studies, I would by Gods assistance
prosecute that knowledge and kinde of literature, the doores
whereof (after a sort) were so happily opened before me.

According to which my resolution, when, not long after,
I was removed to Christ-church in Oxford, my exercises of
duety first performed, I fell to my intended course, and by
degrees read over whatsoever printed or written discoveries
and voyages I found extant either in the Greeke, Latine,

[1] For purposes of illustration, the spelling of an early edition has
been kept.

Italian, Spanish, Portugall, French, or English languages, and in my publike lectures was the first, that produced and shewed both the olde imperfectly composed, and the new lately reformed Mappes, Globes, Spheares, and other instruments of this Art for demonstration in the common schooles, to the singular pleasure, and general contentment of my auditory. In continuance of time, and by reason principally of my insight in this study, I grew familiarly acquainted with the chiefest Captains at sea, the greatest Merchants, and the best Mariners of our nation: by which meanes having gotten somewhat more then common knowledge, I passed at length the narrow seas into France with sir Edward Stafford, her Majesties carefull and discreet Ligier,[1] where during my five yeeres aboad with him in his dangerous and chargeable[2] residencie in her Highnes service, I both heard in speech, and read in books other nations miraculously extolled for their discoveries and notable enterprises by sea, but the English of all others for their sluggish security, and continuall neglect of the like attempts especially in so long and happy a time of peace, either ignominiously reported, or exceedingly condemned: which singular opportunity, if some other people our neighbors had beene blessed with, their protestations are often and vehement, they would farre otherwise have used. . . .

Thus both hearing, and reading the obloquie of our nation, and finding few or none of our owne men able to replie heerin: and further, not seeing any man to have care to recommend to the world, the industrious labors, and painefull travels of our countrey men: for stopping the mouthes of the reprochers, my selfe being the last winter returned from France with the honorable the Lady Sheffield, *for her passing good behavior highly esteemed in all the French court,* determined notwithstanding all difficulties, to undertake the burden of that worke wherein all others pretended either ignorance, or lacke of leasure, or want of sufficient argument, whereas (to speake truely) the huge toile, and the small profit to insue, were the chiefe causes of the refusall. . . .

[1] *Ligier*, an ambassador who remained for some time at a foreign court.
[2] *chargeable*, responsible.

To harpe no longer upon this string, & to speake a word of that just commendation which our nation doe indeed deserve: it can not be denied, but as in all former ages, they have bene men full of activity, stirrers abroad, and searchers of the remote parts of the world, so in this most famous and peerlesse governement of her most excellent Majesty, her subjects through the speciall assistance, and blessing of God, in searching the most opposite corners and quarters of the world, and to speake plainly, in compassing the vaste globe of the earth more then once, have excelled all the nations and people of the earth. †For, which of the kings of this land before her Majesty, had theyr banners ever seene in the Caspian sea? which of them hath ever dealt with the Emperor of Persia, as her Majesty hath done, and obteined for her merchants large and loving priveleges? who ever saw before this regiment,[1] an English Ligier in the stately porch of the Grand Signor at Constantinople? who ever found English Consuls & Agents at Tripolis in Syria, at Aleppo, at Babylon, at Balsara, and which is more, who ever heard of Englishman at Goa before now? what English shippes did heeretofore ever anker in the mighty river of Plate? passe and repasse the unpassable (in former opinion) straight of Magellan, range along the coast of Chili, Peru, and all the backside of Nova Hispania, further then any Christian ever passed, travers the mighty bredth of the South sea, land upon the Luzones[2] in despight of the enemy, enter into alliance, amity, and traffike with the princes of the Moluccaes, & the Isle of Java, double the famous Cape of Bona Speranza,[3] arive at the Isle of Santa Helena, & last of al returne home most richly laden with the commodities of China, as the subjects of this now flourishing monarchy have done?†

[1] *regiment*, government.   [2] *Luzones*, Philippine Islands.
[3] *Bona Speranza*, Good Hope.

4. THE SPANISH ARMADA

(Based, according to Richard Hakluyt, the author, on an account "recorded in Latine by Emanuel van Meteren in the 15 booke of his history
of the low Countreys")

Upon the 29 of July in the morning, the Spanish Fleet
after the foresayd tumult, having arranged themselves againe
into order, were, within sight of Greveling,[1] most bravely
and furiously encountered by the English, where they once
againe got the winde of the Spaniards: who suffered themselves to be deprived of the commodity of the place in Caleis
rode, and of the advantage of the winde neere unto Dunkerk,
rather then they would change their array or separate their
forces now conjoyned and united together, standing onely
upon their defence.

And albeit there were many excellent and warlike ships in
the English fleet, yet scarse were there 22 or 23 among them
all which matched 90 of the Spanish ships in bignesse, or
could conveniently assault them. Wherefore the English
shippes using their prerogative of nimble stirrage, whereby
they could turne and wield themselves with the winde which
way they listed, came often times very neere upon the
Spaniards, and charged them so sore, that now and then they
were but a pikes length asunder: & so continually giving
them one broad side after another, they discharged all their
shot both great and small upon them, spending one whole
day from morning till night in that violent kinde of conflict,
untill such time as powder and bullets failed them. In regard of which want they thought it convenient not to pursue
the Spaniards any longer, because they had many great
vantages of the English, namely[2] for the extraordinary bignesse of their ships, and also for that they were so neerely
conjoyned, and kept together in so good array, that they
could by no meanes be fought withall one to one. The English
thought therefore, that they had right well acquited themselves,
in chasing the Spaniards first from Caleis, and then from
Dunkerk, and by that meanes to have hindered them from
joyning with the Duke of Parma his forces, and getting the
winde of them, to have driven them from their owne coasts.

[1] *Greveling*, Gravelines.　　　　[2] *namely*, especially.

The Spaniards that day sustained great losse and damage, having many of their shippes shot thorow and thorow, and they discharged likewise great store of ordinance against the English; who indeed sustained some hinderance, but not comparable to the Spaniards losse: for they lost not any one shippe or person of account. For very diligent inquisition being made, the English men all that time wherein the Spanish Navy sayled upon their seas, are not found to have wanted above one hundredth of their people: albeit Sir Francis Drakes shippe was pierced with shot above forty times, and his very cabben was twise shot thorow, and about the conclusion of the fight, the bedde of a certaine gentleman lying weary thereupon, was taken quite from under him with the force of a bullet. Likewise, as the Earle of North-umberland and Sir Charles Blunt were at dinner upon a time, the bullet of a demi-culvering brake thorow the middest of their cabbin, touched their feet, and strooke down two of the standers by, with many such accidents befalling the English shippes, which it were tedious to rehearse. Whereupon it is most apparent, that God miracu-lously preserved the English nation. For the L. Admirall wrote unto her Majestie that in all humane reason, and according to the judgement of all men (every circumstance being duly considered) the English men were not of any such force, whereby they might, without a miracle, dare once to approch within sight of the Spanish Fleet: insomuch that they freely ascribed all the honour of their victory unto God, who had confounded the enemy, and had brought his counsels to none effect....

The 29 of July the Spanish fleet being encountered by the English (as is aforesayd) and lying close together under their fighting sailes, with a Southwest winde sailed past Dunkerk, the English ships stil following the chase. ‡Of whom the day following when the Spaniards had got sea roome, they cut their maine sailes; wherby they sufficiently declared that they meant no longer to fight but to flie. For which cause the L. Admirall of England dispatched the L. Henrie Seymer‡ with his squadron of small ships unto the coast of Flanders, where with the helpe of the Dutch ships, he might stop the Prince of Parma his passage, if perhaps he should

attempt to issue forth with his army. And he himselfe in
the meane space pursued the Spanish fleet untill the second
of August, because he thought they had set saile for Scotland.
And albeit he followed them very neere, yet did he not
assault them any more, for want of powder and bullets. But
upon the fourth of August, the winde arising, when as the
Spaniards had spread all their sailes, betaking themselves
wholly to flight, and leaving Scotland on the left hand,
trended toward Norway (whereby they sufficiently declared
that their whole intent was to save themselves by flight,
attempting for that purpose, with their battered and crazed
ships, the most dangerous navigation of the Northren seas)
the English seeing that they were now proceeded unto the
latitude of 57 degrees, and being unwilling to participate
that danger whereinto the Spaniards plunged themselves,
and because they wanted things necessary, and especially
powder and shot, returned backe for England; leaving be-
hinde them certaine pinasses onely, which they enjoyned to
follow the Spaniards aloofe, and to observe their course.
And so it came to passe that the fourth of August, with great
danger and industry, the English arrived at Harwich: for
they had bene tossed up and downe with a mighty tempest
for the space of two or three dayes together, which it is likely
did great hurt unto the Spanish fleet, being (as I sayd before)
so maimed and battered. The English now going on shore,
provided themselves foorthwith of victuals, gunne-powder,
and other things expedient, that they might be ready at all
assayes to entertaine the Spanish fleet, if it chanced any more
to returne. But being afterward more certainely informed of
the Spaniards course, they thought it best to leave them unto
those boisterous and uncouth[1] Northren seas, and not there
to hunt after them.

The Spaniards seeing now that they wanted foure or five
thousand of their people and having divers maimed and sicke
persons, and likewise having lost 10 or 12 of their principall
ships, they consulted among themselves, what they were best
to doe, being now escaped out of the hands of the English,
because their victuals failed them in like sort, and they began
also to want cables, cordage, ankers, masts, sailes, and other

[1] *uncouth*, unknown, wild.

naval furniture, and utterly despaired of the Duke of Parma
his assistance (who verily hoping and undoubtedly expecting
the returne of the Spanish Fleet, was continually occupied
about his great preparation, commanding abundance of
ankers to be made, & other necessary furniture for a Navy to
be provided) they thought it good at length, so soone as the
winde should serve them, to fetch a compasse about Scotland
and Ireland, and so to returne for Spaine.

For they well understood, that commandement was given
thorowout all Scotland, that they should not have any succour
or assistance there. Neither yet could they in Norway supply
their wants. Wherefore, having taken certaine Scotish and
other fisherboats, they brought the men on boord their owne
ships, to the end they might be their guides and Pilots.
Fearing also least their fresh water should faile them, they
cast all their horses and mules overboord: and so touching no
where upon the coast of Scotland, but being carried with a
fresh gale betweene the Orcades and Faar-Isles, they proceeded farre North, even unto 61 degrees of latitude, being
distant from any land at the least 40 leagues. Heere the Duke of
Medina generall of the Fleet commanded all his followers to
shape their course for Biscay: and he himself with twenty or
five and twenty of his ships which were best provided of
fresh water and other necessaries, holding on his course over
the main Ocean, returned safely home. The residue of his
ships being about forty in number, and committed unto his
Vice-admirall, fell neerer with the coast of Ireland, intending
their course for Cape Clare, because they hoped there to get
fresh water, and to refresh themselves on land. But after
they were driven with many contrary windes, at length, upon
the second of September, they were cast by a tempest arising
from the Southwest upon divers parts of Ireland, where
many of their ships perished....

Thus the magnificent, huge, and mighty fleet of the
Spaniards (which themselves termed in all places invincible)
such as sayled not upon the Ocean sea many hundreth yeeres
before, in the yeere 1588 vanished into smoake; to the great
confusion and discouragement of the authours thereof....

5. CHURCH CEREMONIES

From the *Laws of Ecclesiastical Polity* (1594): Richard Hooker

Such was the ancient simplicity and softness of spirit
which sometimes prevailed in the world, that they whose
words were even as oracles amongst men, seemed evermore
loth to give sentence against any thing publicly received in
the Church of God, except it were wonderful apparently
evil; for that they did not so much incline to that severity
which delighteth to reprove the least things it seeth amiss, as
to that charity which is unwilling to behold any thing that
duty bindeth it to reprove. The state of this present age,
wherein zeal hath drowned charity, and skill meekness,
will not now suffer any man to marvel, whatsoever he shall
hear reproved by whomsoever. Those rites and ceremonies of
the Church therefore, which are the selfsame now that they
were when holy and virtuous men maintained them against
profane and deriding adversaries, her own children have at
this day in derision. Whether justly or no, it shall then appear,
when all things are heard which they have to allege against
the outward received orders of this church. Which inasmuch
as themselves do compare unto "mint and cummin",[1]
granting them to be no part of those things which in the
matter of polity are weightier, we hope that for small things
their strife will neither be earnest nor long.

The sifting of that which is objected against the orders of
the Church in particular, doth not belong unto this place.
Here we are to discuss only those general exceptions, which
have been taken at any time against them.

First therefore to the end that their nature and the use
whereunto they serve may plainly appear, and so afterwards
their quality the better be discerned; we are to note, that in
every grand or main public duty which God requireth at the
hands of his Church, there is, besides that matter and form
wherein the essence thereof consisteth, a certain outward
fashion whereby the same is in decent sort administered.
The substance of all religious actions is delivered from God

[1] Matt. xxiii. 23. "The doctrine and discipline of the Church, as the
weightiest things, ought especially to be looked unto: but the ceremonies
also, as 'mint and cummin', ought not to be neglected."

himself in few words. For example's sake in the sacraments. "Unto the element let the word be added, and they both do make a sacrament", saith St Augustine. Baptism is given by the element of water, and that prescript form of words which the Church of Christ doth use; the sacrament of the body and blood of Christ is administered in the elements of bread and wine, if those mystical words be added thereunto. But the due and decent form of administering those holy sacraments doth require a great deal more.

The end which is aimed at in setting down the outward form of all religious actions is the edification of the Church. Now men are edified, when either their understanding is taught somewhat whereof in such actions it behoveth all men to consider, or when their hearts are moved with any affection suitable thereunto; when their minds are in any sort stirred up unto that reverence, devotion, attention, and due regard, which in those cases seemeth requisite. Because therefore unto this purpose not only speech but sundry sensible means besides have always been thought necessary, and especially those means which being object[1] to the eye, the liveliest and the most apprehensive[2] sense of all other, have in that respect seemed the fittest to make a deep and a strong impression: from hence have risen not only a number of prayers, readings, questionings, exhortings, but even of visible signs also; which being used in performance of holy actions, are undoubtedly most effectual to open such matter, as men when they know and remember carefully, must needs be a great deal the better informed to what effect such duties serve. We must not think but that there is some ground of reason even in nature, whereby it cometh to pass that no nation under heaven either doth or ever did suffer public actions which are of weight, whether they be civil and temporal or else spiritual and sacred, to pass without some visible solemnity: the very strangeness whereof and difference from that which is common, doth cause popular eyes to observe and to mark the same. Words, both because they are common, and do not so strongly move the fancy of man, are for the most part but slightly heard: and therefore with singular wisdom it hath been provided, that the deeds of men which are made

[1] *object*, set prominently before (a latinism).
[2] *apprehensive*, sensitive.

in the presence of witnesses should pass not only with words, but also with certain sensible actions, the memory whereof is far more easy and durable than the memory of speech can be.

The things which so long experience of all ages hath confirmed and made profitable, let not us presume to condemn as follies and toys, because we sometimes know not the cause and reason of them. A wit disposed to scorn whatsoever it doth not conceive, might ask wherefore Abraham should say to his servant, "Put thy hand under my thigh and...swear";[1] was it not sufficient for his servant to shew the religion[2] of an oath by naming the Lord God of heaven and earth, unless that strange ceremony were added? In contracts, bargains, and conveyances, a man's word is a token sufficient to express his will. Yet "this was the ancient manner in Israel concerning redeeming and exchanging, to establish all things; a man did pluck off his shoe and gave it his neighbour; and this was a sure witness in Israel".[3] Amongst the Romans in their making of a bondman free, was it not wondered wherefore so great ado should be made? The master to present his slave in some court, to take him by the hand, and not only to say in the hearing of the public magistrate, "I will that this man become free", but after these solemn words uttered, to strike him on the cheek, to turn him round, the hair of his head to be shaved off, the magistrate to touch him thrice with a rod, in the end a cap and a white garment to be given him. To what purpose all this circumstance? Amongst the Hebrews how strange and in outward appearance almost against reason, that he which was minded to make himself a perpetual servant, should not only testify so much in the presence of the judge, but for a visible token thereof have also his ear bored through with an awle![4] It were an infinite labour to prosecute these things[5] so far as they might be exemplified both in civil and religious actions. For in both they have their necessary use and force. "The sensible things[6] which religion hath hallowed, are resemblances framed according to things spiritually understood, whereunto they serve as a hand to lead, and a way to direct."[7]

[1] Gen. xxiv. 2.   [2] *religion*, see p. 58.   [3] Ruth iv. 7.   [4] Exod. xxi. 6.
[5] *prosecute these things*, pursue this line of argument.
[6] *sensible things*, observances or rites that appeal to the senses.
[7] Dionys. [*de Eccl. Hierarch.*].

COMMENTARY

Often, when people talk of the "dark ages", they allude, with unjust vagueness, to the Middle Ages, a period that witnessed the foundation of our universities, that produced the philosophy of the schoolmen, the scientific researches of Roger Bacon and the poetry of Chaucer. In short, the Middle Ages had ideals; it was the fifteenth century that was, by comparison, "dark". While intercourse with the Continent was hindered by wars domestic and foreign, the centre of culture moved gradually from France to Italy, and England in its isolation fell into a state of moral and intellectual stagnation. Men turned gloomily for solace to a faith which affirmed the vanity of life and the corruptness of natural instinct. "In little business lyeth much rest," says Agnes Paston, "this world is but a thoroughfare and full of woe."

Enlightenment came from contact—strangely belated—with influences that had been at work on the Continent as far back as the time of Chaucer. It was in Italy that reaction against medieval religion and tradition was most marked, and there the movement gained impetus from the revived study of the classics. While England was in the throes of the Wars of the Roses, Italy, under enlightened princes like the Medici, was building schools in which the study of Greek antiquities became an absorbing passion. Scholarship, so long yoked with theology, ceased to be the monopoly of the clergy; the New Learning, the study of the humanities, was for all. Man's faith in the value of human endeavour was restored, quickening the spirit of enquiry that animates life and art. "The essence of humanism", says Pater, is the belief "that nothing which has ever interested living men and women can wholly lose its vitality—no language they have spoken; nor oracle beside which they have hushed their voices, no dream which has once been entertained by actual human minds, nothing about which they have ever been passionate, or expended time and zeal." It is to this revolution in outlook as a whole rather than to classical scholarship, which was merely one of its instruments, that the term Renaissance should be applied. The special part played by the New Learning was to bring to the study of the fine arts a knowledge of the theory and practice of the ancients. The result was a revolution in taste and style and a new criterion of *beauty*.

The widening of the mental horizon coincided with a remarkable extension of geographical boundaries. The famous voyage of Columbus is the most familiar of many episodes in an era of adventure and discovery. The re-awakening in the English of their sense of the sea was to be of great importance in Elizabethan literature.

England's direct contact with humanism occurred late in the fifteenth century. Grocyn was taught Greek by an Italian at Oxford, and he himself lectured there in 1491. In spreading beyond the Alps humanism had come under the influence of a sterner morality, which corrected the sensuous paganism of Italy; and it reached our shores in a form more acceptable to the serious-minded English. At first the study of Greek in England meant simply the study of the New Testament, and as such was but a fresh instrument in the hands of religious controversy. Consequently the English Renaissance cannot be dissociated from the Reformation, and even when religious matters had reached a compromise under Elizabeth, scholarship was not entirely free to devote itself to pure literature.

The tendency of Renaissance learning to shift its centre from the cloister to the court was speeded by the dissolution of the monasteries. The interests of the new gentleman-writers were naturally wider and more varied than those of their clerical predecessors, and so vastly was the scope of literature extended that there is scarcely any type of modern writing that was not at least foreshadowed in the age of

Shakespeare. We find drama, poetry, novels, essays, criticism, history and sermons; and for those who were denied the means of studying the ancients at first hand there was no lack of translations of the classics.

The Italians being the pioneers of the New Learning, the Renaissance in England started with a vogue for all things Italian. It was to Italy that the scholar travelled to learn Greek and the courtier to acquire culture. Shakespeare complied with the fashion, and favoured Venice, Padua or Verona for his scenes; but he was one of the first to ridicule the "Italianate" Englishman. The strong national consciousness, itself a feature of the Renaissance, combined with native common sense, removed the danger of Italian becoming imbedded in the ordinary speech of the country. Apart from adding a number of technical terms to the vocabulary of art and music, Italian left the language of the people quite unchanged.

The English of Malory and Caxton had been quite adequate for purposes of simple narrative, but the new thought was claiming fresh means of expression with an urgency that outstripped the normal rate of expansion. It was from Latin that the new writers supplemented their resources, and they were encouraged to do so because they now realised that many words which had long been used without enquiries into pedigree were really Latin words that had been introduced into the language by the Norman-French. There arose a great parade of learning, which incidentally helped to destroy the phonetic character of English. Old friends like Chaucer's *dette* and *dout* were respelt *debt* and *doubt*. The reckless freedom with which words were borrowed threatened to swamp the Saxon element in our literature, and to change English into a romance language like French or Italian. The result was a chaotic jargon which invited invidious comparison with other languages. Latin had every quality that English appeared to lack—style, standard grammar, definitive vocabulary, fixed orthography; and it was because so many scholars believed with Bacon that "modern languages will at one time or another play the bankrupt with books" that More's *Utopia*, published in 1516, did not appear in English until 1551, and that Bacon himself, as late as 1620, published his *Novum Organum* in Latin.

The individual most tireless in stemming the danger of inundation by Latin was, strangely enough, a schoolmaster, Roger Ascham; but a more powerful force was the rising tide of nationalism, to which the break with Rome had given great impetus. "The Church services were now in English; English translations of the Bible were printed, and the beauty of these services and translations opened men's eyes to the value and expressiveness of their native tongue."[1] Realisation of the latent powers of the language led to experiments in style like those of Lyly and Sidney; in these writers it was no longer fondness for Latin, but their very virtues as Elizabethans, their exuberance of fancy, their delight in words for their own sake—qualities turned to marvellous account by the poet-dramatists—that militated against perfection in prose.

Hitherto there had been little literary biography. In medieval times the artist was, relatively, of slight importance compared with his art, and the authors of much of the literature that has survived are either anonymous or mere names. But the individualistic spirit of the Renaissance developed a sense of personality in writing. With the invention of printing the profession of letters comes into being. The writer conceives the possibility of making a name for himself in his own lifetime, and he becomes self-conscious and jealous of his reputation. Hence the prefaces and explanatory dedications here represented by those of Ascham and Hakluyt. Libraries become the repository of records to which there is always access, and supply the means of gratifying the curiosity about a writer that is excited by the success of his book. Biographical material is sought by the critic,

[1] Pearsall Smith, *The English Language*.

and a knowledge of the particular circumstances which account for a writer's idiosyncrasies becomes a most valuable aid to appreciation.

Toxophilus is a treatise on archery by Roger Ascham (1515–1568), Fellow of St John's College, Cambridge, and tutor to Princess Elizabeth. Not the least interesting feature of the work to the student of prose is its preface. "... To have written... in another tongue", says Ascham, "had been more profit for my study, and also more honest [honourable] for my name.... And as for the Latin or Greek tongue, everything is so excellently done in them that none can do better. In the English tongue contrary, everything in a manner so meanly, both for the matter and handling, that no man can do worse." But, he continues, "he that will write well in any tongue, must follow the counsel of Aristotle, to speak as the common people do, to think as wise men do. Many English writers have not done so, but using strange words as Latin, French and Italian, do make all things dark and hard."

Here in a few words we have a statement of the dilemma that faced the scholars of the period. They had the choice of writing in Latin or in English; if they wrote in Latin they would not be understood by the "common people"; if they wrote in English they would be using homespun material that most scholars despised. Patriotism settled the choice. It was to be English, English in an improved form; but whatever means might be employed to raise its standard, latinising its vocabulary was not, according to Ascham, to be one of them. The stand taken by Ascham is the more creditable because it is so obvious that he appreciated the value of Latin culture. It is Renaissance reverence for classical authority that accounts for the allusions in the text and the references in the margin; and, no doubt, the revived study of Plato suggested the dialogue form, soon to become so popular (cf. *Euphues*). What Ascham did for English prose was to stiffen its texture. He gave it something of the compactness and economy of expression that is found in Latin prose, and which is in such marked contrast with the naïve and loosely knit style of Malory in vogue less than a century before.

The subject-matter of *Toxophilus* required composition that lent itself to accurate and succinct explanation of detail. Note the brevity and compactness of the sentences, the skilful management and close dependence of subordinate clauses, and the more logical punctuation. Note, too, the beginning of a sense of style in the use of balanced and antithetical constructions, an example being supplied by the passage:

> And as | a man both must and will take counsel,
>   of a wise and honest man,
>   though he see not the end of it,
> so | must a shooter of necessity, trust
>   an honest and good bowyer for a bow,
>   afore he know the proof of it.
> And as | a wise man will take plenty of counsel
>   afore hand
>   what soever need,
> so | a shooter should have always three or four bows,
>   in store,
>   what so ever chance.

Here we have artifice in the arrangement of words, which, though more mechanical than subtle, gives emphasis by means of antithesis, and a sort of antiphonic rhythm.

The drawback of Ascham's style, however, is that it can become dull, and a contrast, possibly deliberate, to its severe plainness is to be found in the style of the next extract. Certainly Ascham's methods of raising the standard of English prose did not appeal to John Lyly (1553–1606), whose tastes were those of a courtier rather than a scholar. The success of his first book, *Euphues, the Anatomy of Wit* (1578), was immediate and widespread. Euphues, in Greek, meant what we should call a young man of parts. Lyly, exploiting the Elizabethan fondness for wit, introduced a new Euphues, whose extraordinary medley of quaint conceits and affected devices became the model of conversation in learned and courtly circles. The alacrity with which a style so absurdly artificial was received was due in part to the spirit of the times. That the vernacular might supply the material for delightful word-play was one of the discoveries of the Renaissance, and in Euphuism was found a language as rich in elegant devices and as capable of embellishing an argument as the prose of Cicero, so dear to the new rhetoricians. But Euphuism was only a meteor flash; its brief career is reflected in the plays of Shakespeare, by whom the style was first imitated and then burlesqued. Nowadays it could be recommended only as a model of what to avoid, yet in its time it did such good service that it cannot be ignored by the student.

In the first place, *Euphues*, appearing at a critical period in the evolution of prose, proved that English, without aid from Latin, French, or Italian, could achieve elegance, precision and subtlety. Chaucer had shown that perfection of form was within the scope of English verse, but before 1578 prose writing was not seriously regarded as an art, and Lyly was the first to provide a model embodying a clear conception of the requisite qualities, namely, emphasis, euphony and elegance. He was an adept in the use of the various devices by which later writers have obtained these effects. Where he erred was with his contemporaries, who lost their sanity of judgment and sacrificed matter to manner. Stylistic devices used with such clockwork regularity became monotonous and tiresome, and thus defeated their original object.

Secondly, in his subject and its treatment Lyly gave prose a modern trend. Beneath the thin disguise of classical names we recognise contemporary types of men and women; and the realistic treatment of life and manners was a welcome change from the shadowy characterisation of legendary heroes and from the idealised relations of the sexes found in Arthurian romance. In a rudimentary form many of the elements of the modern novel are to be found in *Euphues*.

Thirdly, in paragraphing and in punctuation, both of which had received scant attention from his predecessors, Lyly improved the craftsmanship of prose. The punctuation in the foregoing extract is that of Lyly himself, and the advance made by him can be judged from a comparison with Caxton's punctuation of Malory:[1]

Thene kynge Arthur lete sende for al the children born on may day begote of lordes and born of ladyes | for Merlyn told kynge Arthur that he that shold destroy him | should be born in may day | wherefore he sent for hem all upon payn of deth and so ther were found many lordes sones | and all were sente unto the kynge | and soo was Mordred sent by kyng Lotts wyf |

It will be seen from the above that whereas Caxton's punctuation was based on phrasing and euphony, with a view, perhaps, to reading aloud, Lyly takes into account the syntactical structure of the sentence.

The chief structural devices found in *Euphues* are the following, which aim chiefly at emphasis:[2]

1. *Antithesis*, one sentence or one part of a sentence being balanced against another, e.g.

   Ah foolish Euphues, why diddest thou leave *Athens the nurse of wisdom*, to inhabit *Naples the nourisher of wantonness?*

2. *Rhetorical questions* in series, e.g.

   Doth not the fire...out of the maple tree by the scorpion?

3. *Repetition*, e.g.

   As therefore I gave a farewell to Lucilla, a farewell to Naples, etc.

Partly for emphasis, and partly for ornament and euphony,

---

[1] This is a copy of a photographic facsimile of the text given in Dr Sommer's edition.

[2] This analysis owes much to the Introduction to *John Lyly*, R. Warwick Bond, Oxford University Press.

Lyly had recourse to devices which modern taste considers more appropriate to verse than to prose:

1. *Alliteration*, simple, e.g.
   ...*l*ife in the *l*aps of *l*adies.
   alternate, e.g.
   ...Athens the *n*urse of *w*isdom...*N*aples the *n*ourisher of *w*antonness.
2. *Rhyme*, e.g.
   to Athens there to toss my *books*, no more in Naples to live with fair *looks*.
3. *Consonance*, a sort of half-rhyme, based on identity of consonant sounds, e.g.
   to see *mine amendm*ent tha*n* be a*nim*ated....
4. *Assonance*, based on identity of vowel sounds, e.g.
   ...tr*ie*d in the f*ire* of z*eal* will sh*i*ne br*i*ght and smell sw*ee*t in the n*o*strils of all young n*o*vices.

For rhetorical ornament Lyly obtains his material from sources which, as every reader of Shakespeare will recognise, were very popular in his day. There are numerous allusions to the classics, and to Greek and Roman history, as seen through the eyes of Plutarch. For the greater number of his illustrations, which are chiefly in the form of similes, often very forced, he draws on the fantastic *Natural History of Pliny* (translated in 1601), e.g. *Is not poison taken out of the honeysuckle by the spider?* etc.; or on the pseudo-science of medicine, with its medieval notions of the humours, e.g. *The physician saith it is dangerous to minister physic unto the patient that hath a cold stomach and a hot liver*....

Richard Hakluyt (1552–1616) returns to a plainer style, the characteristics of which are naturalness and ease; there is no studied striving after simplicity. Ascham's sentences were severely short, and his rhythm abrupt. Though Hakluyt's periods are excessively copious, and contain parentheses which modern usage would not sanction (e.g. *...* p. 37) they are seldom involved and never obscure. Moreover, they subdivide into pleasing phrasal lengths which maintain an even flowing rhythm almost identical with that found in the translation of the Bible from which he quotes, e.g.

From the Mappe | he brought me to the Bible, | and turning to the 107 Psalme, | directed mee to the 23 & 24 verses, | where I read, | that they which go downe to the sea in ships, | and occupy by the great waters, | they see the works of the Lord, | and his woonders in the deepe. |

Though essentially a natural writer, content for the main part to rely on the effect of his own enthusiasms, Hakluyt knew how to give weight to his prose by the judicious use of certain devices, such as the rhetorical question (e.g. †...† p. 38) and the periodic construction.[1]

Not being, like Ascham, a purist or theorist, he never troubled to consider whether a construction was of native or Latin origin. Hence his fondness for words that are relative in form, but weakly demonstrative or merely pronominal in function (cf. of *whom*, *whereby*, for *which* cause, in the passage ‡...‡ p. 40); the frequency of the absolute construction (e.g. *my exercises of duety first performed*); and the excessive use of the participle, which, in an uninflected language, requires closer relation to its noun of reference than it received at the hands of Elizabethan writers.

Richard Hooker (1554–1600) was a learned and saintly divine whose sense of duty forced him from the seclusion he loved into the vortex of religious polemics. On him was imposed the onerous burden of defending the Anglican Church against the two extremes of Romanism and Calvinism. Never, except perhaps in Newman, has so much erudition been combined with such humility and self-effacement; never has sweet reasonableness been exercised with more persuasive charm.

In trying to raise the standard of English prose Ascham gave it purity, economy and compactness; Lyly, euphony

[1] See p. 57.

and an artificial form of elegance. What Hooker gave it was harmony. *Church Ceremonies* is the first example in this book of what may be described, with but little qualification, as great prose. Here, for the first time, we have true eloquence, which has been defined as "the art of exposition animated by the greatness of its theme",[1] and supported, we may add, by nobility of character. Hooker's prose possesses qualities of magnificence that suggest comparison with Milton's verse: the seriousness of his theme and the loftiness of his character raise his style to sublimity and maintain it at the height of a great argument. In such a cause his elaborate high-sounding Latinism seems justified: it gives an organ-like solemnity to the stately march of his periods.

Among features of Hooker's style we may note:

1. *Euphony*, resulting from the use of alliteration and consonance, more common in verse, e.g.
Such was the ancient simplicity and softness of spirit which sometimes prevailed in the world, that they whose words were even as oracles amongst men...
where we have a pleasant interweaving of consonant sounds.

2. *Balance*, by which any particular phrase or clause is made similar in form to some other part of the sentence, e.g.
they did not so much incline

to that severity which delighteth to reprove the least things it seeth amiss	as	to that charity which is unwilling to behold anything that duty bindeth it to reprove.

3. *Cadence*, a preference for certain rhythmical sequences which results in characteristic cadences (see Introduction, p. 6). Hooker's favourite cadence is found in a group of four syllables, in which the first and fourth are stressed: *preváiled in the wórld, delíghteth to repróve, éarnest nor lóng, fóllies and tóys.*

---

[1] Herbert Read, *English Prose Style*.

4. What has been called an "undulating rhythm", produced by varying the length of phrases, and by blending words of native and of Latin origin. Note the undulation in the sentence quoted in section 2.

5. *Periodic construction*, an artificial arrangement of the parts of a sentence by which the meaning remains suspended until the end. The qualifying adjuncts being placed at the beginning, the trend of the main thought is concealed, the reader's attention is gripped, until the close. Used with restraint and good taste, the device gives an effect of gravity; the danger is lest the preliminary accumulation of adjuncts should become a strain, or be wasted on trivial matter. Many of Hooker's sentences have a periodic or partially periodic arrangement, e.g. *First therefore to the end...in decent sort administered.*

Why is it that Renaissance prose, for all its qualities of eloquence, cannot be put forward as a model of style? Why is it that the merits of Hooker, one of its greatest exponents, have been called in question? It is said that his construction is too involved and his meaning obscure; and his greatest admirers must admit that his reasoning, though intelligible in its main drift, is not set out with that clarity attained by later writers in the difficult task of presenting abstract argument. The answer is that Hooker's prose contains the faults of the age, faults typical of all Elizabethan prose, and as such it was an imperfect medium in two respects:

1. *Composition.* Take, for example, the opening sentence, from *Such* to *reprove.* Here we have no less than nine subordinate clauses, each of which introduces some qualification of the main statement. The same principle of criticism can be applied to the paragraph, and by extension to the chapter, and thence to the whole treatise—the writer attempts to say too much. The main cause of these faults of composition was that an average sentence length ideally suited to the syntax of the English language had not

been evolved. Ascham's was too short; Hooker's, too long. Scholars like Hooker attempted to force English into an alien mould; to adapt it to the constructions, the rhythms and the idioms of the language in which they had been trained to think, viz. Latin. The Latin language, with its intricate system of inflections, can bring a greater weight of meaning into a single sentence, and can distribute a larger number of attributes without endangering the clear subordination of parts to the whole.

It is the influence of Latin that accounts for the excess of subordinate clauses; for sentences which begin with a relative, e.g. *Which inasmuch as themselves*...; for idioms like: *it shall then appear, when*... (the correlative) and the comparative *weightier*. In the diction there is a heavy proportion of resonant words of Latin origin: e.g. *profane and deriding adversaries*, and there are many words that are used in an etymological sense unintelligible to those who are read only in their own language, e.g. *prescript form of words*; *religion of an oath*, meaning, the binding nature of an oath.

2. *Rhetoric*. Its imperfection may be attributed to a certain confusion of purpose, arising from an inability, common to Elizabethan writers, to distinguish between two rhetorical aims, that of exposition and that of persuasion. Before one can persuade, one must first explain; but the poetical temper of the Elizabethans reversed the logical course: they had a bias for persuasion. An appeal to the emotions was more congenial than an appeal to the reason, and the precision essential to clear reasoning was sacrificed for the persuasive charm of poetical image and phrase.

Chapter III

The Renaissance and After

1. THE ORATION OF BRUTUS

From *Julius Cæsar* (1601): William Shakespeare

Romans, countrymen, and lovers! hear me for my cause, and be silent, that you may hear: believe me for mine honour, and have respect to mine honour, that you may believe: censure[1] me in your wisdom, and awake your senses, that you may the better judge. If there be any in this assembly, any dear friend of Cæsar's, to him I say, that Brutus' love to Cæsar was no less than his. If then that friend demand why Brutus rose against Cæsar, this is my answer: Not that I loved Cæsar less, but that I loved Rome more. Had you rather Cæsar were living and die all slaves, than that Cæsar were dead, to live all freemen? As Cæsar loved me, I weep for him; as he was fortunate, I rejoice at it; as he was valiant, I honour him: but, as he was ambitious, I slew him. There is tears for his love; joy for his fortune; honour for his valour; and death for his ambition. Who is here so base that would be a bondman? If any, speak; for him have I offended. Who is here so rude that would not be a Roman? If any, speak; for him have I offended. Who is here so vile that will not love his country? If any, speak; for him have I offended. I pause for a reply.

All. None, Brutus, none.

Bru. Then none have I offended. I have done no more to Cæsar than you shall do to Brutus. The question of his death is enrolled in the Capitol; his glory not extenuated, wherein he was worthy, nor his offences enforced, for which he suffered death.

Here comes his body, mourned by Mark Antony: who, though he had no hand in his death, shall receive the benefit of his dying, a place in the commonwealth; as which of you

---

[1] *censure*, judge.

shall not? With this I depart—that, as I slew my best lover for the good of Rome, I have the same dagger for myself, when it shall please my country to need my death.

ADVICE TO THE PLAYERS

From *Hamlet* (1602): William Shakespeare

Ham. Speak the speech, I pray you, as I pronounced it to you, trippingly on the tongue: but if you mouth it, as many of your players do, I had as lief the town-crier spoke my lines. Nor do not saw the air too much with your hand, thus; but use all gently: for in the very torrent, tempest, and, as I may say, whirlwind of your passion, you must acquire and beget a temperance[1] that may give it smoothness. O, it offends me to the soul to hear a robustious periwig-pated fellow tear a passion to tatters, to very rags, to split the ears of the ground-lings, who, for the most part, are capable of[2] nothing but inexplicable dumb-shows and noise: I would have such a fellow whipped for o'erdoing Termagant;[3] it out-herods Herod:[4] pray you, avoid it.

First Play. I warrant your honour.

Ham. Be not too tame neither, but let your own discretion be your tutor: suit the action to the word, the word to the action; with this special observance, that you o'erstep not the modesty[5] of nature: for anything so overdone is from the purpose of playing, whose end, both at the first and now, was and is, to hold, as 'twere, the mirror up to nature; to show virtue her own feature, scorn her own image, and the very age and body of the time[6] his form and pressure.[7] Now this overdone or come tardy off, though it make the unskilful laugh, cannot but make the judicious grieve; the censure of which one must in your allowance o'erweigh a whole theatre

---

[1] *temperance*, moderation.   [2] *capable of*, able to appreciate.

[3] *Termagant*, a supposed deity of the Saracens, often mentioned in the old romances, and thence transported into the Miracle plays. He was "represented as a most violent character, so that a ranting actor might always appear to advantage in it".

[4] *Herod*, a similar type in the Miracle plays.

[5] *modesty*, moderation.   [6] *body of the time*, society.

[7] *pressure*, impression made on others.

of others. O, there be players that I have seen play, and heard others praise, and that highly, not to speak it profanely, that neither having the accent of Christians nor the gait of Christian, pagan, nor man, have so strutted and bellowed, that I have thought some of nature's journeymen had made men, and not made them well, they imitated humanity so abominably.

First Play. I hope we have reformed that indifferently with us, sir.

Ham. O, reform it altogether. And let those that play your clowns speak no more than is set down for them: for there be of them that will themselves laugh, to set on some quantity of barren spectators to laugh too, though in the mean time some necessary question of the play be then to be considered: that 's villainous, and shows a most pitiful ambition in the fool that uses it. Go, make you ready.

2. *OF REVENGE*

From the Essays of Francis Bacon, first published in 1597

Revenge is a kind of wild justice, which the more man's nature runs to, the more ought law to weed it out. For as for the first wrong, it doth but offend the law; but the revenge of that wrong putteth the law out of office.[1] Certainly, in taking revenge, a man is but even with his enemy; but in passing it over, he is superior, for it is a prince's part to pardon. And Salomon,[2] I am sure, saith, *It is the glory of a man to pass by an offence.* That which is past is gone and irrevocable, and wise men have enough to do with things present and to come; therefore they do but trifle with themselves, that labour in past matters. There is no man doth a wrong for the wrong's sake, but thereby to purchase himself profit, or pleasure, or honour, or the like; therefore why should I be angry with a man for loving himself better than me? And if any man should do wrong, merely[3] out of ill-nature, why, yet it is but like the thorn or briar, which prick and scratch, because they can do no other. The most tolerable sort of revenge is for those wrongs which there is no law to remedy; but then let a man take heed the revenge be such as there is no law to punish; else a man's enemy is still beforehand, and it is two for one. Some when they take revenge, are desirous the party should know whence it cometh. This is the more generous. For the delight seemeth to be not so much in doing the hurt as in making the party repent. But base and crafty cowards are like the arrow that flieth in the dark. Cosmus,[4] duke of Florence, had a desperate saying against perfidious or neglecting friends, as if those wrongs were unpardonable: *You shall read* (saith he) *that we are commanded to forgive our enemies; but you never read that we are commanded to forgive our friends.* But yet the spirit of Job[5] was in a better tune: *Shall we* (saith he) *take good at God's hands,*

[1] *putteth the law out of office*, usurps the function of law.
[2] *Salomon*, Proverbs xix. 11.
[3] *merely*, purely, altogether.
[4] *Cosmus*, became duke of Florence in 1537.
[5] *Job*, Job ii. 10.

and not be content to take evil also? And so of friends in a proportion. This is certain, that a man that studieth revenge keeps his wounds green, which otherwise would heal and do well. Public revenges are for the most part fortunate;[1] as that for the death of Caesar; for the death of Pertinax;[2] for the death of Henry the Third[3] of France; and many more. But in private revenges it is not so. Nay rather, vindicative[4] persons live the life of witches; who, as they are mischievous, so end they infortunate.

[1] *fortunate*, prosperous. Augustus, for example, prospered after avenging the death of Julius Caesar.

[2] *Pertinax*, emperor of Rome, was murdered by rebellious soldiers. They were put to death by Severus A.D. 193.

[3] *Henry the Third*, assassinated in 1589 by a friar.

[4] *vindicative*, Latin form of "vindictive".

64

3. THE BIBLE

THE COUNSEL OF THE PREACHER
Ecclesiastes xii

Remember now thy Creator in the days of thy youth, while the evil days come not, nor the years draw nigh, when thou shalt say, I have no pleasure in them; while the sun, or the light, or the moon, or the stars, be not darkened; nor the clouds return after the rain; in the day when the keepers of the house[1] shall tremble, and the strong men shall bow themselves, and the grinders cease because they are few, and those that look out of the windows be darkened, and the doors shall be shut in the streets, when the sound of the grinding[2] is low, and he shall rise up at the voice of the bird,[3] and all the daughters of music[4] shall be brought low; also when they shall be afraid of that which is high,[5] and fears shall be in the way, and the almond tree shall flourish,[6] and the grasshopper shall be a burden,[7] and desire shall fail; because man goeth to his long home, and the mourners go about the streets:[8] or ever the silver cord be loosed,[9] or the golden bowl be broken, or the pitcher be broken at the fountain, or the wheel broken at the cistern. Then shall the dust return to the earth as it was; and the spirit shall return unto God who gave it.

[1] *the keepers of the house*, the armed guard.
[2] *the sound of the grinding.* In Eastern countries corn was ground in each house every evening in preparation for the morrow.
[3] *he shall rise up at the voice of the bird.* The literal translation is: "the bird shall arise for a noise": i.e. perhaps the bird, viz. the swallow, flies twittering at the approach of the tempest.
[4] *daughters of music*, a Hebraism for "birds".
[5] *that which is high*, the storm in the heavens.
[6] *the almond tree shall flourish*, because there is none to pluck its fruit.
[7] *the grasshopper shall be a burden*, literally, "shall be loathed", the locust being edible in the East.
[8] *the mourners go about the streets*, i.e. the professional mourners who hope soon to be hired.
[9] *the silver cord be loosed*, the silver chain that suspends the lamp shall be snapped. Here we have fresh symbols of death, to be read in connection with the words "Remember now thy Creator".

Vanity of vanities, saith the Preacher; all is vanity. And, moreover, because the Preacher was wise, he still taught the people knowledge; yea, he gave good heed, and sought out, and set in order many proverbs. The Preacher sought to find out acceptable words: and that which was written was upright, even words of truth. The words of the wise are as goads,[1] and as nails[2] fastened by the masters of assemblies, which are given from one[3] shepherd. And further, by these, my son, be admonished: of making many books there is no end; and much study is a weariness of the flesh.

Let us hear the conclusion of the whole matter: Fear God, and keep his commandments: for this is the whole duty of man. For God shall bring every work into judgment, with every secret thing, whether it be good, or whether it be evil.

Note. Some commentators, preferring the allegory of the decay of the body and the darkening of life's joys in advancing age, stress different analogies: *while the sun...be not darkened*, before the eyesight fail; *the grinders cease*, a reference to the teeth; *those that look out of the windows*, the eyes; *shall rise up at the voice of the bird*, sleeplessness; *daughters of music...brought low*, deafness; *almond tree*, with its blossoms symbolising white hair of old age.

CONFUSION AT EPHESUS

Acts xix 21–41

After these things were ended, Paul purposed in the spirit, when he had passed through Macedonia and Achaia, to go to Jerusalem, saying, "After I have been there, I must also see Rome." So he sent into Macedonia two of them that ministered unto him, Timotheus and Erastus; but he himself stayed in Asia for a season.

And the same time there arose no small stir about that way. For a certain man named Demetrius, a silversmith, which made silver shrines for Diana, brought no small gain unto the craftsmen; whom he called together with the workmen of like occupation, and said, "Sirs, ye know that by this

[1] *goads*, with which herdsmen prick their cattle to prevent them straying.

[2] *nails*, tent-pegs.

[3] *from one*, by the same, possibly God. This is followed by a warning against heathen literature.

craft we have our wealth. Moreover, ye see and hear, that not alone at Ephesus, but almost throughout all Asia, this Paul hath persuaded and turned away much people, saying that they be no gods, which are made with hands: so that not only this our craft is in danger to be set at nought; but also that the temple of the great goddess Diana should be despised, and her magnificence should be destroyed, whom all Asia and the world worshippeth."

And when they heard these sayings, they were full of wrath, and cried out, saying, "Great is Diana of the Ephesians!" And the whole city was filled with confusion: and having caught Gaius and Aristarchus, men of Macedonia, Paul's companions in travel, they rushed with one accord into the theatre.

And when Paul would have entered in unto the people, the disciples suffered him not. And certain of the chief of Asia, which were his friends, sent unto him, desiring him that he would not adventure himself into the theatre. Some therefore cried one thing, and some another; for the assembly was confused; and the more part knew not wherefore they were come together. And they drew Alexander out of the multitude, the Jews putting him forward. And Alexander beckoned with the hand, and would have made his defence unto the people. But when they knew that he was a Jew, all with one voice about the space of two hours cried out, "Great is Diana of the Ephesians!"

And when the townclerk had appeased the people, he said, "Ye men of Ephesus, what man is there that knoweth not how that the city of the Ephesians is a worshipper of the great goddess Diana, and of the image which fell down from Jupiter? Seeing then that these things cannot be spoken against, ye ought to be quiet, and to do nothing rashly. For ye have brought hither these men, which are neither robbers of churches, nor yet blasphemers of your goddess. Wherefore if Demetrius, and the craftsmen which are with him, have a matter against any man, the law is open, and there are deputies: let them implead one another. But if ye enquire any thing concerning other matters, it shall be determined in a lawful assembly. For we are in danger to be called in question for this day's uproar, there being no cause whereby we may give an account of this concourse." And when he had thus spoken, he dismissed the assembly.

CHARITY

1 Corinthians xiii

Though I speak with the tongues of men and of angels, and have not charity, I am become as sounding brass, or a tinkling cymbal. And though I have the gift of prophecy, and understand all mysteries, and all knowledge; and though I have all faith, so that I could remove mountains, and have not charity, I am nothing. And though I bestow all my goods to feed the poor, and though I give my body to be burned, and have not charity, it profiteth me nothing.

Charity suffereth long, and is kind; charity envieth not; charity vaunteth not itself, is not puffed up, doth not behave itself unseemly, seeketh not her own, is not easily provoked, thinketh no evil; rejoiceth not in iniquity, but rejoiceth in the truth; beareth all things, believeth all things, hopeth all things, endureth all things.

Charity never faileth: but whether there be prophecies, they shall fail; whether there be tongues, they shall cease; whether there be knowledge, it shall vanish away. For we know in part, and we prophesy in part. But when that which is perfect is come, then that which is in part shall be done away. When I was a child, I spake as a child, I understood as a child, I thought as a child: but when I became a man, I put away childish things. For now we see through a glass, darkly; but then face to face: now I know in part; but then shall I know even as also I am known.

And now abideth faith, hope, charity, these three; but the greatest of these is charity.

4. BOOKS

From *Areopagitica*[1] (1644): John Milton

I deny not, but that it is of greatest concernment in the church and commonwealth, to have a vigilant eye how books demean themselves as well as men; and thereafter to confine, imprison, and do sharpest justice on them as malefactors; *for books are not absolutely dead things, but do contain a progeny of life in them to be as active as that soul was whose progeny they are; nay, they do preserve as in a vial the purest efficacy and extraction of that living intellect that bred them.* I know they are as lively, and as vigorously productive, as those fabulous dragon's teeth;[2] and being sown up and down, may chance to spring up armed men. And yet on the other hand, unless wariness be used, as good almost kill a man as kill a good book: who kills a man kills a reasonable creature, God's image; but he who destroys a good book, kills reason itself, kills the image of God, as it were in the eye. Many a man lives a burden to the earth; but *a good book is the precious lifeblood of a master spirit, imbalmed and treasured up on purpose to a life beyond life.* It is true, no age can restore a life, whereof perhaps there is no great loss; and revolutions of ages do not oft recover the loss of a rejected truth, for the want of which whole nations fare the worse. We should be wary therefore what persecution we raise against the living labours of public men, how we spill[3] that seasoned life of man, preserved and stored up in books; since we see a kind of homicide may be thus committed, sometimes a martyrdom; and if it extend to the whole impression, a kind of massacre, whereof the execution ends not in the slaying of an elemental life, but strikes at the æthereal and fifth

[1] The title is based on the *Areopagiticus* of Isocrates, 355 B.C., a speech in which he urged on the Areopagus, the supreme court of Athens, the recovery of its ancient powers.

[2] *dragon's teeth*, the teeth of the monster slain by Cadmus. By Athena's advice Cadmus sowed the teeth, out of which sprang up a crop of armed men, who killed each other, with the exception of the five ancestors of the Thebans.

[3] *spill*, O.E. *spillan*, destroy.

essence,[1] the breath of reason itself; slays an immortality rather than a life....

...But I have first to finish, as was propounded, what is to be thought in general of reading books, whatever sort they be, and whether be more the benefit or the harm that thence proceeds....Dionysius[2] Alexandrinus was, about the year 240, a person of great name in the church, for piety and learning, who had wont to avail himself much against heretics, by being conversant in their books; until a certain presbyter laid it scrupulously to his conscience, how he durst venture himself among those defiling volumes. The worthy man, loath to give offence, fell into a new debate with himself what was to be thought; when suddenly a vision sent from God (it is his own Epistle that so avers it) confirmed him in these words: "Read any books whatever come to thy hands, for thou art sufficient both to judge aright, and to examine each matter." To this revelation he assented the sooner, as he confesses, because it was answerable to that of the apostle to the Thessalonians: "Prove all things, hold fast that which is good." And he might have added another remarkable saying of the same author: "To the pure, all things are pure"; not only meats and drinks, but all kinds of knowledge, whether of good or evil: the knowledge cannot defile, nor consequently the books, if the will and conscience be not defiled. For books are as meats and viands are; some of good, some of evil substance; and yet God in that unapocryphal[3] vision said without exception, "Rise, Peter; kill, and eat"; leaving the choice to each man's discretion. Wholesome meats to a vitiated stomach differ little or nothing from unwholesome; and best books to a naughty mind are not unapplicable to occasions of evil. Bad meats will scarce breed good nourishment in the healthiest concoction; but herein the difference is of bad books, that they to a discreet and judicious reader serve in many respects to discover, to confute, to forewarn, and to illustrate....Good and evil we know in the field of this

---

[1] *æthereal and fifth essence.* "Alluding to the hypothesis of four elements which compose the material world, and a fifth element peculiar to God and to the human soul." (Note to Pitt Press Edition.)

[2] *Dionysius*, bishop of Alexandria.

[3] *unapocryphal*, of unquestioned authority.

world grow up together almost inseparably; and the knowledge of good is so involved and interwoven with the knowledge of evil, and in so many cunning resemblances hardly to be discerned, that those confused seeds which were imposed upon Psyche[1] as an incessant labour to cull out, and sort asunder, were not more intermixed. It was from out the rind of one apple tasted, that the knowledge of good and evil, as two twins cleaving together, leaped forth into the world. And perhaps this is that doom which Adam fell into of knowing good and evil, that is to say, of knowing good by evil. As therefore the state of man now is; what wisdom can there be to choose, what continence to forbear, without the knowledge of evil? He that can apprehend and consider vice with all her baits and seeming pleasures, and yet abstain, and yet distinguish, and yet prefer that which is truly better, he is the true wayfaring Christian. *I cannot praise a fugitive and cloistered virtue, unexercised, and unbreathed, that never sallies out and sees her adversary, but slinks out of the race, where that immortal garland is to be run for, not without dust and heat.* Assuredly we bring not innocence into the world, we bring impurity much rather; that which purifies us is trial, and trial is by what is contrary. That virtue therefore which is but a youngling in the contemplation of evil, and knows not the utmost that vice promises to her followers, and rejects it, is but a blank virtue, not a pure; her whiteness is but an excremental[2] whiteness; which was the reason why our sage and serious poet Spenser, whom I dare be known to think a better teacher than Scotus[3] or Aquinas,[4] describing true temperance under the person of Guion, brings him in with his palmer through the cave of Mammon, and the bower of earthly bliss, that he might see and know, and yet abstain. Since therefore the knowledge and survey of vice is in this world so necessary to the constituting of human virtue, and the scanning of error to the confirmation of truth, how can we more safely, and with less danger, scout into the regions of sin and falsity, than by reading all manner of tractates, and hearing all manner of reason?...

[1] *imposed upon Psyche*, i.e. by Venus, who was jealous of Cupid's love for her.   [2] *excremental*, superficial (Lat. *excrementum*, outgrowth).

[3] *Scotus*, Duns Scotus, the schoolman, 1265–1308.

[4] *Aquinas*, the "angelic doctor", 1224–1274.

COMMENTARY

The ripe fruits of the Renaissance were gathered in the early years of the seventeenth century. It was the golden age of English drama, and the imaginative passion of the Elizabethans attained its highest expression in Shakespeare. In Milton artistic beauty was blended with the moral strength of the Reformation. The resolve of Bacon to take all knowledge as his province was the last phase of the New Learning, which was summing up its gains, and inaugurating an era of philosophy and science.

The importance of the drama in developing the quality of ease and naturalness in prose style cannot be overestimated. In typical prose fiction such as Lodge's *Rosalynde* the dialogue consists of long addresses in a style generally frigid and always affected; it never gives the illusion of natural conversation. Shakespeare wrote as the musician composes, hearing the actual sound of his instrument, in this case, the human voice. Because he wrote in the tradition that made verse the normal language of the stage, we are apt to overlook the fact that a collection of his prose passages would fill a fair-sized volume, and would show that in his command of the less familiar medium he was as superior to his contemporaries as he surpassed them in his poetry. On the stage, where no two characters should think or speak alike, the dramatist requires —at least as a theoretical ideal—as many styles as there are characters. How closely Shakespeare approached this ideal can be appreciated by comparing his dialogue with that of Ben Jonson, in whose plays so many characters talk alike that we must assume that they all talked like Ben Jonson.

Shakespeare's treatment of prose was not only more varied but more subtle than that of his contemporaries. The accepted principle was that certain situations, as, for instance, those of low comedy, were too prosaic to justify verse. But Shakespeare has a higher use for prose; he contrasts it with verse in episodes where conventional practice would have preferred verse throughout. A good illustration is the speech of Brutus, which is contrasted with that of Antony, immediately following. This passage is in prose, not because the situation lacked dignity, but because verse, to be good, must address itself to the emotions: its theme must be poetical. Brutus's defence of the murder of Cæsar was the plea of abstract patriotism, an appeal to the reason, a brilliant piece of rhetoric that left the vulgar audience impressed but not deeply moved. The rhetorical devices used are those of a philosophical pedant who tries to animate a cold abstraction with the artifices of the schools; they are a refinement of some of those which Lyly had made familiar:

> Balance and antithesis: *Not that I loved Cæsar less, but that I loved Rome more.*
>
> Climax: *As Cæsar...I slew him,* emphasised by a parallel climax in the next sentence.
>
> Rhetorical question: *Who is here so base...?* etc.
>
> Verbal ornament, such as alliteration and consonance: *so base that would be a bondman; so rude that would not be a Roman; so vile that will not love; his offences enforced, for which he suffered death.*

The dialogue from *Hamlet* is one of the earliest notable examples of modern idiomatic English fully developed, colloquial without being vulgar. The groundwork of Shakespeare's familiar speech is homely Saxon, but the sprinkling of Latin words (*capable* of nothing but *inexplicable* dumb-shows) has no trace of pedantry. The coinage of new words and phrases is the touchstone of genius. Shakespeare's "contribution to our phraseology", according to Professor Weekley, "is ten times greater than that of any writer to any language in the history of the world". This passage alone, brief as it is, has given currency to a number of expressions, such as *mouth it, saw the air, suit the action to the word, hold the mirror up to nature.*

A careful analysis of the diction reveals something of the measure in which language depends for its effectiveness on the mere manipulation of consonant sounds. Note the incisive emphasis of: *Sp*eak the *sp*eech, I *p*ray you, as I *p*ronounced i*t t*o you, *t*rippingly on the *t*ongue; and the explosive violence of: hea*r* a robus*t*ious *p*e*r*iwig-*p*a*t*ed *f*ellow *t*ear a *p*assion *t*o *tatt*ers, to ve*r*y *r*ags.

As a philosopher Bacon's claim to immortality rests on the immense project by which he hoped to inaugurate a new era of science; as a writer he will be remembered for his introduction into English of the Essay, a prose form to which he himself attached little importance. The term "essay" was used by Bacon in the literal sense of a first trial or weighing of a subject. The suggestion came from Montaigne, but Bacon's reflections were different from the pensées of his master, who spoke about himself and his foibles with the frankness to which the modern fashion in essays has reverted. Bacon's essays are less intimate. They reveal the worldly side of a profound thinker who turned sometimes from philosophy to politics, and wished to give his fellow men practical advice "of a nature whereof much should be found in experience and little in books".

The modern essay aims at a high standard of art, demanding a definite plan and careful attention to style. Bacon, having a poor opinion of the future of English as a language, set down his "brief notes of life's experience... rather significantly than curiously",—by which he meant that his concern was with meaning and not style. He was impatient of "curious" stylists like Lyly, and his terseness is in wholesome contrast with their extravagance. But, like most reactionaries, he went to the other extreme; thought followed thought with bewildering rapidity and with a disjointedness more apparent than real. Bacon had not the easy flowing rhythm which is half the charm of the modern essay, but he had some admirable qualities superlatively developed. There has been no finer master of the aphorism, the pithy and proverbial saying. His short pointed sentences have a memorable or quotable quality that is rarer in prose than in verse; they are pregnant in meaning and in thought-provoking quality. His philosophic fondness for analogies supplied him with a rich fund of imagery, which was no vain adornment, or even evidence of poetical feeling, but was a means of illuminating his topic with similitudes taken from familiar objects.

The *Authorised Version* is that rare phenomenon in literature —a translation which has the vital idiom of an original work. The form in which we have it represents the piety and scholarship of many men and many generations, and perhaps no individual could have produced a work so characteristic of, and so acceptable to, the nation as a whole. The germ was Wyclif's translation of the *Vulgate* (*c.* 1378). The work, carried on by Tyndale, Coverdale and Cranmer, was completed in 1611 by a commission appointed by James I, under whom no less than forty-seven leading divines were engaged in assiduous labour over a period of five years. Its influence, both moral and literary, in an age of few books, cannot be overestimated. Almost at once it was adopted by all sects, irrespective of creed. For the Puritans it was the only book, and the rock of their moral strength; without the Bible the career of Cromwell is inconceivable. As literature it "consolidated and established the English idiom which had gradually been formed during the fourteenth and fifteenth centuries;...it is the greatest single influence on the development of English prose style".[1] The novel and varied interests of the New Learning and the strong individuality of its writers had bred an excessive ornateness and idiosyncrasy. The translators of 1611 were expressly enjoined to preserve the simple idiom of the pre-Renaissance versions; they worked with single-minded sincerity to bring the Bible within reach of the unlearned, and in so doing returned to the direct simplicity of Malory, since whose time there had been few writers that could tell a story with the concreteness and

[1] Herbert Read, *English Prose Style*.

economy of the account of Demetrius the silversmith. Nor
has there since been any period when the Bible has not been
recognised as a wholesome corrective of style, as many of
our writers have borne testimony. "Once knowing", says
Ruskin, "the 32nd of Deuteronomy, the 119th Psalm, 15th of
the 1st Corinthians, the Sermon on the Mount, and most of
the Apocalypse, every syllable by heart...it was not possible
for me, even in the foolishest time of youth, to write entirely
superficial or formal English."

But the Bible has done more than prune extravagances of
style, whether of the Renaissance or of later periods. Its
effects were much deeper and wider. Compared with that
of the classics, its appeal was more direct and intimate, as
well as more widespread. Culturally, it interpreted the
manners and philosophy of an ancient race justly celebrated
for its wisdom; and by rendering literally into English the
verbal devices of Hebrew literature it lent freshness and
vigour to the language. Though the whole of the translation
is set out in the form of prose, a large portion of the original
is poetry; and this poetry was embodied in a verse system
which, being neither rhymed nor metrical, could be rendered
into a foreign tongue with little loss. The essential features
of Hebrew poetry were those of a people that loved analogies
and similitudes such as parable and allegory. This racial
characteristic accounted for their fondness for imagery,
expressed in simile, metaphor and personification. But
most prominent was parallelism, a device by which phrase
was made to correspond with phrase, idea rhyming, as it
were, with idea. These parallel expressions are arranged with
rhythmic effect in a roughly strophic pattern:

> Charity never faileth:
> But whether there be prophecies,
> They shall fail;
> Whether there be tongues,
> They shall cease;
> Whether there be knowledge,
> It shall vanish away.

Accentual rhythm is strongly marked; but the exact repetition found in verse is avoided. The passage from *Ecclesiastes* reveals an even closer approach to the movement of verse, the predominant foot being an anapæst: *in the dáys | of thy yoúth | ...while the sún, | or the líght, | or the móon, | or the stárs, | be not dárkened; | nor the clóuds | retúrn | àfter the ráin. |*

Note, too, the similarity of the cadences:

> gólden bòwl be bróken
> bróken at the fóuntain
> bróken at the cístern.

Ecclesiastes well illustrates the Hebrew fondness for imagery. Employing the image of a tempest breaking on an Eastern city as night falls, the Preacher depicts the gloom of old age, the decay of the bodily powers and the terrors of death. If some of the phrases of the translation convey but a blurred picture, it is partly because the richness of inter-mingled metaphor peculiar to the Oriental imagination is confusing; and partly because in the seventeenth century the sense of local colour had not been developed by travel, and it was hard for writers to visualise and render in correct detail a scene so remote from their experience.

To sum up—parallelism and imagery, already by no means foreign to English poetry, were now introduced into the prose of everyday life. The effect was greatly to increase the native capacity for vivid and arresting turns of expression, and to develop the potentialities of rhythm in prose.

A fashionable pose of melancholy was among the early signs of a reaction from the astounding enthusiasm and vitality of Renaissance times. It was ridiculed by Shake-speare in the character of Jaques in *As You Like It*, but the reaction developed in the master himself into the tragic seriousness of *Hamlet* and *King Lear*; and by about 1640 it had become widespread. Questions of conscience and in-dividual liberty led to a sharp cleavage of opinion in politics, and gave a darker tinge to the old religious controversies. It was the call of duty that impelled Milton to wander for nearly twenty of the best years of his life in the arid wastes of polemics. The subjects of many of his pamphlets were of merely transient interest, but as he was drawn into controversy only when principles and ideals were at issue, he wrote with a fervour of passionate conviction that raised the topical to a higher plane, and inspired many a passage with that quality of universal appeal which we associate with great literature.

Areopagitica (1644) was a protest against parliamentary control of printing, but Milton's plea was too advanced for those times, and the ban on unlicensed printing was not removed until 1695. In this pamphlet Milton is seen at his best. Its prose is "the swan-song of the old eloquence".[1] In the extract there are at least three passages (cf. *for books are not absolutely...that bred them*, p. 68; *a good book...life beyond life*, p. 68; *I cannot praise...dust and heat*, p. 70) in which lofty style is so moulded to nobility of thought as to recall the sublimity of *Paradise Lost*, and under the spell of such passages one inclines to the opinion that it is poets who write the greatest prose.

But a more extensive reading of the pamphlets exposes Milton's limitations as a tractarian. He has no sense of humour, no deftness of touch. Released from the restraint imposed on him as a poet by his art, and lacking the suaver taste of more tolerant ages, he lapses into the crude scurrility which then passed for satire. Before Milton's death it was commonly recognised that there was a place in literature for feelings less intense, and for a style less pedantic, less disdainful of our ordinary needs.

[1] Bailey, *John Milton*.

THE COMPOSITION OF THE PERIOD

In our brief sketch of the history of composition we have noted the old synthetic or inflectional system gradually falling into disuse, and the native vocabulary being supplemented or replaced by extensive borrowings from Latin and French. Changes in grammar, diction and spelling proceeded so rapidly that Chaucer would not have understood the language of Alfred, and Shakespeare could not have read Chaucer with ease. Malory, however, would have given Shakespeare little difficulty. It is clear, then, that somewhere about the middle of the fifteenth century the rate of change was arrested, the language was in process of fixation, and the Middle English of Chaucer had merged into the language we use now.

The greatest single influence in fixing the form of the language was the spread of printing, with the consequent multiplication of books and diffusion of learning. We see the same result in other European countries. It is no mere coincidence that after the fifteenth century Romance languages like French and Italian made no further progress along analytical lines, that German adhered to its synthetic character, and that English became reluctant to shed any of the surviving inflections. Spelling, which had hitherto represented the spoken sound, became fixed, and thus helped to protect the form and appearance of words from such extreme changes as they had previously undergone. Being powerless, however, to prevent the shifting of sounds, it has long ceased to be phonetic.

An instance of the way in which printing has resulted in the fixation of language is seen in the survival in modern English of certain forms which were already obsolete during Elizabethan times, notably the -*eth* termination of the verb in the third person singular. -*Eth* was the usual form till the sixteenth century, when the Northern -*s*, which is non-syllabic, began to find favour. From the extracts in this book it will be seen that *-eth* is used by Ascham, Lyly, Hooker, and in the Authorised Version. Milton uses *-s*, and after his time *-eth* was an archaism. Its revival in the poetry of the nineteenth century is due to its preservation in print, particularly in the Bible.

If the introduction of printing tended to check changes in grammar and spelling, it had the opposite effect on vocabulary, because it increased the opportunities of intercourse with foreign literatures, ancient and modern. From the early days of the New Learning until quite recent times Latin and Greek have been the chief subjects of literary study, and words of classical origin have poured into the language. Purists like Ascham protested in vain; the habit of borrowing was too deeply ingrained. A large proportion of the familiar vocabulary consisted of Latin words which had been taken into French during the Middle Ages, and then adopted into English. Literary words were naturalised by a variety of affixes. The following are taken at random from two pages of Chaucer: noun suffixes, *-ion, -ence, -ment, -ity, -y*; adjective suffixes, *-ous, -able, -ent, -ary*. The scholars of the Renaissance made use of affixes of this kind already familiar to anglicise almost any Latin word for which there seemed to be no equivalent in English. They did this with the greater freedom because there was no authoritative dictionary of the language, and because any word from a familiar classical passage would be certain to be understood.

The practice of coining words from Latin and Greek, though sometimes injudicious, had on the whole a beneficial effect on the language, more especially on the literary side. Philosophy, criticism, history and the fine arts were supplied with terms that were badly needed for their development. The preference for Latin words where native equivalents existed is less easy to defend, and many a passage in Milton, Burton and Browne may justly be criticised on this score. There was a strong reaction against their practice during the Restoration period, but they are by no means the last of our great writers to latinise their style.

The chief changes since Elizabethan days are: the gradual disappearance of the subjunctive, of the verbal termination *-eth*, of the use of *thou*, and of the old distinction between *you* and *ye* (*you* being originally an oblique case); the restriction of the auxiliaries *do* and *did* to negative, interrogative and emphatic uses (cf. Hakluyt's *I do remember that being a youth*... p. 36); the distinction that has arisen between *who* and *which*, used until the eighteenth century to refer indifferently to persons and things (cf. Hooker's *he which was minded*, p. 45); the development of new tenses, notably of what we now call the continuous, e.g. *You know not what you do* (*Julius Caesar*), where *do* represents the modern *are doing*; the growing use (or abuse) of the attributive noun, e.g. *the woman suffrage problem*. Otherwise the syntax and accidence of modern English are substantially what they were in Shakespeare's time.

But it would be absurd to conclude that because such changes have become rare the language has lost its faculty of development. A language ceases to be a living force when it can no longer change with changing taste, or expand with the growth of intellect. With accidence fixed and syntax static, other means have been found of increasing expressiveness. Such are new idioms, new words, new compounds, and the enrichment of existing words by their accretion of historical and literary associations. The development of English along these lines is due in no small measure to the advantage it possesses over more highly inflected languages in its unique elasticity, in the ease with which any part of speech may be used as almost any other, and with almost any other to form a compound. In Shakespeare's *But me no buts*, we have what is normally a conjunction used first as a verb and secondly as a noun. The sentence is perfectly clear in meaning, and yet it defies translation into any other language, as does also the startling compound *periwig-pated*, which occurs in our *Hamlet* passage. Such freedom is only possible in a flexionless language in which the various parts of speech are not distinguished by their terminations, and in which the normal order of words is itself a clue to the meaning. It is this characteristic fluidity of English that enables Shakespeare to coin an expression like *it out-herods Herod*, where the compounding of an adverb with a noun results in a new verb of peculiar force.

When we come to consider changes of meaning we find that the use of a word in a certain context may have given it a connotation entirely different from that which first attached to it. Thus, owing to association of ideas, the parable of the Prodigal Son (in which, incidentally, the word *prodigal* does not appear) has given rise to the impression that *prodigal* means *repentant*, and it is conceivable that the latter may supersede the original meaning of *spendthrift*. The more usual phenomenon, however, is not a complete change but a partial modification, which is conveniently termed a *nuance*. The foregoing section contains an abundance of words that have since undergone subtle and elusive changes of meaning. One selected from the *Hamlet* passage will suffice as an illustration. *Censure* occurs twice, in each instance bearing mainly the original meaning of *judge*; but it also has a slight leaning, more pronounced in the second case, towards what has since become its meaning, viz. *blame*, *condemn*. The vocabulary of Shakespeare and his contemporaries needs close scrutiny for such changes; while to appreciate the exact significance of many a sentence in Hooker or Milton depends on the reader's ability to associate one particular word with its classical origin or context.

Chapter IV

The Renaissance and After (*cont.*)

1. *RELIGIO MEDICI* (1643)

SIR THOMAS BROWNE

I thank God, amongst those millions of vices I do inherit and hold from Adam, I have escaped one, and that a mortal enemy to charity, the first and father-sin, not only of man, but of the devil—pride; a vice whose name is comprehended in a monosyllable, but in its nature not circumscribed with a word. I have escaped it in a condition that can hardly avoid it. Those petty acquisitions and reputed perfections that advance and elevate the conceits of other men, add no feathers unto mine. I have seen a grammarian tower and plume himself over a single line in Horace, and show more pride in the construction[1] of one ode, than the author in the composure of the whole book. For my own part, besides the jargon and patois of several provinces, I understand no less than six languages; yet I protest I have no higher conceit of myself than had our fathers before the confusion of Babel, when there was but one language in the world, and none to boast himself either linguist or critic. I have not only seen several countries, beheld the nature of their climes, the chorography[2] of their provinces, topography of their cities, but understood their several laws, customs, and policies; yet cannot all this persuade the dulness of my spirit unto such an opinion of myself, as I behold in nimbler and conceited heads, that never looked a degree beyond their nests. I know the names, and somewhat more, of all the constellations in my horizon, yet I have seen a prating mariner, that could only name the pointers and the north star, out-talk me, and conceit himself a whole sphere above me. I know most of the plants of my country,[3] and of

---

[1] *construction*, from *construe*.
[2] *chorography*, description of geographical features.
[3] *country*, district.

those about me; yet methinks I do not know so many as when I did but know a hundred, and had scarcely ever simpled[1] further than Cheapside. For indeed, heads of capacity, and such as are not full with a handful, or easy measure of knowledge, think they know nothing till they know all, which being impossible, they fall upon the opinion of Socrates, and only know they know not anything. I cannot think that Homer pined away upon the riddle of the fisherman,[2] or that Aristotle, who understood the uncertainty of knowledge, and confessed so often the reason of man too weak for the works of nature, did ever drown himself upon the flux and reflux of the Euripus.[3] We do but learn to-day, what our better advanced judgments will unteach to-morrow; and Aristotle doth not instruct us as Plato did him, that is, to confute himself. I have run through all sorts, yet find no rest in any; though our first studies and junior endeavours may style us peripatetics,[4] stoics, or academics, yet I perceive the wisest heads prove, at last, almost all sceptics, and stand like Janus[5] in the field of knowledge. I have therefore one common and authentic philosophy I learned in the schools, whereby I discourse and satisfy the reason of other men; another more reserved, and drawn from experience, whereby I content mine own. Solomon, that complained of ignorance in the height of knowledge, hath not only humbled my conceits, but discouraged my endeavours. There is yet another conceit that hath sometimes made me shut my books, which tells me it is a vanity to waste our days in the blind pursuit of knowledge; it is but attending a little longer, and we shall enjoy that by instinct and infusion, which we endeavour at here by labour

---

[1] *simpled*, gathered herbs.
[2] *riddle of the fisherman*. According to Plutarch, Homer died of chagrin because he could not solve a certain riddle.
[3] *Euripus*, a narrow channel between Eubœa and Bœotia where the tide ebbed and flowed with great violence.
[4] Here the author alludes to various schools of Athenian philosophy: *peripatetics*, followers of Aristotle, who gave his instruction while *walking* in the Lyceum; *stoics*, members of the school of Zeno, who taught under a *porch* (stoa); *academics*, followers of Plato, whose school was named after a *grove*.
[5] *stand like Janus*, that is, facing both ways, Janus being a Roman god with two opposite faces.

and inquisition. It is better to sit down in a modest ignorance, and rest contented with the natural blessing of our own reasons, than buy the uncertain knowledge of this life, with sweat and vexation, which death gives every fool gratis, and is an accessory of our glorification.

* * * * * * *

Now for my life, it is a miracle of thirty years, which to relate were not a history but a piece of poetry, and would sound to common ears like a fable; for the world, I count it not an inn but an hospital, and a place not to live, but to die in. The world that I regard is myself; it is the microcosm of my own frame that I cast mine eye on; for the other, I use it but like my globe, and turn it round sometimes for my recreation. Men that look upon my outside, perusing only my condition and fortunes, do err in my altitude, for I am above Atlas's shoulders. The earth is a point not only in respect of the heavens above us, but of that heavenly and celestial part within us; that mass of flesh that circumscribes me limits not my mind; that surface that tells the heaven it hath an end cannot persuade me I have any. I take my circle to be above three hundred and sixty. Though the number of the arc do measure my body it comprehendeth not my mind. Whilst I study to find how I am a microcosm, or little world, I find myself something more than the great. There is surely a piece of divinity in us, something that was before the elements, and owes no homage unto the sun. Nature tells me I am the image of God, as well as Scripture. He that understands not thus much hath not his introduction, or first lesson, and is yet to begin the alphabet of man. Let me not injure the felicity of others, if I say I am as happy as any; *Ruat cœlum, fiat voluntas tua*, salveth all; so that whatsoever happens it is but what our daily prayers desire. In brief, I am content, and what should Providence add more? Surely this is it we call happiness, and this do I enjoy; with this I am happy in a dream, and as content to enjoy a happiness in a fancy, as others in a more apparent truth and reality.

2. A FISHERMAN'S PHILOSOPHY

From *The Compleat Angler* (1653): Izaak Walton

Venator.[1] O my good master, this morning walk has been spent to my great pleasure and wonder: but, I pray, when shall I have your direction how to make artificial flies, like to those that the Trout loves best; and, also, how to use them?

Piscator. My honest scholar, it is now past five of the clock: we will fish till nine; and then go to breakfast. Go you to yonder sycamore-tree, and hide your bottle of drink under the hollow root of it; for about that time, and in that place, we will make a brave breakfast with a piece of powdered beef, and a radish or two, that I have in my fish-bag: we shall, I warrant you, make a good, honest, wholesome hungry breakfast. And I will then give you direction for the making and using of your flies: and in the meantime, there is your rod and line; and my advice is, that you fish as you see me do, and let's try which can catch the first fish.

Venator. I thank you, master. I will observe and practice your direction as far as I am able.

Piscator. Look you, scholar; you see I have hold of a good fish: I now see it is a Trout. I pray, put that net under him; and touch not my line, for if you do, then we break all. Well done, scholar; I thank you.

Now, for another. Trust me, I have another bite. Come, scholar, come lay down your rod, and help me to land this as you did the other. So now we shall be sure to have a good dish of fish for supper.

Venator. I am glad of that: but I have no fortune: sure, master, yours is a better rod and better tackling.

Piscator. Nay, then, take mine; and I will fish with yours. Look you, scholar, I have another. Come, do as you did before. And now I have a bite at another. Oh me! he has broke all: there's half a line and a good hook lost.

Venator. Ay, and a good Trout too.

Piscator. Nay, the Trout is not lost; for pray take notice, no man can lose what he never had.

[1] Dialogue between the huntsman and the angler.

Venator. Master, I can neither catch with the first nor second angle: I have no fortune.

Piscator. Look you, scholar, I have yet another. And now, having caught three brace of Trouts, I will tell you a short tale as we walk towards our breakfast. A scholar, a preacher I should say, that was to preach to procure the approbation of a parish that he might be their lecturer, had got from his fellow-pupil the copy of a sermon that was first preached with great commendation by him that composed it: and though the borrower of it preached it, word for word, as it was at first, yet it was utterly disliked as it was preached by the second to his congregation, which the sermon-borrower complained of to the lender of it: and was thus answered: "I lent you, indeed, my fiddle, but not my fiddle-stick; for you are to know, that everyone cannot make music with my words, which are fitted for my own mouth." And so, my scholar, you are to know, that as the ill pronunciation or ill accenting of words in a sermon spoils it, so the ill carriage of your line, or not fishing even to a foot in a right place, makes you lose your labour: and you are to know, that though you have my fiddle, that is, my very rod and tacklings with which you see I catch fish, yet you have not my fiddle-stick, that is, you yet have not skill to know how to carry your hand and line, nor how to guide it to a right place: and this must be taught you; for you are to remember, I told you Angling is an art, either by practice or a long observation, or both. But take this for a rule, When you fish for a Trout with a worm, let your line have so much, and not more lead than will fit the stream in which you fish; that is to say, more in a troublesome stream than in a smaller which is quieter; as near as may be, so much as will sink the bait to the bottom and keep it still in motion, and not more.

But now, let's say grace, and fall to breakfast. What say you, scholar, to the providence of an old angler? Does not this meat taste well? and was not this place well chosen to eat it? for this sycamore-tree will shade us from the sun's heat.

Venator. All excellent good; and my stomach excellent good, too. And now I remember, and find true which devout Lessius says, "that poor men, and those that fast often, have much more pleasure in eating than rich men and gluttons, that always feed before their stomachs are empty of their last meat and call for more; for by that means they rob themselves of that pleasure that hunger brings to poor men." And I do seriously approve of that saying of yours, "that you had rather be a civil, well-governed, well grounded, temperate, poor angler, than a drunken lord": but I hope there is none such. However, I am certain of this, that I have been at many very costly dinners that have not afforded me half the content that this has done; for which I thank God and you.

* * * * * * *

Piscator. Well, scholar, having now taught you to paint your rod, and we having still a mile to Tottenham High-Cross, I will, as we walk towards it in the cool shade of this sweet honeysuckle hedge, mention to you some of the thoughts and joys that have possessed my soul since we two met together. And these thoughts shall be told you, that you also may join with me in thankfulness to the Giver of every good and perfect gift, for our happiness. And that our present happiness may appear to be the greater, and we the more thankful for it, I will beg you to consider with me how many do, even at this very time, lie under the torment of the stone, the gout, and tooth-ache; and this we are free from. And every misery that we miss is a new mercy; and therefore let us be thankful. There have been, since we met, others that have met disasters or broken limbs; some have been blasted, others thunder-stricken: and we have been freed from these, and all those many other miseries that threaten human nature; let us there-fore rejoice and be thankful. Nay, which is a far greater mercy, we are free from the insupportable burthen of an accusing tormenting conscience; a misery that none can bear: and therefore let us praise Him for His preventing grace, and say, Every misery that I miss is a new mercy. Nay, let me tell you, there be many that have forty times our estates, that would give the greatest part of it to be healthful and cheerful like us, who, with the expense of a little money, have eat and drunk, and laughed, and angled, and sung, and slept securely; and rose next day and cast away care, and sung, and laughed, and angled again; which are blessings rich men cannot pur-chase with all their money. Let me tell you, scholar, I have

a rich neighbour that is always so busy that he has no leisure
to laugh; the whole business of his life is to get money, and
more money, that he may still get more and more money; he
is still drudging on, and says, that Solomon says "The
diligent hand maketh rich"; and it is true indeed: but he
considers not that it is not in the power of riches to make a
man happy; for it was wisely said, by a man of great observation, "That there be as many miseries beyond riches as on
this side of them." And yet God deliver us from pinching
poverty; and grant, that having a competency, we may be
content and thankful. Let not us repine or so much as think
the gifts of God unequally dealt, if we see another abound
with riches; when, as God knows, the cares that are the keys
that keep those riches hang often so heavily at the rich man's
girdle, that they clog him with weary days and restless nights,
even when others sleep quietly. We see but the outside of the
rich man's happiness: few consider him to be like the silk-
worm, that, when she seems to play, is, at the very same time,
spinning her own bowels, and consuming herself; and this
many rich men do, loading themselves with corroding cares,
to keep what they have, probably, unconscionably got. Let
us, therefore, be thankful for health and a competence; and
above all, for a quiet conscience.

Let me tell you, scholar, that Diogenes walked on a day,
with his friend, to see a country fair; where he saw ribbons,
and looking-glasses, and nutcrackers, and fiddles, and hobby-
horses, and many other gimcracks; and having observed
them, and all the other finnimbruns that make a complete
country-fair, he said to his friend, "Lord, how many things
are there in this world of which Diogenes hath no need!"
And truly it is so, or might be so, with very many who vex
and toil themselves to get what they have no need of....

My honest scholar, all this is told to incline you to thankfulness; and to incline you the more, let me tell you, and
though the prophet David was guilty of murder and adultery,
and many other of the most deadly sins, yet he was said to be
a man after God's own heart, because he abounded more with
thankfulness than any other that is mentioned in holy
scripture, as may appear in his book of Psalms; where there
is such a commixture, of his confessing of his sins and

unworthiness, and such thankfulness for God's pardon and mercies, as did make him to be accounted, even by God himself, to be a man after His own heart: and let us, in that, labour to be as like him as we can; let not the blessings we receive daily from God make us not to value, or not praise Him, because they be common; let us not forget to praise Him for the innocent mirth and pleasure we have met with since we met together. What would a blind man give to see the pleasant rivers, and meadows, and flowers, and fountains, that we have met with since we met together? I have been told, that if a man that was born blind could obtain to have his sight for but only one hour during his whole life, and should at the first opening of his eyes, fix his sight upon the sun when it was in its full glory, either at the rising or the setting of it, he would be so transported and amazed, and so admire the glory of it, that he would not willingly turn his eyes from that first ravishing object, to behold all the other various beauties this world could present to him. And this, and many other like blessings, we enjoy daily. And for the most of them, because they be so common, most men forget to pay their praises: but let not us; because it is a sacrifice so pleasing to Him that made that sun and us, and still protects us, and gives us flowers, and showers, and stomachs, and meat, and content, and leisure to go a-fishing.

3. CONTENTEDNESS

From *Holy Living* (1650): Jeremy Taylor

Contentedness in all estates is a duty of religion; it is the great reasonableness of complying with the Divine Providence which governs all the world, and hath so ordered us in the administration of His great family. He were a strange fool that should be angry because dogs and sheep need no shoes, and yet himself is full of care to get some. God hath supplied those needs to them, by natural provisions, and to thee by an artificial: for He hath given thee reason to learn a trade, or some means to make or buy them; so that it only differs in the manner of our provision: and which had you rather want, shoes or reason? And my patron that hath given me a farm is freer to me than if he gives a loaf ready baked. But, however, all these gifts come from Him, and therefore it is fit He should dispense them as He pleases; and if we murmur here, we may at the next melancholy be troubled that God did not make us to be angels or stars. For, if that which we are or have do not content us, we may be troubled for everything in the world which is besides our being or our possessions.

God is the master of the scenes; we must not choose which part we shall act; it concerns us only to be careful that we do it well, always saying *if this please God, let it be as it is*: and we, who pray that God's will may be done in earth as it is in heaven, must remember that the angels do whatsoever is commanded them, and go wherever they are sent, and refuse no circumstances: and if their employment be crossed by a higher decree, they sit down in peace and rejoice in the event; and when the Angel of Judæa could not prevail in behalf of the people committed to his charge, because the Angel of Persia opposed it, he only told the story at the command of God, and was as content, and worshipped with as great an ecstasy in his proportion as the prevailing Spirit. Do thou so likewise: keep the station where God hath placed you, and you shall never long for things without, but sit at home feasting upon the Divine Providence and thy own reason, by which we are taught that it is necessary and reasonable to submit to God.

For, is not all the world God's family? Are not we His

creatures? Are we not as clay in the hand of the potter? Do not we live upon His meat, and move by His strength, and do our work by His light? Are we anything but what we are from Him? And shall there be a mutiny among the flocks and herds because their Lord or their Shepherd chooses their pastures, and suffers them not to wander into deserts and unknown ways? If we choose, we do it so foolishly that we cannot like it long, and most commonly not at all: but God, who can do what He pleases, is wise to choose safely for us, affectionate to comply with our needs, and powerful to execute all His wise decrees. Here therefore is the wisdom of the contented man, to let God choose for him: for when we have given up our wills to Him, and stand in that station of the battle where our great General hath placed us, our spirits must needs rest while our conditions have for their security the power, the wisdom, and the charity of God.

Contentedness in all accidents brings great peace of spirit, and is the great and only instrument of temporal felicity. It removes the sting from the accident, and makes a man not to depend upon chance and the uncertain dispositions of men for his well-being, but only on God and his own spirit. We ourselves make our own fortunes good or bad; and when God lets loose a tyrant upon us, or a sickness, or scorn, or a lessened fortune, if we fear to die, or know not to be patient, or are proud, or covetous, then the calamity sits heavy on us. But if we know how to manage a noble principle, and fear not death so much as a dishonest action, and think impatience a worse evil than a fever, and pride to be the biggest disgrace, and poverty to be infinitely desirable before the torments of covetousness; then we who now think vice to be so easy, and make it so familiar, and think the cure so impossible, shall quickly be of another mind, and reckon these accidents among things eligible.[1]

But no man can be happy that hath great hopes and great fears of things without, and events depending upon other men, or upon the chances of fortune. The rewards of virtue are certain, and our provisions for our natural support are certain; or if we want meat till we die, then we die of that disease, and there are many worse than to die with an atrophy or consumption, or unapt and coarser nourishment. But he

[1] *eligible*, desirable.

that suffers a transporting passion concerning things within the power of others is free from sorrow and amazement no longer than his enemy shall give him leave; and it is ten to one but he shall be smitten then and there where it shall most trouble him: for so the adder teaches us where to strike, by her curious and fearful defending of her head. The old Stoics when you told them of a sad story, would still answer: "τί πρὸς μέ; *What is that to me?*" "Yes, for the tyrant hath sentenced you also to prison." "Well, what is that? He will put a chain upon my leg, but he cannot bind my soul." "No: but he will kill you." "Then I'll die. If presently,[1] let me go, that I may presently be freer than himself: but if not till anon or to-morrow, I will dine first, or sleep, or do what reason and nature calls for, as at other times." This in Gentile philosophy is the same with the discourse of St Paul, *I have learned in whatsoever state I am therewith to be content. I know both how to be abased, and I know how to abound: everywhere and in all things I am instructed, both how to be full and how to be hungry, both to abound and suffer need.*

We are in the world like men playing at tables; the chance is not in our power, but to play it is; and when it is fallen we must manage it as we can; and let nothing trouble us, but when we do a base action, or speak like a fool, or think wickedly: these things God hath put into our powers; but concerning those things which are wholly in the choice of another, they cannot fall under our deliberation, and therefore neither are they fit for our passions. My fear may make me miserable, but it cannot prevent what another hath in his power and purpose: and prosperities can only be enjoyed by them who fear not at all to lose them; since the amazement and passion concerning the future takes off all the pleasure of the present possession. Therefore if thou hast lost thy land, do not also lose thy constancy: and if thou must die a little sooner, yet do not die impatiently. For no chance is evil to him that is content, and *to a man nothing miserable, unless it be unreasonable.* No man can make another man to be his slave, unless he hath first enslaved himself to life and death, to pleasure or pain, to hope or fear: command these passions, and you are freer than the Parthian kings.

[1] *presently*, immediately.

4. GEORGE MONCK

From *The Worthies of England* (1662): Thomas Fuller

Some will say he being (and long may he be) alive, belongs not to your pen, according to your premised rules. But, know, he is too high to come under the roof of my regulations, whose merit may make laws for me to observe. Besides, it is better that I should be censured, than he not commended. Pass we by his high birth (whereof hereafter) and hard breeding in the Low Countries, not commencing a captain *per saltum* (as many in our civil wars), but proceeding by degrees from a private soldier, in that martial university. Pass we also by his employment in Ireland, and imprisonment in England, for the king; his sea service against the Dutch; posting to speak of his last performance; which, should I be silent, would speak of itself.

Being made governor of Scotland, no power or policy of Oliver Cromwell could fright or flatter him thence. Scotland was his castle, from the top whereof he took the true prospect of our English affairs. He perceived that, since the martyrdom of king Charles, several sorts of government (like the sons of Jesse before Samuel) passed before the English people; but "neither God nor our nation had chosen them". He resolved, therefore, to send for despised David out of a foreign field; as well assured that the English loyalty would never be at rest till fixed in the centre thereof. He secured Scotland in faithful hands, to have all his foes before his face, and leave none behind his back.

He entered England with excellent foot; but his horse so lean, that they seemed tired at their first setting forth. The chiefest strength of his army consisted in the reputation of the strength thereof, and wise conduct of their general. The loyal English did rather gaze on, than pray for him, as ignorant of his intentions; and as the apostle observeth, "that the private man knoweth not how to say Amen to what is spoken in an unknown language".

Now the scales began to fall down from the eyes of the English nation (as from Saul, when his sight was received), sensible that they were deluded, with the pretences of religion and liberty, into atheism and vassalage. They had learnt also from the soldiers (whom they so long had quartered) to cry out "one and all"; each shire setting forth a remonstrance of their grievances, and refusing further payment of taxes.

Lambert cometh forth of London, abounding with more outward advantages than general Monck wanted; dragon-like, he breathed out nought but fire and fury, chiefly against the church and clergy. But he met with a Saint George, who struck him neither with sword nor spear; but gave his army a mortal wound, without wounding it. His soldiers dwindled away; and indeed a private person (Lambert at last was little more) must have a strong and long hand on his own account, to hold a whole army together.

The hinder part of the Parliament sitting still at Westminster, plied him with many messengers and addresses. He returned an answer, neither granting nor denying their desires; giving them hope, too little to trust, yet too much to distrust, him. He was an absolute riddle; and no ploughing with his heifer to expound him.[1] Indeed, had he appeared what he was, he had never been what he is, a deliverer of his country. But such must be as dark as midnight, who mean to achieve actions as bright as noon-day.

Then he was put on the unwelcome office to pluck down the gates of London, though it pleased God that the odium did not light on him that acted, but those who employed him. Henceforward he sided effectually with the City; I say the City, which, if well or ill affected, was then able to make us a happy or unhappy nation.

Immediately followed that turn of our times, which all the world with wonder doth behold. But let us not look so long on second causes, as to lose the sight of the principal, Divine Providence. Christ, on the cross, said to his beloved disciple, "Behold thy mother;" and said to her, "Behold thy son." Thus was he pleased effectually to speak to the hearts of the English, "Behold your sovereign;" which inspirited them with loyalty, and a longing desire of his presence; saying likewise to our gracious sovereign, "Behold thy subjects;" which increased his ardent affection to return; and now, blessed be God, both are met together, to their mutual comfort.

[1] *no ploughing with his heifer* ....From the story of Samson, Judges xiv. 18.

Since, the honours which he first deserved have been conferred upon him, completed with the title of "the Duke of Albemarle, and Master of his majesty's horse," &c. Nor must it be forgotten that he carried the sceptre with the dove thereupon (the emblem of peace) at the king's coronation. But abler pens will improve these short memoirs into a large history.

COMMENTARY

After the strenuous ardours of the Renaissance, and the heat and turmoil of Reformation controversy, it is restful to turn to the work of certain later Elizabethan writers who had the talent for quiet meditation devoid of bitterness and passion.

Sir Thomas Browne (1605–1682) settled at Norwich, where he acquired a reputation as a physician and antiquarian. His *Religio Medici* (1643) owes its charm to its richly poetic imaginativeness, its quaint erudition and marked individuality. In many respects it is a work typical of the English Renaissance; in it are united the inquiring spirit of a Bacon and the firm faith of a Milton. But the atmosphere is changed: the abounding vitality of the Renaissance has begun to flag, and Browne retires to the study to contemplate the "microcosm of his own frame". From his wide experience and profound knowledge of ancient lore he compounds a faith of his own, of which *Religio Medici* is the whimsical confession.

The new atmosphere is reflected in his style. Meditation has curbed that passionate impetuosity which could carry sentences of Milton's to the inordinate length of half a page. The prose of Browne is still that of a poetical age, and retains that picturesque quality which came of using words with a physical signification in preference to abstract or general terms (*I have seen a grammarian tower and plume himself*; *heads...such as are not full with a handful...of knowledge*); but it is more even, more restrained; its structure is more carefully balanced, its rhythm more cadenced. Browne's immense learning does not make him dogmatic. His diction is that of a classical scholar, but he is not a pedant: his sentence structure is easy and idiomatic. (Note the number of sentences ending with a preposition, e.g. *a place...to die in*; *cast my eye on*.)

In prose harmony Browne is one of our greatest masters: his language is magnificent, the accentual rhythm strongly marked and full of subtle variations, the distribution of pauses most skilful. He derives rhythmical effects from balance: *comprehended in a monosyllable...circumscribed with a word*; *petty acquisitions...reputed perfections*; and from the practice, common in the Prayer Book, of pairing synonyms: *inherit and hold*; *sweat and vexation*; *heavenly and celestial*. It is from considerations of rhythm that he wavers between the present tense with and without *do*: *Men that look upon my outside...do err*; and between the terminations *-eth* and *-s*: *comprehendeth not my mind*. Here the *-eth* form gives him the oft-recurring cadence –∪–∪–, as in *álphabét of mán, fírst and fáther sín, coúnt it nót a críme*.

A pious and reflective habit and a most lovable character are revealed in the *Compleat Angler*. *Izaak Walton*, a linen-draper, finding London during the troubled times of the Civil War little to his taste, retired into the country on a modest competency, and devoted himself to his interest in biography and fishing. The *Compleat Angler* was immediately popular, and in its own day was regarded as a useful manual. What he has to say about the handling of rod and line is still instructive; for the rest there is too little about fly-fishing and too much fantastic tradition mingled with his gossip about the habits of fish. But in his temperament Walton is the ideal companion of anglers, and his book has remained one of the choicest manuals on contentedness in our literature. "It breathes", says Lamb, "the very spirit of innocence, purity and simplicity of heart; it would sweeten a man's temper at any time to read it."

Walton's sentences have the length and diffuseness common in gossipy writers. His diction shows clearly the influence of the Bible. His style in general has the lyrical quality often found where men write more to please themselves than others. He had read much and could be very aptly reminiscent. His descriptions of rural life and scenery are like prose-versions of Elizabethan songs, and as long as men love the country Walton's words will sing in their hearts.

Jeremy Taylor (1613–1667) was the son of a barber. He went to Caius College, Cambridge, and at the early age of

twenty-two, obtained through Archbishop Laud a fellowship
at All Souls, Oxford. He was for a short time chaplain to
Charles I. During the Civil War and afterwards he lived in
South Wales under the protection of the Earl of Carbery,
but could not altogether escape the persecution of the Round-
heads. In 1657 he went to Ulster as a lecturer, but was
driven out by the Presbyterians. Under Charles II he went
back as Bishop of Dromore.

He combined nobility of character with great charm of
personality. He was a most persuasive preacher and a writer
of amazing diligence. In the spirit of contentedness which
he preached he bore his misfortunes during the Commonwealth with true Christian fortitude, and when the turn of
events put his persecutors in his power, he behaved with
laudable forbearance.

Holy Living (1650) vied with *Pilgrim's Progress* as a book
of devotion. There is the same very human quality of imagination, and in his similitudes the same freshness and homeliness.
(*God is the master of the scenes...* ; *And shall there be a mutiny
among the flocks and herds...?*; *We are in the world like men
playing at tables....*)

The style of Taylor is a curious blend: sometimes we are
startled with the Saxon forthrightness of the practical
preacher (*He were a strange fool...*); at other times we hear
echoes of the latinised splendour and magnificence of the
Elizabethan scholar, and of the rich imagery, melody and
lyrical quality of the poets. He stands somewhere between
Hooker and Bunyan, but he is not a model in either the plain
or the ornate manner. His sentences are too long and loosely
constructed. His eloquence was spontaneous and inspired
by genuine feeling, but he paid too little attention to the arts
by which harmony is attained.

Dr Thomas Fuller (1608–1661) was Rector of Broad Windsor
in Dorsetshire. He was a man of immense learning and an
eloquent preacher of great moderation. In 1643 he became
a chaplain in the King's army, and the roving nature of his

calling gave him ample opportunities of proceeding with a work which appeared (posthumously) in 1662 under the title of *The Worthies of England*. He took the death of the king so much to heart that he never completed the book. After the Restoration Charles II rewarded his loyalty by making him his chaplain, but he died soon after the appointment.

The Worthies of England is a curious work, original in plan and execution, with an individual style that reflects the personality of the author. The self-imposed task of honouring the distinguished men of England is reminiscent of what Hakluyt did for its mariners, and the methods he pursued were similar. "In what place soever...he came," says his biographer, "he spent most of his time in views and researches of their antiquities and church monuments; insinuating himself into the acquaintance...of the learnedst and gravest persons residing within the place." The way he handled the mass of information so obtained was a triumph of orderly arrangement that would have been a credit to the scientific mind of a Bacon. County by county he proceeds, in a fixed order, with brief biographies of the local notabilities, supplemented with jottings on topography and genealogy.

The structure of his prose, too, suggests comparison with Bacon. His sentences, never involved or intricate, have the same pregnant brevity; he has the same fondness for similes. But there the resemblance ceases. The most salient features of his style are the outcome of his eccentric character. The fact that he was a learned divine with antiquarian interests is reflected in his latinism, in his archaic and pedantic diction, strongly flavoured with biblical phraseology, and in his obscure allusions. He was a wit whose strong sense of the ludicrous led him to indulge in the most ingenious conceits and the quaintest mannerisms; he was fond of alliterative jingles, and he could not resist a pun, however outrageous (...*his high birth and hard breeding in the Low Countries*). He could give plain words an odd twist that made even truth look incongruous. No wonder he was to be an endless source of delight to Charles Lamb.

Chapter V

The Restoration

1. RESTORATION REFINEMENT

From *An Essay on the Dramatic Poetry of the Last Age* (1672):
John Dryden

And this leads me to the last and greatest advantage of our writing, which proceeds from *conversation....* Now, if they ask me, whence it is that our conversation is so much refined? I must freely, and without flattery, ascribe it to the court; and, in it, particularly to the king, whose example gives a law to it. His own misfortunes, and the nation's, afforded him an opportunity, which is rarely allowed to sovereign princes, I mean of travelling, and being conversant in the most polished courts of Europe; and thereby, of cultivating a spirit which was formed by nature to receive the impressions of a gallant and generous education. At his return, he found a nation lost as much in barbarism as in rebellion; and, as the excellency of his nature forgave the one, so the excellency of his manners reformed the other. The desire of imitating so great a pattern first awakened the dull and heavy spirits of the English from their natural reservedness; loosened them from their stiff forms of conversation, and made them easy and pliant to each other in discourse. Thus, insensibly, our way of living became more free; and the fire of the English wit, which was before stifled under a constrained, melancholy way of breeding, began first to display its force, by mixing the solidity of our nation with the air and gaiety of our neighbours....

Let us therefore admire the beauties and the heights of Shakespeare, without falling after him into a carelessness, and, as I may call it, a lethargy of thought, for whole scenes together. Let us imitate, as we are able, the quickness and easiness of Fletcher, without proposing him as a pattern to us, either in the redundancy of his matter, or the incorrectness of his language.... Let us ascribe to Jonson, the height and accuracy of judgment in the ordering of his plots, his choice of characters, and maintaining what he had chosen to the end. But let us not think him a perfect pattern of imitation, except it be in humour; for love, which is the foundation of all comedies in other languages, is scarcely mentioned in any of his plays; and for humour itself, the poets of this age will be more wary than to imitate the meanness of his persons. Gentlemen will now be entertained with the follies of each other; and, though they allow Cobb and Tib[1] to speak properly, yet they are not much pleased with their tankard or with their rags. And surely their conversation can be no jest to them on the theatre, when they would avoid it in the street.

To conclude all, let us render to our predecessors what is their due, without confining ourselves to a servile imitation of all they writ; and, without assuming to ourselves the title of better poets, let us ascribe to the gallantry and civility of our age the advantage which we have above them, and to our knowledge of the customs and manner of it the happiness we have to please beyond them.

[1] *Cobb and Tib*, a water-bearer and his wife, in Ben Jonson's *Everyman in His Humour*.

2. CHAUCER

From *Preface to Fables* (1700): John Dryden

In the first place, as he is the father of English poetry, so I
hold him in the same degree of veneration as the Grecians
held Homer, or the Romans Virgil. He is a perpetual
fountain of good sense; learned in all sciences; and therefore
speaks properly on all subjects. As he knew what to say, so
he knows also when to leave off, a continence which is
practised by few writers, and scarcely by any of the ancients,
excepting Virgil and Horace....

* * * * * * *

Chaucer followed nature everywhere; but was never so
bold to go beyond her: and there is a great difference of being
Poeta and *nimis Poeta*,[1] if we believe Catullus, as much as
betwixt a modest behaviour and affectation. The verse of
Chaucer, I confess, is not harmonious to us; but is like the
eloquence of one whom Tacitus commends, it was *auribus
istius temporis accommodata*: they who lived with him, and
some time after him, thought it musical; and it continues so,
even in our judgment, if compared with the numbers of
Lydgate and Gower, his contemporaries: there is the rude
sweetness of a Scotch tune in it, which is natural and pleasing,
though not perfect. 'Tis true, I cannot go so far as he who
published the last edition of him; for he would make us
believe the fault is in our ears, and that there were really ten
syllables in a verse where we find but nine: but this opinion
is not worth confuting; 'tis so gross and obvious an error, that
common sense (which is a rule in everything but matters of
Faith and Revelation) must convince the reader, that equality
of numbers, in every verse which we call heroic, was either
not known, or not always practised in Chaucer's age.[2] It

[1] *nimis Poeta*, overmuch a poet. The quotation is to be found not in
Catullus but in Martial. The next quotation, "adapted to the ears of that
period", is inaccurate, for Dryden, as he admits earlier in his preface,
relies on a memory which is impaired by years.

[2] Dryden's erroneous criticism of Chaucer's prosody is due to ignorance
of Middle English (see p. 15), in which the final -e was syllabic except
before another vowel. For example, Chaucer's

As lenë was his hors(e) as is a rake

is a perfect "heroic verse", but to Dryden it was "lame for want of half
a foot".

were an easy matter to produce some thousands of his verses, which are lame for want of half a foot, and sometimes a whole one, and which no pronunciation can make otherwise. We can only say, that he lived in the infancy of our poetry, and that nothing is brought to perfection at the first. We must be children before we grow men.

* * * * * * *

Chaucer must have been a man of a most wonderful comprehensive nature, because, as it has been truly observed of him, he has taken into the compass of his *Canterbury Tales* the various manners and humours (as we now call them) of the whole English nation, in his age. Not a single character has escaped him. All his pilgrims are severally distinguished from each other; and not only in their inclinations, but in their very physiognomies and persons. Baptista Porta[1] could not have described their natures better than by the marks which the poet gives them. The matter and manner of their tales and of their telling are so suited to their different educations, humours, and callings, that each of them would be improper in any other mouth. Even the grave and serious characters are distinguished by their several sorts of gravity: their discourses are such as belong to their age, their calling, and their breeding; such as are becoming of them, and of them only. Some of his persons are vicious, and some virtuous; some are unlearned or (as Chaucer calls them) lewd, and some are learned. Even the ribaldry of the low characters is different: the Reeve, the Miller, and the Cook are several men, and distinguished from each other, as much as the mincing lady Prioress and the broad-speaking gaptoothed Wife of Bath. But enough of this: there is such a variety of game springing up before me, that I am distracted in my choice, and know not which to follow. 'Tis sufficient to say, according to the proverb, that here is God's plenty. We have our forefathers and great-grandames all before us, as they were in Chaucer's days; their general characters are still remaining in mankind, and even in England, though they are called by other names than those of Monks, and Friars, and Canons, and Lady Abbesses, and Nuns: for mankind is ever the same, and nothing lost out of nature, though everything is altered.

[1] *Baptista Porta*, a famous Italian physiognomist.

3. CHRISTIAN IN DOUBTING CASTLE

From *The Pilgrim's Progress* (1678): John Bunyan

Now, there was, not far from the place where they lay, a castle, called Doubting Castle, the owner whereof was Giant Despair, and it was in his grounds they were now sleeping; whereof he, getting up in the morning early, and walking up and down in his fields, caught Christian and Hopeful asleep in his grounds. Then, with a grim and surly voice, he bid them awake, and asked them whence they were, and what they did in his grounds. They told him that they were pilgrims, and that they had lost their way. Then said the giant, "You have this night trespassed on me by trampling in and lying on my grounds, and therefore must ye go along with me." So they were forced to go, because he was stronger than they. They also had but little to say, for they knew themselves in fault. The giant, therefore, drove them before him, and put them into his castle, into a very dark dungeon, nasty, and stinking to the spirit of these two men. Here, then, they lay from Wednesday morning till Saturday night, without one bit of bread or drop of drink, or light, or any to ask how they did....

Now, Giant Despair had a wife, and her name was Diffidence: so, when he was gone to bed, he told his wife what he had done; to wit, that he had taken a couple of prisoners, and cast them into his dungeon for trespassing on his grounds. Then he asked her also what he had best to do further to them. So she asked him what they were, whence they came, and whither they were bound; and he told her. Then she counselled him, that when he arose in the morning, he should beat them without any mercy. So when he arose, he getteth him a grievous crab-tree cudgel, and goes down into the dungeon to them, and there first falls to rating of them as if they were dogs, although they never gave him a word of distaste. Then he falls upon them, and beats them fearfully, in such sort that they were not able to help themselves, or to turn them upon the floor. This done, he withdraws and leaves them there to condole their misery, and to mourn under their

distress; so all that day they spent their time in nothing but
sighs and bitter lamentations. The next night she, talking
with her husband about them further, and understanding
that they were yet alive, did advise him to counsel them to
make away with themselves. So, when morning was come,
he goes to them in a surly manner as before, and, perceiving
them to be very sore with the stripes that he had given them
the day before, he told them that, since they were never like
to come out of that place, their only way would be forthwith
to make an end of themselves, either with knife, halter, or
poison: "For why", said he, "should you choose life, seeing
it is attended with so much bitterness?" But they desired
him to let them go. With that, he looked ugly upon them, and
rushing to them, had doubtless made an end of them himself,
but that he fell into one of his fits (for he sometimes, in sun-
shiny weather, fell into fits), and lost for a time the use of his
hand; wherefore he withdrew, and left them as before to
consider what to do....Towards evening, the giant goes
down into the dungeon again, to see if his prisoners had
taken his counsel. But, when he came there, he found them
alive; and truly, alive was all; for now, what for want of
bread and water, and by reason of the wounds they received
when he beat them, they could do little but breathe. But I
say, he found them alive; at which, he fell into a grievous rage,
and told them, that, seeing they had disobeyed his counsel,
it should be worse with them than if they had never been born.
   At this they trembled greatly, and I think that Christian
fell into a swoon; but, coming a little to himself again, they
renewed their discourse about the giant's counsel, and
whether yet they had best take it or no. Now, Christian again
seemed for doing it; but Hopeful made his reply as followeth:
   "My brother," said he, "rememberest thou not how valiant
thou hast been heretofore? Apollyon could not crush thee,
nor could all that thou didst hear, or see, or feel in the Valley
of the Shadow of Death. What hardship, terror, and amazement hast thou already gone through! and art thou now
nothing but fear? Thou seest that I am in the dungeon with
thee, a far weaker man by nature than thou art. Also this
giant has wounded me as well as thee, and hath also cut off
the bread and water from my mouth, and, with thee, I mourn

without the light. But let us exercise a little more patience. Remember how thou playedst the man at Vanity Fair, and wast neither afraid of the chain, nor cage, nor yet of bloody death: wherefore, let us (at least to avoid the shame that it becomes not a Christian to be found in) bear up with patience as well as we can."

Now, night being come again, and the giant and his wife being in bed, she asked him concerning the prisoners, and if they had taken his counsel: to which he replied, "They are sturdy rogues; they choose rather to bear all hardship than to make away with themselves." Then said she, "Take them into the castle-yard to-morrow, and show them the bones and skulls of those thou hast already despatched; and make them believe, ere a week comes to an end, thou wilt tear them also in pieces, as thou hast done their fellows before them."

So, when the morning was come, the giant goes to them again, and takes them into the castle-yard, and shows them as his wife had bidden him. "These", said he, "were pilgrims, as you are, once, and they trespassed in my grounds as you have done; and, when I thought fit, I tore them in pieces; and so, within ten days, I will do you: go, get you down to your den again." And, with that, he beat them all the way thither. They lay, therefore, all day on Saturday in a lamentable case as before. Now, when night was come, and when Mrs Diffidence and her husband, the giant, were got to bed, they began to renew their discourse of their prisoners; and withal, the old giant wondered, that he could neither by his blows nor counsel bring them to an end. And, with that, his wife replied, "I fear", said she, "that they live in hope that some will come to relieve them; or that they have pick-locks about them, by the means of which they hope to escape." "And sayest thou so, my dear?" said the giant: "I will therefore search them in the morning."

Well, on Saturday, about midnight, they began to pray, and continued in prayer till almost break of day.

Now, a little before it was day, good Christian, as one half amazed, brake out into this passionate speech: "What a fool", quoth he, "am I to lie in a stinking dungeon, when I may as well walk at liberty! I have a key in my bosom called Promise, that will, I am persuaded, open any lock in Doubting Castle."

Then said Hopeful, "That's good news; good brother, pluck it out of thy bosom and try."

Then Christian pulled it out of his bosom, and began to try at the dungeon-door, whose bolt, as he turned the key, gave back, and the door flew open with ease, and Christian and Hopeful both came out. Then he went to the outward door that leads into the castle-yard, and with his key opened that door also. After, he went to the iron gate, for that must be opened too; but that lock went damnable hard, yet the key did open it. Then they thrust open the gate to make their escape with speed; but that gate, as it opened, made such a creaking, that it waked Giant Despair, who, hastily rising to pursue his prisoners, felt his limbs to fail; for his fits took him again, so that he could by no means go after them. Then they went on, and came to the King's highway again, and so were safe, because they were out of his jurisdiction.

4. A MARRIAGE BARGAIN

From *The Way of the World* (1700): William Congreve

Enter MIRABELL

Mirabell. "Like Daphne she, as lovely and as coy." Do you lock yourself up from me, to make my search more curious? or is this pretty artifice contrived to signify that here the chase must end, and my pursuits be crowned? For you can fly no further.

Mrs Millamant. Vanity! no—I'll fly, and be followed to the last moment. Though I am upon the verge of matrimony, I expect you should solicit me as much as if I were wavering at the grate of a monastery, with one foot over the threshold. I'll be solicited to the very last, nay, and afterwards.

Mir. What, after the last?

Mrs Mil. Oh, I should think I was poor and had nothing to bestow, if I were reduced to an inglorious ease, and freed from the agreeable fatigues of solicitation.

Mir. But do not you know, that when favours are conferred upon instant[1] and tedious solicitation, that they diminish in their value, and that both the giver loses the grace, and the receiver lessens his pleasure?

Mrs Mil. It may be in things of common application; but never sure in love. Oh, I hate a lover that can dare to think he draws a moment's air, independent of the bounty of his mistress. There is not so impudent a thing in nature, as the saucy look of an assured man, confident of success. The pedantic arrogance of a very husband has not so pragmatical[2] an air. Ah! I'll never marry, unless I am first made sure of my will and pleasure....My dear liberty, shall I leave thee? my faithful solitude, my darling contemplation, must I bid you then adieu? Ay-h adieu—my morning thoughts, agreeable wakings, indolent slumbers, all ye *douceurs*,[3] ye *sommeils du matin*,[4] adieu?—I can't do't, 'tis more than impossible— positively, Mirabell, I'll lie abed in a morning as long as I please.

[1] *instant*, pressing, insistent.　　　　[2] *pragmatical*, self-important.
[3] *douceurs*, all that is soft and soothing.
[4] *sommeils du matin*, morning slumbers.

Mir. Then I'll get up in a morning as early as I please.

Mrs Mil. Ah! idle creature, get up when you will—and d'ye hear, I won't be called names after I'm married; positively I won't be called names.

Mir. Names!

Mrs Mil. Ay, as wife, spouse, my dear, joy, jewel, love, sweetheart, and the rest of that nauseous cant, in which men and their wives are so fulsomely familiar—I shall never bear that—good Mirabell, don't let us be familiar or fond, nor kiss before folks, like my Lady Fadler and Sir Francis: nor go to Hyde-park together the first Sunday in a new chariot, to provoke eyes and whispers, and then never to be seen there together again; as if we were proud of one another the first week, and ashamed of one another ever after. Let us never visit together, nor go to a play together; but let us be very strange and well bred: let us be as strange as if we had been married a great while; and as well bred as if we were not married at all.

Mir. Have you any more conditions to offer? Hitherto your demands are pretty reasonable.

Mrs Mil. Trifles!—As liberty to pay and receive visits to and from whom I please; to write and receive letters, without interrogatories or wry faces on your part; to wear what I please; and choose conversation with regard only to my own taste; to have no obligation upon me to converse with wits that I don't like, because they are your acquaintance; or to be intimate with fools, because they may be your relations. Come to dinner when I please; dine in my dressing-room when I'm out of humour, without giving a reason. To have my closet inviolate; to be sole empress of my tea-table, which you must never presume to approach without first asking leave. And lastly, wherever I am, you shall always knock at the door before you come in. These articles subscribed, if I continue to endure you a little longer, I may by degrees dwindle into a wife.

Mir. Your bill of fare is something advanced in this latter account.—Well, have I liberty to offer conditions—that when you are dwindled into a wife, I may not be beyond measure enlarged into a husband?

Mrs Mil. You have free leave; propose your utmost, speak and spare not.

Mir. I thank you.—*Imprimis* then, I covenant, that your acquaintance be general; that you admit no sworn confidant, or intimate of your own sex; no she-friend to screen her affairs under your countenance, and tempt you to make trial of a mutual secrecy. No decoy duck to wheedle you a fop-scrambling to the play in a mask—then bring you home in a pretended fright, when you think you shall be found out—and rail at me for missing the play, and disappointing the frolic which you had to pick me up, and prove my constancy.

Mrs Mil. Detestable *imprimis*! I go to the play in a mask!

Mir. *Item*,[1] I article, that you continue to like your own face, as long as I shall: and while it passes current with me, that you endeavour not to new-coin it. Lastly, to the dominion of the tea-table I submit—but with proviso, that you exceed not in your province; but restrain yourself to native and simple tea-table drinks, as tea, chocolate, and coffee: as likewise to genuine and authorised tea-table talk—such as mending of fashions, spoiling reputations, railing at absent friends, and so forth—but that on no account you encroach upon the men's prerogative, and presume to drink healths, or toast fellows; for prevention of which I banish all foreign forces, all auxiliaries to the tea-table, as orange-brandy, all aniseed, cinnamon, citron, and Barbadoes waters,[2] together with ratafia,[3] and the most noble spirit of clary[4]—but for cowslip wine, poppy water, and all dormitives,[5] those I allow. —These provisos admitted, in other things I may prove a tractable and complying husband.

Mrs Mil. O horrid provisos! filthy strong-waters! I toast fellows! odious men! I hate your odious provisos.

Mir. Then we are agreed! shall I kiss your hand upon the contract?

---

[1] *Item*, moreover.
[2] *Barbadoes waters*, a cordial flavoured with orange peel.
[3] *ratafia*, a liqueur flavoured with fruit kernels.
[4] *spirit of clary*, made from steeping clary flowers in brandy.
[5] *dormitives*, medicines causing sleep.

COMMENTARY

To do justice to the literature of the Restoration one must be prepared to make allowances for the licentious frivolity of the times. This was but a passing phase which can be readily accounted for. During the Civil War, letters had fallen into a decline, and the party which afterwards came into power had a puritanical bias against the arts. When, amidst national rejoicings, Charles II and the companions of his long exile were welcomed back to England, the pent-up flood of literature hurled itself with the violence of reaction against the intolerance of the Puritans. The most powerful influence was that of the court, to which time-serving writers were only too prone to pander, and the new fashion, led by the king, to mock at virtue and to regard sound morals as tedious, was tolerated by the whole of society.

This cynical disregard for virtue was coupled with a worldly-wiseness which set greater store by the reason than the imagination. Conditions were inimical to the true spirit of poetry; good verse was written, but there was no place for the joyous enthusiasms, for the wide and splendid vision of the Elizabethans. In comparison, therefore, the outlook of Restoration writers appears narrow and limited, and their work pedestrian.

The changes in literature that were the response to the new outlook were hastened by external events. The court had spent many years at Versailles, acquiring an intense admiration for the sprightliness and elegance of the French. So long as English prose aped the floridity of the Italian or the magnificence of the Latin, it would have continued to be marred by ingenious conceits and excessive ornateness. In taking the French for their model, the new writers, whatever their shortcomings, initiated a reform already overdue. At last it was realised that the first duty of prose is the clear and concise expression of correct thinking.

The result is the birth of modern prose. The literature of

the Elizabethans had been an appeal to the imagination and emotions. Its poetical qualities overflowed into its prose; its strength was an impassioned eloquence; its weakness, an inability to tell a plain story in a plain way. Two factors combined to prepare the ground for the new prose: firstly, the matter-of-fact mentality that engendered a scientific and critical habit; and secondly, the fact that the arbiters of taste were no longer scholars or mere pedants, but wits of the court, who, though an exclusive class, brought literature a stage nearer to everyday interests. What they wrote was more like the spoken language than ever before, a refinement of the natural idiom. A point had occurred when suddenly it was realised that the influences which had been moulding the language had "resulted in an appropriateness: in a fit relation of sound, sense, and conversational ease".[1] Hence the new style was adopted with unanimity; it is common to Dryden discussing Dramatic Poesy and to Congreve laughing at the foibles of the smart set. The ideals of the Royal Society, "positive expressions, clear sense, and a native easiness", became the tradition by which English prose has since been guided. The previous century had been experimental and formative, a period of idiosyncrasy, each writer a law unto himself. Syntax had been elastic, vocabulary capable of infinite expansion. From round about 1660 the language tends to become fixed in form, and more prone to discard what is superfluous and eccentric than eager to welcome innovation; its growth is by development of existing resources within the limits of tradition.

Almost the whole of the prose of *John Dryden* (1631-1700) consists of literary criticism found in the dedications and prefaces to his poetry. "Restoration Refinement" is rather complacent in tone, but Dryden's assumption of superior qualities is much suaver than that of the dogmatic Milton. His eulogy of Chaucer is proof of catholic taste and unusual independence of judgment.

[1] Herbert Read, *English Prose Style*, chap. XIV.

To read Dryden immediately after Milton gives one the measure of the change that had come about in style. With the slight alteration of a word or phrase here and there, what Dryden wrote might easily pass for the prose of a present-day writer. His sentences have, as he claims for those of his contemporaries, the easy flow of good conversation; they combine vigour with urbanity, familiarity with dignity; they blend the solidity of the English with the "air and gaiety" of the French. He is in conscious revolt against the excessive length of the sentences of his predecessors, breaking them up with heavy pauses, which ensure clarity. (Cf. *The verse of Chaucer...though not perfect*, p. 102.) Conscious of the newly realised distinction between the scope of prose and that of poetry, he avoids poetical expressions, and is less figurative than many writers who never penned a line of verse.

John Bunyan (1628–1688), the son of a tinker, was born at Elstow, near Bedford. He served as a soldier during the Civil War. After the Restoration he was "converted", was arrested for unlicensed preaching, and spent the greater part of eleven years in Bedford jail. There he is believed to have written *Pilgrim's Progress*, published in 1678. He owed less to literary training than any other English writer, but he had the Bible by heart. Within the narrow limits of his experience he was a shrewd observer of men and manners, with a penetrating insight into character. The spiritual phenomenon of his conversion had been as vivid as that of St Paul, and he thought and felt with the intensity of one who lives in the presence of the miraculous. His Puritan convictions forced on him a sense of the overwhelming burden of guilt, and he became obsessed with the moral obligation to repress the natural instincts and the impulses of a sanguine heartiness.

Pilgrim's Progress is the record of this inner conflict; it is a chain of adventures in which the hero is at war with himself. Though not the first allegory of its kind, it is the greatest, because it carries the conviction of immediate experience. So unstrained are the analogies on which its symbolism is based, so life-like are the objective forms with which he clothes his abstractions, that the story has all the moving force of reality. In addition to this faculty of creative imagination, Bunyan has the dramatist's gift of delineating character progressively in racy colloquial dialogue, enlivened by gleams of humour and touches of satire; he has the novelists' ease of invention both of character and incident, and a command of telling phrase. In his taste for fact he is a child of the age; even his visions have a background of English landscape. He can be as realistic as Defoe, and like the latter he knew the power to convince that lies in the use of minute detail.

His writing is a model of the plain style. He knew no Latin and no foreign language. Hence his diction is predominantly Saxon and monosyllabic. His sentences, without being diffuse, have an easy flow, and their structure is devoid of conscious artifice. His idiom is that of the spoken language coloured by the phraseology and imagery of the Bible, and illuminated by natural wit and a genius for compelling phrase.

Note, in the passage selected, the clever delineation of character. Giant Despair might so easily have remained a mere abstraction, or at best a figure out of a fairy tale. But he is a real landowner, who rises early to guard his rights, and who has the law on his side as he proceeds against trespassers; in private he is a very ordinary mortal, who talks to his wife in bed, and, for all his bluster, is subject to fainting-fits. Note also the naturalness of the dialogue; the touches of realism in the use of detail: the mention of the exact days, "from Wednesday morning till Saturday night"; the "grievous *crab-tree* cudgel"; the lock "that went *damnable* hard"; "the *King's highway*".

William Congreve was born in 1670 at Bardsey, near Leeds. He came of good Cavalier stock settled in Ireland. From the University of Dublin he came to London, ostensibly to study law, but he had few interests outside the world of literature and fashion. His reputation as a wit was established with his first play, produced in 1693. In 1698 Jeremy Collier wrote his famous pamphlet, *A Short View of the Profaneness and Immorality of the English Stage*, as the result of which Restoration comedy, never really popular, ceased to be fashionable. Hence *The Way of the World* was only a partial success, and the author, at the age of thirty, retired from literature. Thereafter he lived on government sinecures, and remained till his death in 1729 a notable figure in society, and the friend of great writers like Addison and Pope.

Congreve is our most brilliant exponent of the kind of drama known as the comedy of repartee, a type as artificial as the glittering society it portrays. If it is true that he, in the words of Macaulay, "knew human nature only as it appears between Hyde Park and The Tower", it was because his aims and interest extended no further. The portrayal of the passions, the delineation of the humours, the correction of manners and morals by means of serious satire were aims inconsistent with the suavity of the well-bred. His comedies have for their chief claim to distinction the brilliance of the dialogue, which is the quintessence of Restoration prose. It is trenchant without straining after effect and brilliant without mechanical artifices of style. It has a lightness and deftness of touch, a variety of rhythm and pace that had never been achieved before. "It exhibits", says Hazlitt, "all the sprightliness, ease and animation of familiar conversation with the correctness and delicacy of the most finished composition."

Chapter VI

The Eighteenth Century

1. *A TALE OF A TUB* (1704)[1]

Jonathan Swift

We left Lord Peter[2] in open rupture[3] with his two brethren; both for ever discarded from his house, and resigned to the wide world, with little or nothing to trust to.... The two exiles, so nearly united in fortune and interest, took a lodging together, where, at their first leisure, they began to reflect on the numberless misfortunes and vexations of their life past, and could not tell on the sudden, to what failure in their conduct they ought to impute them, when, after some recollection, they called to mind the copy of their father's will,[4] which they had so happily recovered.[5] This was immediately produced, and a firm resolution taken between them, to alter whatever was already amiss, and reduce all their future measures to the strictest obedience prescribed therein. The main body of the will...consisted in certain admirable rules about the wearing of their coats,[6] in the perusal whereof, the two brothers, at every period, duly comparing the doctrine with the practice, there was never seen a wider difference between two things, horrible downright transgressions of every point. Upon which they both resolved, without further delay, to fall immediately upon reducing the whole, exactly after their father's model....

[1] (S.) is appended to notes taken from the edition of Sir Walter Scott.
[2] *Lord Peter*, Roman Catholicism.
[3] *in open rupture*, at the time of the Reformation.
[4] *their father's will*, the New Testament.
[5] *so happily recovered.* The will had been "locked up in a strong box, brought out of Greece or Italy", an allusion to the ban on the use of scripture in the vernacular.
[6] *wearing of their coats*, the coats bequeathed to the sons, with an implied injunction not to alter them, are the original doctrines of Christianity.

These two brothers began to be distinguished at this time by certain names. One of them desired to be called MARTIN,[1] and the other took the appellation of JACK.[2] These two had lived in much friendship and agreement, under the tyranny of their brother Peter, as it is the talent of fellow-sufferers to do; men in misfortune being like men in the dark, to whom all colours are the same. But when they came forward into the world, and began to display themselves to each other, and to the light, their complexions appeared extremely different, which the present posture of their affairs gave them sudden opportunity to discover....

I ought in method to have informed the reader, about fifty pages ago, of a fancy Lord Peter took, and infused into his brothers, to wear on their coats whatever trimmings came up in fashion; never pulling off any, as they went out of the mode, but keeping on altogether, which amounted in time to a medley the most antic[3] you can possibly conceive, and this to a degree, that upon the time of their falling out, there was hardly a thread of the original coat to be seen, but an infinite quantity of lace and ribbons, and fringe, and embroidery, and points;[4] (I mean only those tagged with silver, for the rest fell off). Now this material circumstance having been forgot in due place, as good fortune hath ordered, comes in very properly here, when the two brothers were just going to reform their vestures into the primitive state, prescribed by their father's will.

They both unanimously entered upon this great work, looking sometimes on their coats, and sometimes on the will. Martin laid the first hand; at one twitch brought off a large handful of points; and, with a second pull, stripped away ten dozen yards of fringe.[5] But when he had gone thus far, he demurred a while: he knew very well there yet remained a great deal more to be done; however, the first heat being over, his violence began to cool, and he resolved to proceed more

---

[1] *Martin*, Martin Luther.

[2] *Jack*, John Calvin.

[3] *antic*, old and quaint.

[4] *embroidery, and points.* Points of doctrine for which, it is suggested, there is no authority; and particularly those (*tagged with silver*) by which the revenue of the Church is increased.

[5] *ten dozen yards of fringe.* "Alluding to the commencement of the Reformation in England, by seizing on the abbey lands." (S.)

moderately in the rest of the work; having already narrowly escaped a swinging rent,[1] in pulling off the points, which, being tagged with silver (as we have observed before) the judicious workman had, with much sagacity, double sewn, to preserve them from falling. Resolving therefore to rid his coat of a great quantity of gold-lace, he picked up the stitches with much caution, and diligently gleaned out all the loose threads as he went, which proved to be a work of time. Then he fell about the embroidered Indian figures of men, women, and children,[2] against which...their father's testament was extremely exact and severe: these, with much dexterity and application, were, after a while, quite eradicated, or utterly defaced. For the rest, where he observed the embroidery to be worked so close, as not to be got away without damaging the cloth, or where it served to hide or strengthen any flaw in the body of the coat, contracted by the perpetual tampering of workmen upon it; he concluded, the wisest course was to let it remain,[3] resolving in no case whatsoever, that the substance of the stuff should suffer injury, which he thought the best method for serving the true intent and meaning of his father's will. And this is the nearest account I have been able to collect of Martin's proceedings upon this great revolution.

But his brother Jack, whose adventures will be so extraordinary, as to furnish a great part of the remainder of this discourse, entered upon the matter with other thoughts, and a quite different spirit. For the memory of Lord Peter's injuries, produced a degree of hatred and spite, which had a much greater share of inciting him, than any regards after his father's commands, since these appeared, at best, only secondary and subservient to the other. However, for this medley of humour, he made a shift to find a very plausible name, honouring it with the title of zeal; which is perhaps the most significant word that has been ever yet produced in any language;...

[1] *a swinging rent.* "The dissolution of the monasteries occasioned several insurrections and much convulsion, during the reign of Edward VI." (S.)
[2] *Indian figures of men, women, and children.* The images of saints, the Virgin and the infant child. "The abolition of the worship of saints was the second grand step in the English reformation." (S.)
[3] *to let it remain.* An allusion to the spirit of compromise which brought about religious settlement under Elizabeth.

I record, therefore, that brother Jack, brimful of this miraculous compound, reflecting with indignation upon Peter's tyranny, and farther provoked by the despondency of Martin, prefaced his resolutions to this purpose. "What!" said he, "a rogue that locked up his drink,[1] turned away our wives,[2] cheated us of our fortunes; palmed his damned crusts[3] upon us for mutton; and, at last, kicked us out of doors; must we be in his fashions, with a pox? A rascal, besides, that all the street cries out against." Having thus kindled and inflamed himself, as high as possible, and by consequence in a delicate temper for beginning a reformation, he set about the work immediately; and in three minutes made more dispatch than Martin had done in as many hours. For, (courteous reader), you are given to understand, that zeal is never so highly obliged, as when you set it a-tearing; and Jack, who doated on that quality in himself, allowed it at this time its full swing. Thus it happened, that, stripping down a parcel of gold lace a little too hastily, he rent the main body[4] of his coat from top to bottom; and whereas his talent was not of the happiest in taking up a stitch, he knew no better way, than to darn it again with packthread and a skewer. But the matter was yet infinitely worse (I record it with tears) when he proceeded to the embroidery: for, being clumsy by nature, and of temper impatient; withal, beholding millions of stitches that required the nicest hand, and sedatest constitution, to extricate; in a great rage he tore off the whole piece, cloth and all, and flung them into the kennel,[5] and furiously thus continuing his career. "Ah! good master Martin," said he, "do as I do,[6] for the love of God; strip,

[1] *locked up his drink.* The withholding of the cup from the laity.

[2] *turned away our wives.* The celibacy of the clergy.

[3] *palmed...crusts.* An allusion to the doctrine of transubstantiation.

[4] *rent the main body.* "The reformers in Scotland left their established clergy in an almost beggarly condition, from the hasty violence with which they seized on all the possessions of the Romish Church." (S.)

[5] *flung them into the kennel.* "The presbyterians, in discarding forms of prayers, and unnecessary church ceremonies, disused even those founded in scripture." (S.) *Kennel*, drain.

[6] *do as I do.* "The presbyterians were particularly anxious to extend their church government into England. This was the bait held out by the English parliament to prevail on the Scots to invade England in 1643." (S.)

tear, pull, rend, flay off all, that we may appear as unlike the rogue Peter as it is possible. I would not, for a hundred pounds, carry the least mark about me, that might give occasion to the neighbours of suspecting that I was related to such a rascal." But Martin, who at this time happened to be extremely phlegmatic and sedate, begged his brother, of all love, not to damage his coat by any means; for he never would get such another: desired him to consider, that it was not their business to form their actions by any reflection upon Peter, but by observing the rules prescribed in their father's will. That he should remember, Peter was still their brother, whatever faults or injuries he had committed; and therefore they should, by all means, avoid such a thought as that of taking measures for good and evil, from no other rule than of opposition to him. That it was true, the testament of their good father was very exact in what related to the wearing of their coats; yet it was no less penal, and strict, in prescribing agreement, and friendship, and affection between them. And therefore, if straining a point were at all dispensible, it would certainly be so, rather to the advance of unity, than increase of contradiction.

2. THE SPECTATOR CLUB (1710)

Richard Steele

The first of our society is a gentleman of *Worcestershire*, of antient descent, a baronet, his name Sir ROGER DE COVERLEY. His great grandfather was inventor of that famous country-dance which is call'd after him. All who know that shire are very well acquainted with the parts[1] and merits of Sir ROGER. He is a gentleman that is very singular in his behaviour, but his singularities proceed from his good sense, and are contradictions to the manners of the world, only as he thinks the world is in the wrong. However, this humour creates him no enemies, for he does nothing with sourness or obstinacy; and his being unconfined to modes and forms, makes him but the readier and more capable to please and oblige all who know him. When he is in town he lives in *Soho-Square*: It is said, he keeps himself a batchelor by reason he was crossed in love, by a perverse beautiful widow of the next county to him. Before this disappointment, Sir ROGER was what you call a fine gentleman, had often supped with my Lord *Rochester*[2] and Sir *George Etherege*,[3] fought a duel upon his first coming to town, and kick'd Bully *Dawson* in a publick coffee-house for calling him youngster. But being ill used by the above-mentioned widow, he was very serious for a year and a half; and though, his temper being naturally jovial, he at last got over it, he grew careless of himself, and never dressed afterwards; he continues to wear a coat and doublet of the same cut that were in fashion at the time of his repulse, which, in his merry humours, he tells us, has been in and out twelve times since he first wore it. He is now in his fifty sixth year, cheerful, gay, and hearty, keeps a good house both in town and country; a great lover of mankind; but there is such a mirthful cast in his behaviour, that he is rather beloved than esteemed: his tenants grow rich, his servants look satisfied, all the young women profess love to him, and the young men

[1] *parts*, qualities.
[2] *Lord Rochester*, a licentious poet, died in 1680.
[3] *Etherege*, a Restoration dramatist.

are glad of his Company: when he comes into a house he calls the servants by their names, and talks all the way up stairs to a visit. I must not omit that Sir Roger is a justice of the *quorum*;[1] that he fills the chair at a Quarter-Session with great abilities, and three months ago gain'd universal applause by explaining a passage in the Game-Act.

The gentleman next in esteem and authority among us, is another batchelor, who is a member of the *Inner Temple*; a man of great probity, wit, and understanding; but he has chosen his place of residence rather to obey the direction of an old humoursom[2] father, than in pursuit of his own inclinations. He was placed there to study the laws of the land, and is the most learned of any of the house in those of the stage. *Aristotle*[3] and *Longinus*[4] are much better understood by him than *Littleton* or *Cooke*.[5] The father sends up every post questions relating to marriage-articles, leases, and tenures, in the neighbourhood; all which questions he agrees with an attorney to answer and take care of in the lump: He is studying the passions themselves, when he should be inquiring into the debates among men which arise from them. He knows the argument of each of the orations of *Demosthenes* and *Tully*, but not one case in the reports of our own courts. No one ever took him for a fool, but none, except his intimate friends, know he has a great deal of wit. This turn makes him at once both disinterested and agreeable: As few of his thoughts are drawn from business, they are most of them fit for conversation. His taste of books is a little too just for the age he lives in; he has read all, but approves of very few. His familiarity with the customs, manners, actions, and writings of the antients, makes him a very delicate observer of what occurs to him in the present world. He is an excellent critick, and the time of the play is his hour of business; exactly at five he passes thro' *New-Inn*, crosses thro' *Russel-Court*, and takes a turn at *Will's* till the play begins; he has his shoes rubbed and his perriwig powder'd at the barber's as

[1] *justice of the quorum*, a county magistrate.
[2] *humoursom*, whimsical.
[3] *Aristotle*: an allusion to Aristotle's *Poetics*.
[4] *Longinus*, a Greek philosopher who wrote *On the Sublime*.
[5] *Littleton or Cooke*. Chief Justice Coke, who served under James I, wrote a commentary on Littleton's *Tenures*, a much earlier work.

you go into the *Rose*. It is for the good of the audience when he is at a play, for the actors have an ambition to please him.

The person of next consideration is Sir ANDREW FREEPORT, a merchant of great eminence in the city of *London*. A person of indefatigable industry, strong reason, and great experience. His notions of trade are noble and generous, and (as every rich man has usually some sly way of jesting, which would make no great figure were he not a rich man) he calls the sea the *British Common*. He is acquainted with commerce in all its parts, and will tell you that it is a stupid and barbarous way to extend dominion by arms; for true power is to be got by arts and industry. He will often argue, that if this part of our trade were well cultivated, we should gain from one nation; and if another, from another. I have heard him prove, that diligence makes more lasting acquisitions than valour, and that sloth has ruined more nations than the sword. He abounds in several frugal maxims, among which the greatest favourite is, "A penny saved is a penny got". A general trader of good sense, is pleasanter company than a general scholar; and Sir ANDREW having a natural unaffected eloquence, the perspicuity of his discourse gives the same pleasure that wit would in another man. He has made his fortunes himself; and says that *England* may be richer than other kingdoms, by as plain methods as he himself is richer than other men; tho' at the same time I can say this of him, that there is not a point in the compass but blows home a ship in which he is an owner.

Next to Sir ANDREW in the club-room sits Captain SENTRY, a gentleman of great courage, good understanding, but invincible modesty. He is one of those that deserve very well, but are very awkward at putting their talents within the observation of such as should take notice of them. He was some years a captain, and behaved himself with great gallantry in several engagements, and at several sieges; but having a small estate of his own, and being next heir to Sir ROGER, he has quitted a way of life in which no man can rise suitably to his merit, who is not something of a courtier as well as a soldier. I have heard him often lament, that in a profession where merit is placed in so conspicuous a view, impudence should get the better of modesty. When he has talked to this purpose I never heard him make a sour expression, but frankly confess that he left the world, because he was not fit for it. A strict honesty and an even regular behaviour, are in themselves obstacles to him that must press through crowds, who endeavour at the same end with himself, the favour of a commander. He will however in his way of talk excuse generals, for not disposing according to mens desert, or inquiring into it: For, says he, that great man who has a mind to help me, has as many to break through to come at me, as I have to come to him: therefore he will conclude, that the man who would make a figure, especially in a military way, must get over all false modesty, and assist his patron against the importunity of other pretenders,[1] by a proper assurance in his own vindication. He says it is a civil cowardice to be backward in asserting what you ought to expect, as it is a military fear to be slow in attacking when it is your duty. With this candour does the gentleman speak of himself and others. The same frankness runs through all his conversation. The military part of his life has furnish'd him with many adventures, in the relation of which he is very agreeable to the company; for he is never overbearing, though accustomed to command men in the utmost degree below him; nor ever too obsequious, from an habit of obeying men highly above him.

But that our society may not appear a set of humourists[2] unacquainted with the gallantries and pleasures of the age, we have among us the gallant WILL. HONEYCOMB, a gentleman who according to his years should be in the decline of his life, but having ever been very careful of his person, and always had a very easie fortune, time has made but very little impression, either by wrinkles on his forehead, or traces in his brain. His person is well turn'd, of a good height. He is very ready at that sort of discourse with which men usually entertain women. He has all his life dressed very well, and remembers habits[3] as others do men. He can smile when one speaks to him, and laughs easily. He knows the history of every mode, and can inform you from which of the *French* king's wenches our wives and daughters had this manner of

---

[1] *pretenders*, claimants.   [2] *humourists*, cranks.
[3] *habits*, fashions in dress.

curling their hair, that way of placing their hoods; and whose vanity to show her foot made petticoats so short in such a year. In a word, all his conversation and knowledge has been in the female world: as other men of his age will take notice to you what such a minister said upon such and such an occasion, he will tell you when the Duke of *Monmouth* danced at court such a woman was then smitten, another was taken with him[1] at the head of his troop in the *Park*. In all these important relations, he has ever about the same time received a glance or a blow of a fan from some celebrated beauty, mother of the present lord such-a-one. This way of talking of his very much enlivens the conversation among us of a more sedate turn; and I find there is not one of the company but my self, who rarely speak at all, but speaks of him as that sort of man, who is usually called a well-bred fine gentleman.... These are my ordinary companions.

[1] *was taken with him*, was captivated by his appearance.

3. SIR ROGER AT THE PLAY

Joseph Addison

My friend Sir ROGER DE COVERLY, when we last met together
at the club, told me that he had a great mind to see the new
tragedy with me, assuring me at the same time, that he had
not been at a play these twenty years. The last I saw, says
Sir ROGER, was the *Committee*,[1] which I should not have gone
to neither, had I not been told before-hand that it was a good
Church of *England* comedy. He then proceeded to enquire
of me who this Distress'd Mother[2] was, and upon hearing
that she was *Hector's* widow, he told me, that her husband
was a brave man, and that when he was a school-boy, he had
read his life at the end of the dictionary. My friend asked me,
in the next place, if there would not be some danger in coming
home late, in case the *Mohocks*[3] should be abroad. I assure
you, says he, I thought I had fallen into their hands last night,
for I observ'd two or three lusty black men that followed me
half way up *Fleet-street*, and mended their pace behind me,
in proportion as I put on to get away from them. You must
know, continued the knight with a smile, I fancied they had
a mind to *hunt* me; for I remember an honest gentleman in
my neighbourhood, who was serv'd such a trick in King
Charles the Second's time; for which reason he has not
ventured himself in town ever since. I might have shown
them very good sport, had this been their design, for as I am
an old fox-hunter, I should have turned and dodged, and have
play'd them a thousand tricks they had never seen in their
lives before. Sir ROGER added, that if these gentlemen had
any such intention, they did not succeed very well in it; for
I threw them out, says he, at the end of *Norfolk-street*, where

[1] *the Committee.* A play by Sir Robert Howard, which was written
soon after the Restoration, and was full of strong cavalier prejudices.

[2] *Distress'd Mother.* An adaptation of Racine's *Andromaque*, by Ambrose
Phillips.

[3] *Mohocks.* "...a set of men who have lately erected themselves into a
nocturnal fraternity, under the title of the *Mohock* Club, a name borrowed,
it seems, from a sort of cannibals in India, who subsist by plundering and
devouring all the nations about them..." (extract from *The Spectator* of
March, 1712).

I doubled the corner, and got shelter in my lodgings before they could imagine what was become of me. However, says the Knight, if Captain SENTRY will make one with us to morrow night, and if you will both of you call upon me about four a-clock, that we may be at the house before it is full, I will have my own coach in readiness to attend you, for *John* tells me he has got the fore-wheels mended.

The Captain, who did not fail to meet me there at the appointed hour, bid Sir ROGER fear nothing, for that he had put on the same sword which he made use of at the battel of *Steenkirk*.[1] Sir ROGER's servants, and among the rest my old friend the butler, had, I found, provided themselves with good oaken plants, to attend their master upon this occasion. When we had plac'd him in his coach, with my self at his left hand, the Captain before him, and his butler at the head of his footmen in the rear, we convoy'd him in safety to the play-house; where, after having march'd up the entry in good order, the Captain and I went in with him, and seated him betwixt us in the pit. As soon as the house was full, and the candles lighted, my old friend stood up and looked about him with that pleasure, which a mind seasoned with humanity naturally feels in it self, at the sight of a multitude of people who seem pleased with one another, and partake of the same common entertainment. I could not but fancy to my self, as the old man stood up in the middle of the pit, that he made a very proper center to a tragick audience. Upon the entring of *Pyrrhus*, the Knight told me, that he did not believe the King of *France* himself had a better strut. I was indeed very attentive to my old friend's remarks, because I looked upon them as a piece of natural criticism, and was well pleased to hear him at the conclusion of almost every scene, telling me that he could not imagine how the play would end. One while he appear'd much concerned for *Andromache*; and a little while after as much for *Hermione*; and was extremely puzzled to think what would become of *Pyrrhus*.

When Sir ROGER saw *Andromache's* obstinate refusal to her lover's importunities, he whispered me in the ear, that he was sure she would never have him; to which he added, with a more than ordinary vehemence, You can't imagine,

[1] *Steenkirk*, in which William III was defeated by the French, in 1692.

Sir, what 'tis to have to do with a widow. Upon *Pyrrhus* his
threatening afterwards to leave her, the Knight shook his
head, and muttered to himself, Ay, do if you can. This part
dwelt so much upon my friend's imagination, that at the close
of the third act, as I was thinking of something else, he
whispered in my ear, These widows, Sir, are the most perverse
creatures in the world. But pray, says he, you that are a
critick, is the play according to your dramatick rules, as you
call them? Should your people in tragedy always talk to be
understood? Why, there is not a single sentence in this play
that I do not know the meaning of.

The fourth act very luckily begun before I had time to
give the old gentleman an answer; Well, says the Knight,
sitting down with great satisfaction, I suppose we are now to
see *Hector's* ghost. He then renewed his attention, and, from
time to time, fell a praising the widow. He made, indeed, a
little mistake as to one of her pages, whom at his first entring,
he took for *Astyanax*; but he quickly set himself right in that
particular, though, at the same time, he owned he should have
been very glad to have seen the little boy, who, says he, must
needs be a very fine child by the account that is given of him.
Upon *Hermione's* going off with a menace to *Pyrrhus*, the
audience gave a loud clap, to which Sir ROGER added, On my
word, a notable young baggage.

As there was a very remarkable silence and stillness in the
audience during the whole action, it was natural for them to
take the opportunity of these intervals between the acts, to
express their opinion of the players, and of their respective
parts. Sir ROGER hearing a cluster of them praise *Orestes*,
struck in with them, and told them, that he thought his friend
Pylades was a very sensible man; as they were afterwards
applauding *Pyrrhus*, Sir ROGER put in a second time, And let
me tell you, says he, though he speaks but little, I like the old
fellow in whiskers as well as any of them. Captain SENTRY,
seeing two or three waggs who sat near us lean with an attentive ear towards Sir ROGER, and fearing lest they should
smoak the Knight, pluck'd him by the elbow, and whispered
something in his ear, that lasted till the opening of the fifth
act. The Knight was wonderfully attentive to the account
which *Orestes* gives of *Pyrrhus* his death, and at the con-

clusion of it, told me it was such a bloody piece of work, that he was glad it was not done upon the stage. Seeing afterwards *Orestes* in his raving fit, he grew more than ordinary serious, and took occasion to moralize (in his way) upon an evil conscience, adding that *Orestes, in his madness, looked as if he saw something.*

As we were the first that came into the house, so we were the last that went out of it; being resolved to have a clear passage for our old friend, whom we did not care to venture among the justling of the crowd. Sir ROGER went out fully satisfy'd with his entertainment, and we guarded him to his lodgings in the same manner that we brought him to the playhouse; being highly pleased, for my own part, not only with the performance of the excellent piece which had been presented, but with the satisfaction which it had given to the good old man.

4. THE MAKING OF A THIEF

From *Moll Flanders* (1721): Daniel Defoe

I went out now by daylight, and wandered about I knew not whither, and in search of, I knew not what, when the devil put a snare in my way of a dreadful nature indeed, and such a one as I have never had before or since. Going through Aldersgate Street, there was a pretty little child had been at a dancing-school, and was agoing home all alone; and my prompter, like a true devil, set me upon this innocent creature. I talked to it, and it prattled to me again, and I took it by the hand and led it along till I came to a paved alley that goes into Bartholomew Close, and I led it in there. The child said, that was not its way home. I said, "Yes, my dear, it is; I'll show you the way home." The child had a little necklace on of gold beads, and I had my eye upon that, and in the dark of the alley I stooped, pretending to mend the child's clog that was loose, and took off her necklace, and the child never felt it, and so led the child on again. Here, I say, the devil put me upon killing the child in the dark alley, that it might not cry, but the very thought frighted me so that I was ready to drop down; but I turned the child about and bade it go back again, for that was not its way home; the child said, so she would; and I went through into Bartholomew Close, and then turned round to another passage that goes into Long Lane, so away into Charterhouse Yard, and out into St John's street; then crossing into Smithfield, went down Chick Lane, and into Field Lane, to Holborn Bridge, when, mixing with the crowd of people usually passing there, it was not possible to have been found out, and thus I made my second sally into the world.

The thoughts of this booty put out all the thoughts of the first, and the reflections I had made wore quickly off; poverty hardened my heart, and my own necessities made me regardless of anything. The last affair left no great concern upon me, for as I did the poor child no harm, I only thought I had given the parents a just reproof for their negligence, in leaving the poor lamb to come home by itself, and it would teach them to take more care another time.

This string of beads was worth about £12 or £14. I suppose it might have been formerly the mother's, for it was too big for the child's wear, but that, perhaps, the vanity of the mother to have her child look fine at the dancing-school, had made her let the child wear it; and no doubt the child had a maid sent to take care of it, but she, like a careless jade, was taken up perhaps with some fellow that had met her, and so the poor baby wandered till it fell into my hands.

However I did the child no harm; I did not so much as fright it, for I had a great many tender thoughts about me yet, and did nothing but what, as I may say, mere necessity drove me to.

I had a great many adventures after this, but I was young in the business, and did not know how to manage, otherwise than as the devil put things into my head; and, indeed, he was seldom backward to me. One adventure I had which was very lucky to me. I was going through Lombard Street in the dusk of the evening, just by the end of Three King Court, when on a sudden comes a fellow running by me as swift as lightning, and throws a bundle that was in his hand just behind me, as I stood up against the corner of the house at the turning into the alley. Just as he threw it in, he said, "God bless you, mistress, let it lie there a little", and away he runs. After him comes two more, and immediately a young fellow without his hat, crying, "Stop thief!" They pursued the two last fellows so close, that they were forced to drop what they had got, and one of them was taken into the bargain; the other got off free.

I stood stock-still all this while, till they came back, dragging the poor fellow they had taken, and lugging the things they had found, extremely well satisfied that they had recovered the booty and taken the thief; and thus they passed by me, for I looked only like one who stood up while the crowd was gone.

Once or twice I asked what was the matter, but the people neglected answering me, and I was not very importunate; but after the crowd was wholly passed, I took my opportunity to turn about and take up what was behind me and walk away. This, indeed, I did with less disturbance than I had done formerly, for these things I did not steal, but they were stolen to my hand. I got safe to my lodgings with this cargo, which was a piece of fine black lustring silk, and a piece of velvet; the latter was but part of a piece of about eleven yards; the former was a whole piece of near fifty yards. It seems it was a mercer's shop they had rifled. I say rifled, because the goods were so considerable that they had lost; for the goods that they recovered were pretty many, and I believe came to about six or seven several pieces of silk. How they came to get so many I could not tell; but as I had only robbed the thief, I made no scruple at taking these goods, and being very glad of them too.

COMMENTARY

The eighteenth century witnessed the rapid growth of prose in scope and importance. Milton had shown the potentialities of the prose pamphlet, but its appeal had been restricted by dogmatic pedantry and a ponderous style. It was not until Dryden, in *Absalom and Achitophel* and other works, applied his mastery of the art of satire to topical matters that the political value of the writer was fully revealed. It was soon recognised, too, that the new prose was a vehicle that could carry satire almost as neatly and compactly as the rhyming verse of Dryden. But the free expression of political opinion was shackled by the censorship, against which Milton had penned his vain protest. After the Revolution of 1688, however, the censorship became less stringent, and was finally abandoned in 1693. There was an immediate increase of prose output, particularly of the newspaper, which had been hitherto under the control of a "surveyor of the press". Our "first journalistic writer of national importance" was Defoe. In 1704 he began *The Review*, a four-page publication appearing anonymously three times a week. It is on record that by 1711 about 44,000 copies of various newspapers were in weekly circulation. Defoe's *Review* presented its news in good style and with fair accuracy; but few of its contemporaries reached so high a standard, and it was with a desire to give the public something more literary and less irresponsible than the current news sheets that Steele launched his *Tatler*, 1709. He made news a feature of secondary importance, but what journalism lost in this way was more than counterbalanced by a greatly improved standard of style and taste.

This condition of affairs coincided with the rise of the party system of government, and Whig and Tory, realising that the pen of the pamphleteer and journalist could do much to influence public opinion, vied with each other in the search for writers of talent. Such a discovery was Swift, the most influential contributor to *The Examiner* (1710), the organ of the Tory party. He has been called "the father of the leading article". The power he exercised could reverse the current of public opinion, and it was his influence "that enabled the ministers to conclude the Peace of Utrecht".[1] In such circumstances authorship under official patronage not only began to pay, but was capable of opening the door to the highest offices; Addison, for example, became one of the two Secretaries of State.

Certain changes in the structure of society were also favourable to the development of prose. The growth of commerce increased the prosperity and power of the middle classes, in whom a strong desire for self-improvement led to a wider diffusion of culture and to an extension of the reading public. At the London coffee-houses, men of varied interests and of different ranks of life met on terms of comparative equality; newspapers were read and discussed; and the free exchange of ideas laid the foundation of a more democratic culture and of an easier style of intercourse. The embodiment of the spirit of the coffee-house is to be found in the pages of Steele and Addison.

In an age pre-eminent in the history of prose the most powerful and most vital writer was *Jonathan Swift* (1667–1745). As a satirist he was devastating. As a thinker he was gifted with a superior intellect that annihilated all sides of a controversy but his own; his arguments were unassailable in their logic and force. His style was so clear that it gave to an intricate problem the illusion of simple truth, and to a perverse or distorted point of view an air of reasonableness. These are qualities one expects to find highly developed in an age of reason, but Swift would not have been the great writer he was, had it not been for certain other qualities, the clue to which is to be found in his letters and journals. In these he is revealed as a man of deep passions and fine susceptibilities. His *Journal to Stella* is an idyll of tender

[1] Lecky, *Introduction to Prose Works of Swift*. G. Bell.

sentiment, and he knew what it was to love and be loved. He had a rare capacity for disinterested friendship, and to individuals and worthy causes he showed kindness and charity. What is it that made the fruit of these wholesome qualities so harsh and bitter? It is true that he sacrificed, by his own indiscretion, all prospect of preferment; that in politics he threw in his lot with the losing side; and that his love affairs involved him in tragedy. But other men have experienced disappointments as great, and have retained their sweetness and sanity. There can be no doubt that the germ of Swift's misanthropy was morbidly present from the first, that it fed on the decay of his hopes, and was brought to monstrous growth by the unspirituality and scepticism of the times. What makes the savagery of Swift's indignation at all tolerable is our knowledge that there was much in the state of society to excuse it. His life was the tragedy of a great-hearted man, whose intense feelings were either repressed or misdirected, and it is from this smothered fire as much as from his intellectual qualities that the volcanic force of his writing is derived.

The *Tale of a Tub* seems to have been written in 1696, but was not published till 1704. In his preface the author says that just as "seamen have a custom, when they meet a whale, to fling him an empty tub by way of amusement, to divert him from laying hands upon the ship", so the object of this tale is "to prevent the wits of the present age from tossing and sporting with the commonwealth and from picking holes in the weak sides of religion". The plan of the book is simplicity itself. A father leaves to each of his three sons a coat (a system of worship) which will last as long as the wearer needs it. He enjoins in his will (the New Testament) that the coat shall never be altered. The three sons, Peter, Martin and Jack, stand respectively for the Church of Rome, the Reformed Church, and the Dissenters. The disputes between the brothers over their father's will are an allegory of the dissensions that have divided the Christian Church; whilst the unseemly conduct of the brothers and the unlovely traits in their character are double-edged satire both on the abuses that have disfigured religion and on the pettiness and depravity of mankind. The scathing manner in which Swift dealt with religious questions has cast doubt on the sincerity of his Christianity. Queen Anne felt so strongly on the subject that she resolutely opposed Swift's preferment to a bishopric. The writer himself contended that his object was to defend the Church of England by ridiculing its opponents; but the best that can be said in support of this plea is that of three unlikeable figures the least disagreeable is Martin.

As an allegory on a religious theme, the *Tale of a Tub* invites comparison with *Pilgrim's Progress*. Bunyan's allegory is in the form of a well-sustained narrative, with a straightforward symbolism, easily interpreted; in the *Tale of a Tub* the story (unlike that of Gulliver) is little in itself, but it owes its grip on the reader to the extraordinary aptness and ingenuity with which every detail is made parallel with the historical facts that are satirised. No other work of its kind is so pervaded with irony.

Both writers have a simple Saxon style; it was natural to Bunyan, because he was a homely man who wrote as he spoke, in the language of the Bible; in Swift it was employed with the deliberate purpose of a great artist. Common to both are the qualities of the best narrative prose, viz. directness and clear definition, attained by the sparing use of epithets, figurative language and poetical imagery, and by the complete suppression of idiosyncrasy and studied ornament. In Bunyan this simplicity was instinctive; in Swift it was the stalking-horse under cover of which he approached the victims of his irony: almost every sentence was barbed with his sardonic wit.

The names of *Richard Steele* and *Joseph Addison*, close companions in life, will always be coupled in literature, because the most enduring portion of their work was produced in collaboration. Their friendship started at Charterhouse, and was continued during their university career at Oxford. The first number of *The Tatler* was issued in 1709, Steele being the sole author of the project, but Addison, as his friend, was at first an occasional, and, later, a frequent contributor. *The Spectator* (1711) was a joint concern. The partnership was an ideal one, rare in the annals of literature. By education and upbringing they both belonged to the new middle class, and it was to this class that they specially addressed themselves. Their common aim was to leave society the better for their writing, and so nicely were they attuned to the spirit of the age, in their limitations no less than in their virtues, that they succeeded, where greater idealism and genius might have failed, in raising the moral tone of their contemporaries: they spoke to and for the average man. Their weapon was satirical humour, which, if it did not probe ignorance and vice as deeply as they claimed, was really efficacious in the correction of manners and fashions, and in separating laughter from immorality.

The parallel between the two writers extends also to their style; so close is the resemblance in vocabulary, turn of phrase and sentence structure, that it is not always possible to say with certainty of a particular passage whether it is Steele's or Addison's. But where there is so much talent there must also be individuality, and each possessed qualities complementary to those of his partner. Steele had the more lively imagination; it is to him, for instance, that we must give credit for the invention of the Spectator Club. His special virtue is an artless fluency that has its springs in enthusiasm and sympathy, and there is far more sentiment in his composition than in Addison's. The latter had more restraint: his strength lay in a moderation that was not the outcome of mediocrity but of a fine balance of qualities. He had great learning without pedantry. His natural taste was refined by culture, and he was a more finished and more conscious artist than Steele.

It would be difficult to overstate the indebtedness of posterity to Steele and Addison. In the first place their literary journalism did more than anything else in the eighteenth century to create and satisfy a demand for prose of good quality. The circulation of *The Spectator* rose in a few months from three thousand to thirty thousand copies, and its readers were the nucleus of the vast reading-public of modern times. Already by the middle of the century, and in spite of the imposition of the Stamp Tax, over seven million copies of newspapers were sold annually. In these the general pattern of style was the prose of *The Spectator*, and its influence continued to be felt for several generations. "Whoever writes", says Johnson, "to attain an English style, familiar but not coarse, and elegant but not ostentatious, must give his days and nights to the volumes of Addison." Thus was founded a standard literary style which was accepted almost without question until Macaulay and Carlyle broke away from it. Secondly, Steele and Addison gave to the essay, which had hitherto been tentative and experimental, its distinctive form. Thirdly, in respect of subject-matter no less than of style, *The Spectator* Essays were the final preparation for the modern novel. There had been no lack of tales in which incident bore little relation to character, and there had been character-sketches which were mere enumerations of qualities unenlivened by incident. But in the portrayal of Sir Roger and his friends there is movement among the familiar scenes of everyday life; their traits of character emerge from their actions and conversation. In short, the *Coverley Papers* contain all the ingredients of the modern novel except that continuity of incident which we call plot.

Daniel Defoe (1659–1730), one of the most prolific writers of all time, preceded Steele and Addison as a journalist; but he was nearly sixty when he began a succession of eight novels (the first and best known of which is *Robinson Crusoe*), and thus carried a stage further the process of enlarging the circle of readers which was set in motion by public interest in *The Spectator*. By birth and conviction a dissenter, and by occupation a tradesman, he was instrumental in making literature more democratic. His keen interest in public questions led him to take up journalism, at first in the Whig interests. He prospered until the accession of Queen Anne brought the High Church party into power. For his ironical pamphlet *The Shortest Way with Dissenters* he was pilloried, and imprisoned for two years in Newgate. Here he acquired that intimate knowledge of the criminal underworld that gave him material for his later novels. In prison, too, he started his famous *Review*, which he kept going single-handed for nine years (1704–1713). His success as a journalist was immense. He had unique qualities, a valiant zest for life, boundless curiosity, a nimble intelligence, and a flair for what was likely to interest his readers. Had he remained only a journalist, his name would still be recalled with interest, but it is as the author of *Robinson Crusoe* that he has won imperishable fame. Yet English literature is indirectly the richer for his thirty years of journalism, for when, by a happy accident, he turned to fiction, he could write stories only in one way, and that was a new way. As a political agent he had not been overscrupulous in defining the border between fact and invention; and when he became a novelist it was second nature to him to buttress invention with fact. The partition between the two is thin enough in his fictitious histories to have deceived good critics. There had been tales of adventure before *Robinson Crusoe*, but there had never been a tale with so convincing an air of actuality. Moreover, as it was founded on an incident which was known to have occurred, few contemporaries were able to judge where invention began and fact ended. But whether there is an initial incident of fact or not, Defoe's method is always the same. First he comes forward as the editor, introducing the narrator. With a number of business-like statements, marshalled in the manner of circumstantial evidence, he establishes the authenticity of the memoirs. The story is then told in the first person, and the illusion of truth is complete. The plot follows the simple plan of autobiography. In this form of fiction interest in the story cannot be separated from interest in the personality of the narrator, and Defoe's development of the psychological element marks an important advance in the art of fiction. His predilection for humble characters and a sordid milieu, such as we have in *Moll Flanders*, gave to the novels of the next generation a pronounced realistic trend.

Hackwork and journalism had formed Defoe's style long before the refinements of Addison had come into fashion, and his writing is so plain that it has been said that he had no style at all. He had not Addison's classical training to teach him the careful choice of words and the art to conceal art. His sentences are hastily constructed, innocent of artifice, and occasionally ungrammatical; but his style, though colloquial and lacking in refinement, and devoid of passion and idealism, is on the whole eminently suitable for its homespun purpose.

The passage from *Moll Flanders* illustrates the type of character in which Defoe had a curious interest; it reveals, too, his subtlety in the dissection of character (note how the theft is defended as a just reproof for the laxity of the parents) and his skill in the use of circumstantial details to give verisimilitude to a situation.

Chapter VII

The Eighteenth Century (*cont.*)

1. UNCLE TOBY AND THE WIDOW WADMAN

From *Tristram Shandy* (*c.* 1765): Laurence Sterne

—I am half distracted, Captain Shandy, said Mrs Wadman, holding up her cambric handkerchief to her left eye, as she approached the door of my uncle Toby's sentry-box—a mote—or sand—or something—I know not what, has got into this eye of mine—do look into it—it is not in the white—

In saying which, Mrs Wadman edged herself close in beside my uncle Toby, and squeezing herself down upon the corner of his bench, she gave him an opportunity of doing it without rising up—Do look into it—said she.

Honest soul! thou didst look into it with as much innocency of heart, as ever child looked into a raree-show-box; and 'twere as much a sin to have hurt thee.—If a man will be peeping of his own accord into things of that nature—I've nothing to say to it—

My uncle Toby never did: and I will answer for him, that he would have sat quietly upon a sofa from June to January (which, you know, takes in both the hot and cold months), with an eye as fine as the Thracian[1] Rhodope's[2] beside him, without being able to tell, whether it was a black or blue one.

The difficulty was to get my uncle Toby to look at one at all.

'Tis surmounted. And

I see him yonder with his pipe pendulous in his hand, and the ashes falling out of it—looking—and looking—then

[1] Rhodope Thracia tam inevitabili fascino instructa, tam exactè oculis intuens attraxit, ut si in illam quis incidisset, fieri non posset quin caperetur. —I know not who.

[2] Thracian Rhodope, endowed with irresistible witchcraft, had such fascination in the power of her eyes that no one who came under her influence could help being her slave.

rubbing his eyes—and looking again, with twice the good nature that ever Galileo looked for a spot in the sun.

—In vain! for by all the powers which animate the organ—Widow Wadman's left eye shines this moment as lucid as her right—there is neither mote, or sand, or dust, or chaff, or speck, or particle of opaque matter floating in it—There is nothing, my dear paternal uncle! but one lambent delicious fire, furtively shooting out from every part of it, in all directions, into thine—

—If thou lookest, uncle Toby, in search of this mote one moment longer—thou art undone.

An eye is for all the world exactly like a cannon, in this respect; That it is not so much the eye or the cannon, in themselves, as it is the carriage of the eye—and the carriage of the cannon, by which both the one and the other are enabled to do so much execution. I don't think the comparison a bad one; However, as 'tis made and placed at the head of the chapter, as much for use as ornament, all I desire in return, is, that whenever I speak of Mrs Wadman's eyes (except once in the next period), that you keep it in your fancy.

I protest, Madam, said my uncle Toby, I can see nothing whatever in your eye.

It is not in the white; said Mrs Wadman: my uncle Toby looked with might and main into the pupil—

Now of all the eyes which ever were created—from your own, Madam, up to those of Venus herself, which certainly were as venereal a pair of eyes as ever stood in a head—there never was an eye of them all, so fitted to rob my uncle Toby of his repose, as the very eye, at which he was looking—it was not, Madam, a rolling eye—a romping or a wanton one—nor was it an eye sparkling—petulant or imperious—of high claims and terrifying exactions, which would have curdled at once that milk of human nature, of which my uncle Toby was made up—but 'twas an eye full of gentle salutations—and soft responses—speaking—not like the trumpet stop of some ill-made organ, in which many an eye I talk to, holds coarse converse—but whispering soft—like the last low accents of an expiring saint—How can you live comfortless, Captain

Shandy, and alone, without a bosom to lean your head on—
or trust your cares to?

It was an eye—

But I shall be in love with it myself, if I say another word
about it.

—It did my uncle Toby's business.

2. *LETTER TO LORD CHESTERFIELD*

Samuel Johnson. Quoted in Boswell's *Life*

February 7, 1755.

MY LORD,—I have been lately informed, by the proprietor of "The World", that two papers, in which my Dictionary is recommended to the public, were written by your lordship. To be so distinguished is an honour, which, being very little accustomed to favours from the great, I know not well how to receive, or in what terms to acknowledge.

When, upon some slight encouragement, I first visited your lordship, I was overpowered, like the rest of mankind, by the enchantment of your address, and could not forbear to wish that I might boast myself *Le vainqueur du vainqueur de la terre*;—that I might obtain that regard for which I saw the world contending; but I found my attendance so little encouraged, that neither pride nor modesty would suffer me to continue it. When I had once addressed your lordship in public, I had exhausted all the art of pleasing which a retired and uncourtly scholar can possess. I had done all that I could; and no man is well pleased to have his all neglected, be it ever so little.

Seven years, my lord, have now past, since I waited in your outward rooms, or was repulsed from your door; during which time I have been pushing on my work through difficulties, of which it is useless to complain, and have brought it, at last, to the verge of publication, without one act of assistance, one word of encouragement, or one smile of favour. Such treatment I did not expect; for I never had a patron before.

The shepherd in Virgil grew at last acquainted with Love, and found him a native of the rocks.

Is not a patron, my lord, one who looks with unconcern on a man struggling for life in the water, and, when he has reached ground, encumbers him with help? The notice which you have been pleased to take of my labours, had it been early, had been kind; but it has been delayed till I am indifferent, and cannot enjoy it; till I am solitary, and cannot impart it;[1] till I am known and do not want it. I hope it is no very cynical asperity not to confess my obligations where no benefit has been received, or to be unwilling that the public should consider me as owing that to a patron, which Providence has enabled me to do for myself.

Having carried on my work thus far with so little obligation to any favourer of learning, I shall not be disappointed though I should conclude it, if less be possible, with less; for I have been long wakened from that dream of hope, in which I once boasted myself with so much exultation,

MY LORD,

Your lordship's most humble, most obedient servant,

SAM. JOHNSON.

[1] In this passage Dr Johnson evidently alludes to the loss of his wife. (Note to Everyman edition.)

3. JOHNSON'S *DICTIONARY*
An excerpt from the fifth edition of 1784

NÉPOTISM. *n.s.* [*nepotisme*, French; *nepos*, Latin]. Fondness for nephews.

To this humour of *nepotism* Rome owes its present splendour; for it would have been impossible to have furnished out so many glorious places with such a profusion of pictures and statues, had not the riches of the people fallen into different families.

Addison on Italy.

NÉRVELESS. *adj.* [from *nerve*]. Without strength.

There sunk Thalia, *nerveless*, faint and dead,
Had not her sister Satire held her head. *Dunciad.*

NÉRVOUS. *adj.* [*nervosus*, Latin].

1. Well strung; strong; vigorous.

What *nervous* arms he boasts, how firm his tread,
His limbs how turn'd. *Pope's Odyssey.*

2. Relating to the nerves; having the seat in the nerves.

The venal torrent, murm'ring from afar,
Whispered no peace to calm this *nervous* war;
And Philomel, the siren of the plain,
Sung soporific unisons in vain. *Harte.*

3. [In medical cant.] Having weak or diseased nerves.

Poor, weak, *nervous* creatures. *Cheyne.*

NÉRVY. *adj.* [from *nerve*]. Strong; vigorous. Not in use.

Death, that dark spirit, in his *nervy* arm doth lie,
Which being advanc'd, declines, and then men die.
Shakespeare.

NÉSCIENCE. *n.s.* [from *nescio*, Latin]. Ignorance; the state of not knowing.

Many of the most accomplished wits of all ages, have resolved their knowledge into Socrates his sum total, and after all their pains in quest of science, have sat down in a professed *nescience*. *Glanville's Scepsis.*

NESH. *adj.* [*nesc*, Saxon]. Soft; tender; easily hurt. *Skinner*.

NESS.

1. A termination added to an adjective to change it into a substantive, denoting *state* or *quality*; as *poisonous, poisonousness*; *turbid, turbidness*; *lovely, loveliness*; from nisse, Saxon.

2. The termination of many names of places where there is a headland or promontory; from nese, Saxon; a *nose of land* or headland: as INVERNESS.

NEST. *n.s.* [*nest*, Saxon].

1. The bed formed by the bird for incubation and feeding her young.

> If a bird's *nest* chance to be before thee in the way, thou shalt not take the dam with the young. *Deut.* xxii. 6.

> Th' example of the heav'nly lark,
> Thy fellow poet, Cowley, mark,
> Above the skies let thy proud musick sound,
> Thy humble *nest* build on the ground. *Cowley*.

2. Any place where animals are produced.

> Redi found that all kinds of putrefaction did only afford a *nest* and aliment for the eggs and young of those insects he admitted. *Bentley*.

3. An abode; place of residence; a receptacle. Generally in a bad sense: as, a *nest* of rogues and thieves.

> Come from that *nest*
> Of death, contagion, and unnatural sleep.
> *Shakespeare*.

4. A warm close habitation, generally in contempt.

> Some of our ministers having livings offered unto them, will neither, for zeal of religion, nor winning souls to God, be drawn forth from their warm *nests*. *Spenser*.

5. Boxes or drawers; little pockets or repositories.

To NEST. *v.n.* [from the noun]. To build nests.

> The cedar stretched his branches as far as the mountains of the moon, and the king of birds *nested* within his leaves. *Howel's Vocal Forest*.

NÉSTEGG. *n.s.* [*nest* and *egg*]. An egg left in the nest to keep the hen from forsaking it.

> Books and money laid for shew,
> Like *nesteggs*, to make clients lay.   *Hudibras*.

To NÉSTLE. *v.n.* [from *nest*]. To settle; to harbour; to lie close and snug, as a bird in her nest.

> Their purpose was, to fortify in some strong place of the wild country, and there *nestle* 'till succours came.
>   *Bacon*.

> A cock got into a stable was *nestling* in the straw among the horses.   *L'Estrange*.

> The king's fisher wonts commonly by the waterside, and *nestles* in hollow banks.   *L'Estrange*.

> Fluttering there they *nestle* near the throne,
> And lodge in habitations not their own.   *Dryden*.

> The floor is strowed with several plants, amongst which the snails *nestle* all the winter.   *Addison on Italy*.

> Mark where the shy directors creep,
> Nor to the shore approach too nigh;
> The monsters *nestle* in the deep
> To seize you in your passing by.   *Swift's Miscel*.

To NÉSTLE *v.a.*

1. To house, as in a nest.
>   Poor heart!
> That labour'st yet to *nestle* thee,
> Thou think'st by hov'ring here to get a part,
> In a forbidden or forbidding tree.   *Donne*.

> Cupid found a downy bed,
> And *nestl'd* in his little head.   *Prior*.

2. To cherish, as a bird her young.
>   This Ithacus, so highly is endear'd
> To this Minerva, that her hand is ever in his deeds:
> She, like his mother, *nestles* him.   *Chapman's Iliad*.

NÉSTLING. *n.s.* [from *nestle*]. A bird just taken out of the nest.

NET. *n.s.* [*nati*, Gothick; *net*, Saxon].

1. A texture woven with large interstices or meshes, used commonly as a snare for animals.

> Poor bird! thou'dst never fear the *net*, nor lime,
> The pitfall or the gin. *Shakespeare's Macbeth.*

Impatience intangles us like the fluttering of a bird in a *net*, but cannot at all ease our trouble.

Taylor's Holy Living.

2. Any thing made with interstitial vacuities.

He made *nets* of chequered work for the chapiters, upon the top of the pillars. 1 *Kings* vii. 17.

> The vegetative tribes,
> Wrapt in a filmy *net*, and clad with leaves.

Thomson.

4. THE HIGHLANDS

From *A Journey to the Western Islands* (1775): Samuel Johnson

Mountainous countries commonly contain the original, at least the oldest race of inhabitants, for they are not easily conquered, because they must be entered by narrow ways, exposed to every power of mischief from those that occupy the heights; and every new ridge is a new fortress, where the defendants have again the same advantages. If the assailants either force the strait, or storm the summit, they gain only so much ground; their enemies are fled to take possession of the next rock, and the pursuers stand at gaze, knowing neither where the ways of escape wind among the steeps, nor where the bog has firmness to sustain them: besides that, mountaineers have an agility in climbing and descending distinct from strength or courage, and attainable only by use.

If the war be not soon concluded, the invaders are dislodged by hunger; for in those anxious and toilsome marches, provisions cannot easily be carried, and are never to be found. The wealth of mountains is cattle, which, while the men stand in the passes, the women drive away. Such lands at last cannot repay the expense of conquest, and therefore perhaps have not been so often invaded by the mere ambition of dominion, as by resentment of robberies and insults, or the desire of enjoying in security the more fruitful provinces.

As the mountains are long before they are conquered, they are likewise long before they are civilised. Men are softened by intercourse mutually profitable, and instructed by comparing their own notions with those of others. Thus Caesar found the maritime parts of Britain made less barbarous by their commerce with the Gauls. Into a barren and rough tract no stranger is brought either by the hope of gain or of pleasure. The inhabitants, having neither commodities for sale, nor money for purchase, seldom visit more polished places, or if they do visit them, seldom return.

It sometimes happens that by conquest, intermixture, or gradual refinement, the cultivated parts of a country change their language. The mountaineers then become a distinct nation, cut off by dissimilitude of speech from conversation with their neighbours. Thus in Biscay, the original Cantabrian, and in Dalecarlia, the old Swedish still subsists. Thus Wales and the Highlands speak the tongue of the first inhabitants of Britain, while the other parts have received first the Saxon, and in some degree afterwards the French, and then formed a third language between them.

That the primitive manners are continued where the primitive language is spoken, no nation will desire me to suppose, for the manners of mountaineers are commonly savage, but they are rather produced by their situation than derived from their ancestors.

Such seems to be the disposition of man, that whatever makes a distinction produces rivalry....A tract intersected by many ridges of mountains, naturally divides its inhabitants into petty nations, which are made by a thousand causes enemies to each other. Each will exalt its own chiefs, each will boast the valour of its men, or the beauty of its women, and every claim of superiority irritates competition; injuries will sometimes be done, and be more injuriously defended; retaliation will sometimes be attempted, and the debt exacted with too much interest.

In the Highlands it was a law, that if a robber was sheltered from justice, any man of the same clan might be taken in his place. This was a kind of irregular justice, which, though necessary in savage times, could hardly fail to end in a feud, and a feud once kindled among an idle people, with no variety of pursuits to divert their thoughts, burnt on for ages, either sullenly glowing in secret mischief, or openly blazing into public violence. Of the effects of this violent judicature, there are not wanting memorials. The cave is now to be seen to which one of the Campbells, who had injured the Macdonalds, retired with a body of his own clan. The Macdonalds required the offender, and being refused, made a fire at the mouth of the cave, by which he and his adherents were suffocated together.

Mountaineers are warlike, because by their feuds and competitions they consider themselves as surrounded with enemies, and are always prepared to repel incursions, or to make them. Like the Greeks in their unpolished state, described by Thucydides, the Highlanders, till lately, went always armed, and carried their weapons to visits and to church.

Mountaineers are thievish, because they are poor, and having neither manufactures nor commerce, can grow richer only by robbery. They regularly plunder their neighbours, for their neighbours are commonly their enemies; and having lost that reverence for property, by which the order of civil life is preserved, soon consider all as enemies, whom they do not reckon as friends, and think themselves licensed to invade whatever.they are not obliged to protect.

By a strict administration of the laws, since the laws have been introduced into the Highlands, this disposition to thievery is very much represt. Thirty years ago no herd had ever been conducted through the mountains, without paying tribute in the night, to some of the clans; but cattle are now driven, and passengers travel without danger, fear, or molestation.

Among a warlike people, the quality of highest esteem is personal courage, and with the ostentatious display of courage are closely connected promptitude of offence and quickness of resentment. The Highlanders, before they were disarmed, were so addicted to quarrels, that the boys used to follow any public procession or ceremony, however festive, or however solemn, in expectation of the battle, which was sure to happen before the company dispersed.

Mountainous regions are sometimes so remote from the seat of government, and so difficult of access, that they are very little under the influence of the sovereign, or within the reach of national justice. Law is nothing without power; and the sentence of a distant court could not be easily executed, nor perhaps very safely promulgated, among men ignorantly proud and habitually violent, unconnected with the general system, and accustomed to reverence only their own lords. It has therefore been necessary to erect many particular jurisdictions, and commit the punishment of crimes, and the decision of right to the proprietors of the country who could enforce their own decrees. It immediately appears that such judges will be often ignorant, and often partial; but in the immaturity of political establishments no better expedient could be found....

In the Highlands, some great lords had an hereditary jurisdiction over counties; and some chieftains over their own lands; till the final conquest of the Highlands afforded an opportunity of crushing all the local courts, and of extending the general benefits of equal law to the low and the high, in the deepest recesses and obscurest corners.

While the chiefs had this resemblance of royalty, they had

little inclination to appeal, on any question, to superior judicatures. A claim of lands between two powerful lairds was decided like a contest for dominion between sovereign powers. They drew their forces into the field, and right attended the strongest. This was, in ruder times, the common practice, which the kings of Scotland could seldom control.

Even so lately as in the last years of King William, a battle was fought at Mull Roy, on a plain a few miles to the south of Inverness, between the clans of Mackintosh and Macdonald of Keppoch. Col. Macdonald, the head of a small clan, refused to pay the dues demanded from him by Mackintosh, as his superior lord. They disdained the interposition of judges and laws, and calling each his followers to maintain the dignity of the clan, fought a formal battle, in which several considerable men fell on the side of Mackintosh, without a complete victory to either. This is said to have been the last open war made between the clans by their own authority.

The Highland lords made treaties, and formed alliances, of which some traces may still be found, and some consequences still remain as lasting evidences of petty regality. The terms of one of these confederacies were, that each should support the other in the right, or in the wrong, except against the king.

The inhabitants of mountains form distinct races, and are careful to preserve their genealogies. Men in a small district necessarily mingle blood by intermarriages, and combine at last into one family, with a common interest in the honour and disgrace of every individual. Then begins that union of affections, and co-operation of endeavours that constitute a clan. They who consider themselves as ennobled by their family, will think highly of their progenitors, and they who through successive generations live always together in the same place, will preserve local stories and hereditary prejudices. Thus every Highlander can talk of his ancestors, and recount the outrages which they suffered from the wicked inhabitants of the next valley.

Such are the effects of habitation among mountains, and such were the qualities of the Highlanders, while their rocks secluded them from the rest of mankind, and kept them an unaltered and discriminated race. They are now losing their distinction, and hastening to mingle with the general community.

5. THE VICAR AT THE FAIR

From *The Vicar of Wakefield* (1766): Oliver Goldsmith

I had, in the usual forms, when I came to the fair, put my horse through all his paces, but for some time had no bidders. At last a chapman[1] approached, and, after he had for a good while examined the horse round, finding him blind of one eye, he would have nothing to say to him; a second came up, but observing he had a spavin,[2] declared he would not take him for the driving home; a third perceived he had a wind-gall,[3] and would bid no money; a fourth knew by his eye that he had the bots;[4] a fifth wondered what a plague I could do at the fair with a blind, spavined, galled hack, that was only fit to be cut up for a dog-kennel. By this time I began to have a most hearty contempt for the poor animal myself, and was almost ashamed at the approach of every customer: for though I did not entirely believe all the fellows told me, yet I reflected that the number of witnesses was a strong presumption they were right, and St Gregory, upon good works, professes himself to be of the same opinion.

I was in this mortifying situation, when a brother clergyman, an old acquaintance, who had also business at the fair, came up, and shaking me by the hand, proposed adjourning to a public-house, and taking a glass of whatever we could get. I readily closed with the offer, and entering an alehouse, we were shown into a little back room, where there was only a venerable old man, who sat wholly intent over a large book, which he was reading. I never in my life saw a figure that prepossessed me more favourably. His locks of silver gray venerably shaded his temples, and his green old-age seemed to be the result of health and benevolence. However, his presence did not interrupt our conversation. My friend and I discoursed on the various turns of fortune we had met, the Whistonian controversy, my last pamphlet, the archdeacon's reply, and the hard measure that was dealt me. But our attention was in a short time taken off by the appearance of a youth, who, entering the room, respectfully said something

[1] *chapman*, merchant.   [2] *spavin*, an enlargement of the hock.
[3] *wind-gall*, a swelling about the fetlock.
[4] *bots*, a disease of the intestines.

softly to the old stranger. "Make no apologies, my child," said the old man; "to do good is a duty we owe to all our fellow-creatures. Take this; I wish it were more; but five pounds will relieve your distress, and you are welcome." The modest youth shed tears of gratitude, and yet his gratitude was scarce equal to mine. I could have hugged the good old man in my arms, his benevolence pleased me so. He continued to read, and we resumed our conversation, until my companion, after some time, recollecting that he had business to transact in the fair, promised to be soon back, adding, that he always desired to have as much of Dr Primrose's company as possible. The old gentleman, hearing my name mentioned, seemed to look at me with attention for some time, and when my friend was gone, most respectfully demanded if I was in any way related to the great Primrose, that courageous monogamist, who had been the bulwark of the Church. Never did my heart feel sincerer rapture than at that moment. "Sir," cried I, "the applause of so good a man, as I am sure you are, adds to that happiness in my breast which your benevolence has already excited. You behold before you, sir, that Dr Primrose, the monogamist, whom you have been pleased to call great. You here see that unfortunate divine who has so long, and it would ill become me to say successfully, fought against the deuterogamy[1] of the age."—"Sir," cried the stranger, struck with awe, "I fear I have been too familiar, but you'll forgive my curiosity, sir; I beg pardon."—"Sir," cried I, grasping his hand, "you are so far from displeasing me by your familiarity, that I must beg you'll accept my friendship, as you already have my esteem."—"Then with gratitude I accept the offer," cried he, squeezing me by the hand, "thou glorious pillar of unshaken orthodoxy; and do I behold"—I here interrupted what he was going to say, for though, as an author, I could digest no small share of flattery, yet now my modesty would permit no more. However, no lovers in romance ever cemented a more instantaneous friendship. We talked upon several subjects: at first I thought he seemed rather devout than learned, and began to think he despised all human doctrine as dross. Yet this no way lessened him in my esteem, for I had for some time begun privately to harbour such an opinion myself. I therefore took

[1] *deuterogamy*, the practice of permitting second marriage.

occasion to observe that the world in general began to be
blamably indifferent as to doctrinal matters, and followed
human speculations too much. "Ay, sir," replied he—as if
he had reserved all his learning to that moment, "Ay, sir, the
world is in its dotage, and yet the cosmogony or creation of
the world has puzzled philosophers of all ages. What a medley
of opinions have they not broached upon the creation of the
world! Sanchoniathon, Manetho, Berosus, and Ocellus
Lucanus, have all attempted it in vain. The latter has these
words *Anarchon ara kai atelutaion to pau*,[1] which imply that
all things have neither beginning nor end. Manetho also,
who lived about the time of Nebuchadon-Asser—Asser being
a Syriac word usually applied as a surname to the kings of
that country, as Teglat Phael-Asser, Nabon-Asser—he, I say,
formed a conjecture equally absurd; for, as we usually say,
ek to biblion kubernetes, which implies that books will never
teach the world; so he attempted to investigate—But, sir,
I ask pardon; I am straying from the question." That he
actually was, nor could I for my life see how the creation of
the world had anything to do with the business I was talking of; but it was sufficient to show me that he was a man
of letters, and I now reverenced him the more. I was resolved, therefore, to bring him to the touchstone; but he was
too mild and too gentle to contend for victory. Whenever I
made any observation that looked like a challenge to controversy, he would smile, shake his head, and say nothing,
by which I understood he could say much if he thought
proper. The subject, therefore, insensibly changed from the
business of antiquity to that which brought us both to the
fair: mine, I told him, was to sell a horse, and very luckily
indeed, his was to buy one for one of his tenants. My horse
was soon produced, and, in fine, we struck a bargain. Nothing
now remained but to pay me, and he accordingly pulled out a
thirty-pound note and bid me change it. Not being in a
capacity of complying with this demand, he ordered his foot-
man to be called up, who made his appearance in a very
genteel livery. "Here, Abraham," cried he, "go and get gold
for this; you'll do it at neighbour Jackson's, or anywhere."
While the fellow was gone, he entertained me with a pathetic

[1] *Anarchon, etc.* The old man's Greek is hardly more intelligible than
his argument.

harangue on the great scarcity of silver, which I undertook to improve by deploring also the great scarcity of gold; so that by the time Abraham returned we had both agreed that money was never so hard to be come at as now. Abraham returned to inform us that he had been over the whole fair, and could not get change, though he had offered half a crown for doing it. This was a great disappointment to us all; but the old gentleman, having paused a little, asked me if I knew one Solomon Flamborough, in my part of the country. Upon replying that he was my next-door neighbour, "If that be the case, then," returned he, "I believe we shall deal. You shall have a draft upon him, payable at sight, and let me tell you he is as warm a man as any within five miles round him. Honest Solomon and I have been acquainted for many years together. I remember I always beat him at three jumps; but he could hop on one leg farther than I." A draft upon my neighbour was to me the same as money, for I was sufficiently convinced of his ability. The draft was signed, and put into my hands, and Mr Jenkinson, the old gentleman, his man Abraham, and my horse, old Blackberry, trotted off, very well pleased with each other.

After a short interval being left to reflection, I began to recollect that I had done wrong in taking a draft from a stranger, and so prudently resolved upon following the purchaser and having back my horse. But this was now too late; I therefore made directly homewards, resolving to get the draft changed into money at my friend's as fast as possible. I found my honest neighbour smoking his pipe at his own door, and, informing him that I had a small bill upon him, he read it twice over. "You can read the name, I suppose," cried I, "Ephraim Jenkinson."—"Yes," returned he, "the name is written plain enough, and I know the gentleman too, the greatest rascal under the canopy of heaven. This is the very same rogue who sold us the spectacles. Was he not a venerable-looking man, with gray hair, and no flaps to his pocket-holes? And did he not talk a long string of learning about Greek, and cosmogony, and the world!" To this I replied with a groan. "Ay," continued he, "he has but that one piece of learning in the world, and he always talks it away whenever he finds a scholar in company; but I know the rogue, and will catch him yet."

6. ENGLAND AND THE COLONIES

From *Speech on Conciliation with the Colonies* (1775): Edmund Burke

But to clear up my ideas on this subject—a revenue from America transmitted hither—do not delude yourselves—you never can receive it—No, not a shilling. We have experience that from remote countries it is not to be expected. If, when you attempted to extract revenue from Bengal, you were obliged to return in loan what you had taken in imposition; what can you expect from North America? For certainly, if ever there was a country qualified to produce wealth, it is India; or an institution fit for transmission, it is the East India Company. America has none of these aptitudes. If America gives you taxable objects, on which you lay your duties here, and gives you, at the same time, a surplus by a foreign sale of her commodities to pay the duties on these objects, which you tax at home, she has performed her part to the British revenue. But with regard to her own internal establishments; she may, I doubt not she will, contribute in moderation. I say, in moderation; for she ought not to be permitted to exhaust herself. She ought to be reserved to a war; the weight of which, with the enemies[1] that we are likely to have, must be considerable in her quarter of the globe. There she may serve you, and serve you essentially.

For that service, for all service, whether of revenue, trade, or empire, my trust is in her interest in the British Constitution. My hold of the Colonies is in the close affection which grows from common names, from kindred blood, from similar privileges, and equal protection. These are ties, which, though light as air, are strong as links of iron. Let the Colonists always keep the idea of their civil rights associated with your government;—they will cling and grapple to you; and no force under heaven will be of power to tear them from their allegiance. But let it be once understood, that your government may be one thing, and their privileges another; that these two things may exist without any mutual relation;—

[1] *with the enemies, etc.* The French and Spaniards had settlements in America.

the cement is gone; the cohesion is loosened; and everything hastens to decay and dissolution. As long as you have the wisdom to keep the sovereign authority of this country as the sanctuary of liberty, the sacred temple consecrated to our common faith, wherever the chosen race and sons of England worship freedom, they will turn their faces towards you. The more they multiply, the more friends you will have; the more ardently they love their liberty, the more perfect will be their obedience. Slavery they can have anywhere. It is a weed that grows in every soil. They may have it from Spain, they may have it from Prussia. But until you become lost to all feeling of your true interest and your natural dignity, freedom they can have from none but you. This is the commodity of price, of which you have the monopoly. This is the true Act of Navigation,[1] which binds to you the commerce of the Colonies, and through them secures to you the wealth of the world. Deny them this participation of freedom, and you break that sole bond, which originally made, and must still preserve, the unity of the Empire. Do not entertain so weak an imagination, as that your registers and your bonds,[2] your affidavits and your sufferances,[3] your cockets[4] and your clearances,[5] are what form the great securities of your commerce. Do not dream that your letters of office,[6] and your instructions,[7] and your suspending clauses, are the things that hold together the great contexture of the mysterious whole. These things do not make your government. Dead instruments, passive tools as they are, it is the spirit of the English communion that gives all their life and efficacy to them. It is the spirit of the English Constitution, which, infused through the mighty mass, pervades, feeds, unites, invigorates, vivifies every part of the empire, even down to the minutest member.

[1] *Act of Navigation*, by which the Colonies were forbidden to trade with any country except England.

[2] *registers...bonds, etc.*, alluding to the routine and regulations of the Customs.

[3] *sufferances*, permits.

[4] *cockets*, sealed warrants that dues have been paid.

[5] *clearances*, documents authorising the passing of goods through the Customs.

[6] *letters of office*, ministerial letters.

[7] *instructions*, viz. to colonial governors.

Is it not the same virtue which does everything for us here in England? Do you imagine then, that it is the Land Tax Act which raises your revenue? that it is the annual vote in the Committee of Supply which gives you your army? or that it is the Mutiny Bill which inspires it with bravery and discipline? No! surely no! It is the love of the people; it is their attachment to their government, from the sense of the deep stake they have in such a glorious institution—which gives you your army and your navy, and infuses into both that liberal obedience, without which your army would be a base rabble, and your navy nothing but rotten timber.

All this, I know well enough, will sound wild and chimerical to the profane herd of those vulgar and mechanical politicians, who have no place among us; a sort of people who think that nothing exists but what is gross and material; and who therefore, far from being qualified to be directors of the great movement of empire, are not fit to turn a wheel in the machine. But to men truly initiated and rightly taught, these ruling and master principles, which, in the opinion of such men as I have mentioned, have no substantial existence, are in truth every thing, and all in all. Magnanimity in politics is not seldom the truest wisdom; and a great empire and little minds go ill together. If we are conscious of our station, and glow with zeal to fill our places as becomes our situation and ourselves, we ought to auspicate[1] all our public proceedings on America with the old warning of the church, *Sursum corda!* We ought to elevate our minds to the greatness of that trust to which the order of Providence has called us. By adverting to the dignity of this high calling, our ancestors have turned a savage wilderness into a glorious empire; and have made the most extensive, and the only honourable conquests, not by destroying, but by promoting the wealth, the number, the happiness, of the human race. Let us get an American revenue as we have got an American empire. English privileges have made it all that it is; English privileges alone will make it all it can be.

---

[1] *auspicate*, give an auspicious beginning to (obs.).

7. THE BATTLE OF CHÂLONS, A.D. 451

From *The Decline and Fall of the Roman Empire*: Edward Gibbon

The discipline and tactics of the Greeks and Romans form an interesting part of their national manners. The attentive study of the military operations of Xenophon, or Caesar, or Frederic, when they are described by the same genius which conceived and executed them, may tend to improve (if such improvement can be wished) the art of destroying the human species. But the battle of Châlons can only excite our curiosity by the magnitude of the object; since it was decided by the blind impetuosity of Barbarians, and has been related by partial writers, whose civil or ecclesiastical profession secluded them from the knowledge of military affairs. Cassiodorus, however, had familiarly conversed with many Gothic warriors, who served in that memorable engagement; "a conflict", as they informed him, "fierce, various, obstinate and bloody; such as could not be paralleled either in the present or in past ages". The number of the slain amounted to one hundred and sixty-two thousand, or, according to another account, three hundred thousand persons; and these incredible exaggerations suppose a real and effective loss, sufficient to justify the historian's remark that whole generations may be swept away, by the madness of kings, in the space of a single hour. After the mutual and repeated discharge of missile weapons, in which the archers of Scythia might signalise their superior dexterity, the cavalry and infantry of the two armies were furiously mingled in closer combat. *The Huns, who fought under the eyes of their king,[1] pierced through the feeble and doubtful centre of the allies,[2] separated their wings from each other, and wheeling, with a rapid effort, to the left, directed their whole force against the Visigoths.* As Theodoric rode along the ranks to animate his troops, he received a mortal stroke from the javelin of Andages, a noble Ostrogoth, and immediately fell from his horse. The wounded

[1] *their king*, Attila.
[2] *the allies*, the Romans under Aetius, general of the Romans of the West, with whom were allied the Visigoths from the southern provinces of Gaul, under Theodoric.

king was oppressed in the general disorder, and trampled under the feet of his own cavalry; and this important death served to explain the ambiguous prophecy[1] of the haruspices.[2] Attila already exulted in the confidence of victory, when the valiant Torismond[3] descended from the hills, and verified the remainder of the prediction. The Visigoths, who had been thrown into confusion by the flight, or defection, of the Alani, gradually restored their order of battle; and the Huns were undoubtedly vanquished, since Attila was compelled to retreat. He had exposed his person with the rashness of a private soldier; but the intrepid troops of the centre had pushed forwards beyond the rest of the line; their attack was faintly supported; their flanks were unguarded; and the conquerors of Scythia and Germany were saved by the approach of the night from a total defeat. They retired within the circle of waggons that fortified their camp; and the dismounted squadrons prepared themselves for a defence, to which neither their arms nor their temper were adapted. The event[4] was doubtful; but Attila had secured a last and honourable resource. The saddles and rich furniture of the cavalry were collected by his order into a funeral pile; and the magnanimous Barbarian had resolved, if his intrenchments should be forced, to rush headlong into the flames, and to deprive his enemies of the glory which they might have acquired by the death or captivity of Attila.

But his enemies had passed the night in equal disorder and anxiety. The inconsiderate courage of Torismond was tempted to urge the pursuit, till he unexpectedly found himself, with a few followers, in the midst of the Scythian waggons. In the confusion of a nocturnal combat, he was thrown from his horse; and the Gothic prince must have perished like his father, if his youthful strength, and the intrepid zeal of his companions, had not rescued him from this dangerous situation. In the same manner, but on the left of

[1] *ambiguous prophecy.* The scrutiny of the entrails of victims had revealed "Attila's defeat, with the death of his principal adversary".

[2] *haruspices.* Haruspex, a soothsayer who interpreted natural prodigies and inspected the entrails of sacrifices.

[3] *Torismond*, son of Theodoric.

[4] *event*, issue.

the line, Aetius himself, *separated from his allies, ignorant of
their victory, and anxious for their fate, encountered and
escaped* the hostile troops that were scattered over the plains
of Châlons; and at length reached the camp of the Goths,
which he could only fortify with a slight rampart of shields,
till the dawn of day. The Imperial general was soon satisfied
of the defeat of Attila, who still remained inactive within his
intrenchments; and, when he contemplated the bloody scene,
he observed, with secret satisfaction, that the loss had principally fallen on the Barbarians. The body of Theodoric,
pierced with honourable wounds, was discovered under a
heap of the slain: his subjects bewailed the death of their
king and father; but their tears were mingled with songs
and acclamations, and his funeral rites were performed in
the face of a vanquished enemy. The Goths, clashing their
arms, elevated on a buckler his eldest son Torismond, to
whom they justly ascribed the glory of their success; and
the new king accepted the obligation of revenge as a sacred
portion of his paternal inheritance. Yet the Goths themselves were astonished by the fierce and undaunted aspect
of their formidable antagonist; and their historian has compared Attila to a lion encompassed in his den, and threatening his hunters with redoubled fury. The kings and nations,
who might have deserted his standard in the hour of distress,
were made sensible that the displeasure of their monarch
was the most imminent and inevitable danger. All his
instruments of martial music incessantly sounded a loud
and animating strain of defiance; and the foremost troops
who advanced to the assault were checked, or destroyed, by
showers of arrows from every side of the intrenchments. It
was determined in a general council of war, to besiege the
king of the Huns in his camp, to intercept his provisions, and
to reduce him to the alternative of a disgraceful treaty or an
unequal combat. But the impatience of the Barbarians soon
disdained these cautious and dilatory measures; and the
mature policy of Aetius was apprehensive that, after the ex-
tirpation of the Huns, the republic would be oppressed by
the pride and power of the Gothic nation. *The patrician
exerted the superior ascendant of authority and reason, to
calm the passions which the son of Theodoric considered as

a duty; represented, with seeming affection, and real truth, the dangers of absence and delay; and persuaded Torismond to disappoint, by his speedy return, the ambitious designs of his brothers,* who might occupy the throne and treasures of Toulouse. After the departure of the Goths and the separation of the allied army, Attila was surprised at the vast silence that reigned over the plains of Châlons; the suspicion of some hostile stratagem detained him several days within the circle of his waggons; and his retreat beyond the Rhine confessed the last victory which was achieved in the name of the Western empire.

COMMENTARY

As the century advanced, the importance of literature in the daily life of the people grew steadily, and the man of letters began to occupy a position in society not unlike that which he holds to-day. The party system being firmly established, politicians like Walpole found means of securing votes which enabled them to dispense with the services of eminent writers. Authors had perforce to look to the publisher and the public for their livelihood, and during the interim they had a hard struggle. Johnson and Goldsmith were slaves to hackwriting for many years before their exceptional gifts won recognition and released them from bondage to Grub Street. In the long run, however, the separation of literature from patronage, aristocratic and political, was of lasting benefit. Literature threw off its fetters, and the author acquired with his independence a self-respect which bred respect in others and raised his status in society. It is doubtful whether, in any case, literature and politics could have continued long in partnership. Politics became more and more corrupt, while the moral tone of literature steadily improved. The reaction against the frivolity of the Restoration became more pronounced. Johnson is as representative of the latter phase of the century as Dryden of its opening years, and the contrast between them is a contrast of character.

The prose-writer, unwanted in politics, was soon provided by changing conditions with new fields to conquer. The stage had fallen into disrepute. The eighteenth century, as the popularity of Defoe's novels proved, had an appetite for the accurate observation of contemporary manners, an appetite which the drama made no attempt to satisfy. Richardson's first novel, *Pamela* (1740), showed how it might be catered for, and the period which followed has more classic fiction to its credit than any other. It was then that fiction, with its greater ease of circulation, established an ascendancy which the drama, until the recent rise of the cinema, seemed unlikely ever to recapture. About the same time there was a revival of interest in the periodical essay. Literature in its more scholarly aspects received additions from the publication of Burke's political treatises, and from the labours of Hume and Gibbon, who gave to the world a new conception of history as an exact science in which philosophy and literary style were important features. The publication of Johnson's *Dictionary* in 1735 was an event in literary history. Johnson's methods, by which "the words are deduced from their originals and illustrated in their different significations by examples from the best writers", happily blend the application of tradition and current usage in determining what is standard English; and these methods have ever since been a guide to lexicographers.

Laurence Sterne (1713–1768), the son of an officer in a line regiment, was born at Clonmel. He graduated at Cambridge, and became rector of Sutton in Yorkshire, in which county he lived uneventfully until the publication of his novel made him a celebrity in London society, and supplied him with the means of travelling on the continent in the hope of improving his never robust health. The hope was vain, and he was only fifty-five when he died.

The extract consists of two consecutive chapters from the eighth book of the bulky *Life and Opinions of Tristram Shandy, Gent*, the publication of which was begun with the issue of books I and II in 1759, and ended, from sheer weariness, with that of book IX in 1767. Such a method of composition does not make for structural perfection, and it would be difficult to find any parallel for such formlessness in fiction. Tristram himself is not born until well into the third book, and there is less about his "life and opinions" than those of any of his relations. The style is as eccentric as the plan. In the composition of chapters, paragraphs and sentences Sterne ignored or defied conventional practice, and observed no laws but those of his whimsical fancy.

His punctuation is anarchical, at least as many sentences ending with a dash as with a full-stop. The fantastic tricks and japes were no doubt welcomed by his contemporaries for their novelty; by us they must be tolerated as the facetiousness of an allowed jester. For Sterne has great qualities both as a narrator and as a stylist. His unorthodox methods are deliberate, and admirably suited for the purpose he had in view, which was not a consecutive narrative shaped into an artistic plot, but the delineation of character as revealed in the daily intimacies of the domestic life of a whole family —conditions that debar what is sensational and give scope for the observation of individual oddities. To sketch the outline of a character in a few bold strokes is to imply that we can get to know a man in a few moments. This is not Sterne's method: human nature is too intricate. The most trifling incidents have their significance. Uncle Toby and the rest are revealed gradually, with an infinite number of minute strokes, subtle and delicate, by their gestures, their conversation, their silences, and even by their misunderstandings.

For purposes such as these the more typical prose of the eighteenth century, stately and sonorous, would have been too weighty an instrument. Something capable of more sensitive manipulation was needed. Before *Tristram Shandy* there had been nothing so flexible, so expressive of delicate distinctions, of mere nuances of feeling; nothing so subtly responsive to varying moods and swift transitions from humour to pathos, and from pathos to poetry.

Johnson's *Letter to Lord Chesterfield* has several claims on our interest. It is a revelation of the character of the writer and a masterpiece of style. However well merited the rebuke, there were few men of letters in Johnson's day with the courage to administer it. With what dignity he refers to his early struggles, and with what restraint he conveys the pathos of success so long delayed! The irony is as devastating as anything in Swift, but the reality of his sufferings absolves him from the charge of "cynical asperity". The letter is, moreover, a document in literary history, and throws a vivid light on the conditions of authorship. To claim that it was the death-blow to patronage would be an exaggeration, for the whole of Johnson's career covers a period when writers were on the verge of independence; but dilettanti like Chesterfield might have continued to strut in the rôle of Maecenas, had not Johnson's action opened men's eyes to the insincerity with which the part had been played.

The passage from the *Journey* is, like all Johnson's writing, highly typical of the eighteenth century. It was a rare event for Johnson to leave the vicinity of Fleet Street, and now, nearly sixty-five years of age, and in indifferent health, he yielded to the importunity of Boswell and undertook the arduous journey to the Highlands, much of which had to be done on horseback. A novel adventure into what would have been considered a little later the most picturesque region of Britain evoked from Johnson few romantic descriptions of particular localities, but much philosophic discourse on mountains and mountaineers in general, such as he could have composed almost as well without leaving the armchair at his club. Johnson, it is true, was shortsighted, but his blindness to the beauties of nature was more temperamental than physical. He represents a period in which the perception of natural beauty was dormant. Moreover, he was incurably urban in his outlook, and the conviction that a region's culture is in inverse ratio to its distance from London accounts for the tone of condescension with which he discusses the Highlands. Where Johnson excels is in the acuteness of his pronouncements on men and manners, and in the clear statement of broad principles deduced from observation of detail.

The style of Johnson and his contemporaries differs from that of the previous generation. Post-Restoration ideals had resulted in a prose that was flat in tone and lacking in distinction (cf. Defoe); Johnson was mainly responsible for a reaction against this pedestrianism, and it appears not im-

probable that the change he effected owed something to a
rather superficial appreciation of the rich qualities of Caroline
writers like Richard Burton and Sir Thomas Browne. The
influence could not have been very profound, for Johnson
had little in common with them except a love of Latin
literature, and had no share in what he might have called the
"anfractuosities of mind" from which the idiosyncrasy of
Browne's style is derived. However, Caroline influence, so
far as it went, coupled with eighteenth-century correctness,
endued Johnson's prose with the dignity that befits formal
occasions. But the well-known witticism that the learned
doctor's little fishes talk like great whales is rather unfair:
Johnsonese is the exception, not the rule. One may smile at
his definition of *net* as *anything made with interstitial vacuities*,
but it is merely an ingenious evasion. What heaviness there
is in his writing must be attributed to the nature of the
thought, to the fondness for abstract generalisations, rather
than to the turn of expression. Johnson never achieved
Addison's lightness of touch, but he responded admirably to
a dignified theme. One has only to examine the *Journey*
to find that he remains true to the tradition of the plain
style. His sentences are short, and his statements direct and
vigorous. Balanced phrase and antithesis are used more for
emphasis than ornament, and to his readers, whose ears were
attuned to the mechanical swing of the heroic couplet, he
must have appeared to employ these devices with restraint.
French had already ceased to be an influence on style, and
Johnson's dislike of it is to be detected in his subtly con-
temptuous use of a French phrase in the letter to Chesterfield.
The influence of Latin is to be seen in his addiction to words
of the length of *dissimilitude*, and to words used in a stricter
etymological sense than was idiomatic (The Macdonalds
required the offender).

"Whatever he touched, he adorned", said Johnson of
Goldsmith, and did no more than justice to his memory.

Oliver Goldsmith (1728–1774) was perhaps the most versatile of eighteenth-century writers: as an essayist he came nearer than anyone else to the popularity of Steele and Addison; his poetry is more widely read than that of Pope; his comedy, *She Stoops to Conquer*, retains its freshness on the modern stage; while his one novel, *The Vicar of Wakefield*, can never cease to charm. When the latter made its casual appearance in 1766, the novel of domestic life and manners, as opposed to the picaresque or rogue novel of Defoe, had been brought to a high stage of development by Richardson, Fielding and Sterne. Goldsmith gave to the new fiction a turn in the direction where his sympathies lay. His life, since he left his father's country vicarage in Ireland, had been one of many vicissitudes. He had traversed Europe, almost a vagabond; he had tried his hand at many professions, and had finally settled down to writing for the booksellers. How often his thoughts must have turned from the harsh realities of life in London to the simple and romantic scenes of his childhood! From fond memories of his own personal experiences he wove a romance, an idyll of country life, rich in sympathetic humour—rare in the eighteenth century—of every variety from rollicking laughter to the smile that "trembles on the edge of tears".

Goldsmith belongs to the school of Johnson in that he was actuated by the same conscious endeavour to redeem English prose from excessive "easiness". In his more serious essays he can attain a slightly formal manner without becoming stiff or ponderous. He knew how to give firmness to his structure by the use of the antithetical form and pointed expression that were so favoured by the eighteenth century, and of which he acquired the habit in writing heroic couplets. But he is at his best when, as in *The Vicar*, he is most natural, when he gives the rein to his high spirits and love of fun; what he then writes is the mirror of his charming and unaffected personality. His wit, however, is never undisciplined; he never relaxes his firm hold on the structure, and his diction, though copious, is always pure.

His sentences have the ease and grace of Addison's, but a more airy lightness of touch. In *The Vicar* there is a limpid flow, a sparkle of animation that we seldom find in the sedater pages of the earlier essayists.

Edmund Burke (1729-1797) enjoyed great prestige in higher political circles, but his success in the House was only moderate. His lofty eloquence soared above the heads of the country squires who composed the bulk of his audience; impatient of his idealism and profound reasoning, they dubbed him "the dinner-bell". But the obtuseness of others was not the only cause of his failure: it has been said that "his rhetoric inclined more to the written than the spoken form".[1] The preparation of his speeches involved writing and rewriting, a method which destroys that effect of spontaneity essential to success on the rostrum. It was only in print that their rich qualities were fully perceived.

A profound political philosophy animates the work of Burke. He conceives of society as an organic whole, the health of which depends on the harmonious relations of its parts. To attain this harmony, abstract principles of right must be sacrificed to a wise expediency. In dealing with the colonies, therefore, true statesmanship would waive legal rights, and obtain its revenue by the friendly consent of the governed.

The greatness of Burke is the result of perfect equipoise of intellect and emotion. There are few writers who have combined such lucidity in exposition and such sanity of outlook with so moving a power of fervid remonstrance and passionate indignation. He never supported a cause at variance with his high ideals or advocated a policy inconsistent with his philosophy. His imagination and learning gave him the key to a Miltonic armoury of imagery and allusion. No matter how impetuous the sweep of his rhythm, he kept his diction under severe control, and chose his words with fastidious regard for the niceties of meaning and euphony.

[1] Saintsbury.

The *Speech on Conciliation* well exemplifies the most marked characteristic of his persuasive style, viz. a form of repetition which consists in presenting the argument in a great variety of ways, with frequent changes of metaphor and a wealth of illustration. Here, for example, the simple idea that affection and common love of liberty are the bonds that hold the Colonies to the Mother Country is amplified and emphasised by every device which enables the orator to repeat without becoming wearisome. Sentences are varied in length and structure. There are short incisive sentences like: *Slavery they can have anywhere. It is a weed that grows in every soil*; lengthy sentences that work up to a climax or gain cohesion from antithesis: *it is their attachment to their government...but rotten timber*; parallel sentences beautifully balanced: *Do not entertain so weak an imagination....Do not dream...mysterious whole*; occasional epigrams that brand themselves on the memory: *a great empire and little minds go ill together*.

Another characteristic of Burke's style is its rich allusiveness. In no respect is his reverence for tradition better exemplified than in the manner in which he has assimilated the phraseology of the Bible and the English poets, particularly Shakespeare. From these he seldom quotes at length, but borrows short phrases with a felicity that more than pays for the loan. Among the biblical phrases we have: *my trust is in her...*; *no force under heaven...*; *turn their faces towards you*; *this high calling*. *Julius Caesar* supplies *as strong as links of iron*, *Hamlet*, *grapple to you*; while the passage *your registers and your bonds...your suspending clauses* is strongly reminiscent of Hamlet's monologue on the skull of a lawyer. But there is scarcely a paragraph in Burke which has not echoes, however faint and elusive, of the music of the past.

The Decline and Fall is one of those monumental works, which result, like *Paradise Lost*, from self-dedication to a task too ambitious for ordinary mortals. *Edward Gibbon* (1737–1794) was in his twenty-seventh year when, "musing amidst the ruins of the Capitol", he conceived the project of his great history. For this he was already partly equipped. Religious difficulties had driven him to Catholicism at Oxford, and back to Protestantism at Lausanne; and, though his enquiries into the origins of Christianity left him even more of a sceptic than a Protestant, the knowledge he had thus acquired was profound. A short term of service with the militia gave him a practical interest in military affairs, which was to be of great value to the future historian of Roman campaigns. The writing of his work extended over a period of twelve years, a great part of which was spent at Lausanne. His familiarity with French and his residence abroad put him in close touch with the thought of continental historians, and gave him a breadth of view that had been denied to his more insular predecessors.

It has been said[1] that the conditions which qualify a history to be regarded as a work of art are three: a comprehensive knowledge of available documents and records; a philosophical plan that gives coherence and unity to a chaos of details; and an appropriate style. The work of Gibbon satisfies all these conditions; that which chiefly concerns us is his style. History is a composite form of writing, in which the art of narration is blended with that of exposition. That is to say, the historian has to tell a story and at the same time to explain and comment on the course of events. The movement of the story is impeded by the necessity of exposition, and even in passages where the narrative intention is uppermost, the movement has not the dramatic speed of events recorded by an eyewitness. The more remote the period of history, the more does the treatment turn to the stately style of the epic. For Gibbon's purpose of unfolding the solemn pageant of Roman

[1] Saintsbury, *Short History of English Literature*.

history the massive prose of the *Decline and Fall* is admirably suited. He obtains graphic pictorial effects from the copious use of epithets, a power well illustrated in the description of the battle-scenes, dying into "the *vast* silence that reigned over the plains of Châlons". A sentence like *After the mutual and repeated discharge of missile weapons, in which the archers of Scythia might signalise their superior dexterity* shows him more pompous than Johnson, but the hint of irony saves him from ridicule. His diction is in the scholarly and rather pedantic tradition of the eighteenth century, e.g. *oppressed*, *event*; he is particularly prone to weighty periphrases. The latter, we should note, however, are seldom mere elegant variations: *the magnanimous Barbarian* for Attila, *the conquerors of Scythia and Germany* for the Huns, lend colour to the narrative; sometimes the device recapitulates information, as in *the Imperial general* (Aetius), or it serves to lend force to the argument: e.g. *to calm the passions which the son of Theodoric considered as a duty*, i.e. to calm the passions which Torismond, as a son of the slain Theodoric, considered etc.... In the structure of his sentences he is not so antithetical as Johnson, but he resembles him in his fondness for a sort of architectural symmetry in the arrangement of masses of words in groups of two's and three's, e.g. *The Huns who... Visigoths* (p. 161); *separated from his allies...escaped* (p. 163); *The patrician...his brothers* (pp. 163–4).

Of the inner qualities of style which reveal the personality of the writer, but which seldom emerge clearly in so short a passage, we have, however, a hint or two. The undertone of grave irony and humour by which he achieved an effect of aloofness is faintly audible in his reference to the art of destroying the human species. The impression of impartiality is enhanced by the sceptical reserve with which he receives the testimony even of eyewitnesses in estimating the number of the slain. His attitude in this matter might well be contrasted with that of Macaulay.

Chapter VIII

The Romantic Movement

1. THE FIGHT

(Extract from an article published in *The New Monthly Magazine* (1822):
William Hazlitt)

The day, as I have said, was fine for a December morning.
The grass was wet, and the ground miry, and ploughed up
with multitudinous feet, except that, within the ring itself,
there was a spot of virgin-green closed in and unprofaned by
vulgar tread, that shone with dazzling brightness in the mid-
day sun. For it was now noon, and we had an hour to wait.
This is the trying time. It is then the heart sickens, as you
think what the two champions are about, and how short a
time will determine their fate. After the first blow is struck,
there is no opportunity for nervous apprehensions; you are
swallowed up in the immediate interest of the scene—but

> Between the acting of a dreadful thing
> And the first motion, all the interim is
> Like a phantasma, or a hideous dream.[1]

I found it so as I felt the sun's rays clinging to my back, and
saw the white wintry clouds sink below the verge of the
horizon. "So, I thought, my fairest hopes have faded from
my sight! so will the Gas-man's glory, or that of his adversary
vanish in an hour." The *swells* were parading in their white
box-coats,[2] the outer ring was cleared with some bruises on
the heads and shins of the rustic assembly (for the *cockneys*
had been distanced by the sixty-six miles[3]); the time drew
near, I had got a good stand; a bustle, a buzz, ran through the
crowd, and from the opposite side entered Neate, between
his second and bottle-holder. He rolled along, swathed in his

---

[1] *Between the acting...*, *Julius Caesar*, II, 1, 63–5.
[2] *box-coat*, a thick overcoat for driving.
[3] *sixty-six miles*. The fight took place at Hungerford, near Newbury.

loose great coat, his knock-knees bending under his huge bulk; and, with a modest cheerful air, threw his hat into the ring. He then just looked round, and began quietly to undress; when from the other side there was a similar rush and an opening made, and the Gas-man came forward with a conscious air of anticipated triumph, too much like the cock-of-the-walk. He strutted about more than became a hero, sucked oranges with a supercilious air, and threw away the skin with a toss of his head, and went up and looked at Neate, which was an act of supererogation. The only sensible thing he did was, as he strode away from the modern Ajax,[1] to fling out his arms, as if he wanted to try whether they would do their work that day. By this time they had stripped, and presented a strong contrast in appearance. If Neate was like Ajax, "with Atlantean shoulders,[2] fit to bear" the pugilistic reputation of all Bristol, Hickman might be compared to Diomed,[3] light, vigorous, elastic, and his back glistened in the sun, as he moved about, like a panther's hide. There was now a dead pause—attention was awe-struck. Who at that moment, big with a great event, did not draw his breath short—did not feel his heart throb? All was ready. They tossed up for the sun, and the Gas-man won. They were led up to the *scratch*—shook hands, and went at it.

In the first round every one thought it was all over. After making play a short time, the Gas-man flew at his adversary like a tiger, struck five blows in as many seconds, three first, and then following him as he staggered back, two more, right and left, and down he fell, a mighty ruin. There was a shout, and I said, "There is no standing this". Neate seemed like a lifeless lump of flesh and bone, round which the Gas-man's blows played with the rapidity of electricity or lightning, and you imagined he would only be lifted up to be knocked down again. It was as if Hickman held a sword or a fire in that right hand of his, and directed it against an unarmed body. They met again, and Neate seemed, not cowed, but particularly cautious. I saw his teeth clenched together

---

[1] *Ajax*, one of the tallest of the Greek heroes.

[2] *with Atlantean shoulders....* Description of Beelzebub in *Paradise Lost*, II, 306.

[3] *Diomed*, another of the Greek heroes before Troy.

and his brows knit close against the sun. He held out both his arms at full length straight before him, like two sledge-hammers, and raised his left an inch or two higher. The Gas-man could not get over this guard—they struck mutually and fell, but without advantage on either side. It was the same in the next round; but the balance of power was thus restored—the fate of the battle was suspended. No one could tell how it would end. This was the only moment in which opinion was divided; for, in the next, the Gas-man aiming a mortal blow at his adversary's neck, with his right hand, and failing from the length he had to reach, the other returned it with his left at full-swing, planted a tremendous blow on his cheek-bone and eyebrow, and made a red ruin of that side of his face. The Gas-man went down, and there was another shout—a roar of triumph as the waves of fortune rolled tumultuously from side to side. This was a settler. Hickman got up, and "grinned horrible a ghastly smile,"[1] yet he was evidently dashed in his opinion of himself; it was the first time he had ever been so punished; all one side of his face was perfect scarlet, and his right eye was closed in dingy blackness, as he advanced to the fight, less confident, but still determined. After one or two rounds, not receiving another such remembrancer, he rallied and went at it with his former impetuosity. But in vain. His strength had been weakened,—his blows could not tell at such a distance,—he was obliged to fling himself at his adversary, and could not strike from his feet; and almost as regularly as he flew at him with his right hand, Neate warded the blow, or drew back out of its reach, and felled him with the return of his left. There was little cautious sparring—no half-hits—no tapping and trifling, none of the *petit-maîtreship* of the art—they were almost all knock-down blows:—the fight was a good stand-up fight. The wonder was the half-minute time. If there had been a minute or more allowed between each round, it would have been intelligible how they should by degrees recover strength and resolution; but to see two men smashed to the ground, smeared with gore, stunned, senseless, the breath beaten out of their bodies; and then, before you recover from the shock, to see them rise up with new strength and courage,

---

[1] *grinned horrible....* Description of Death in *Paradise Lost*, ii, 846.

stand steady to inflict or receive mortal offence, and rush upon each other "like two clouds over the Caspian"[1]—this is the most astonishing thing of all:—this is the high and heroic state of man! From this time forward the event became more certain every round; and about the twelfth it seemed as if it must have been over. Hickman generally stood with his back to me; but in the scuffle, he had changed positions, and Neate just then made a tremendous lunge at him, and hit him full in the face. It was doubtful whether he would fall backwards or forwards; he hung suspended for a second or two, and then fell back, throwing his hands in the air, and with his face lifted up to the sky. I never saw anything more terrific than his aspect just before he fell. All traces of life, of natural expression, were gone from him. His face was like a human skull, a death's head, spouting blood. The eyes were filled with blood, the nose streamed with blood, the mouth gaped blood. He was not like an actual man, but like a preternatural, spectral appearance, or like one of the figures in Dante's *Inferno*. Yet he fought on after this for several rounds, still striking the first desperate blow, and Neate standing on the defensive, and using the same cautious guard to the last, as if he had still all his work to do; and it was not till the Gas-man was so stunned in the seventeenth or eighteenth round, that his senses forsook him, and he could not come to time, that the battle was declared over. Ye who despise the Fancy,[2] do something to shew as much *pluck*, or as much self-possession as this, before you assume a superiority which you have never given a single proof of by any one action in the whole course of your lives!—When the Gas-man came to himself, the first words he uttered were, "Where am I? What is the matter?" "Nothing is the matter, Tom,— you have lost the battle, but you are the bravest man alive." And Jackson whispered to him, "I am collecting a purse for you, Tom." Vain sounds, and unheard at that moment! Neate instantly went up and shook him cordially by the hand, and seeing some old acquaintance, began to flourish with his fists, calling out, "Ah, you always said I couldn't fight—

---

[1] *like two clouds....* Adapted from the description of the encounter of Satan and Death in *Paradise Lost*, II, 714–16.
[2] *the Fancy*, pugilism.

What do you think now?" But all in good humour, and without any appearance of arrogance; only it was evident Bill Neate was pleased that he had won the fight. When it was over, I asked Cribb if he did not think it was a good one? He said, "*Pretty well!*" The carrier-pigeons now mounted into the air, and one of them flew with the news of her husband's victory to the bosom of Mrs Neate. Alas, for Mrs Hickman!

2. MODERN GALLANTRY

From *Essays of Elia*: Charles Lamb
(First published in *London Magazine*, November, 1822)

In comparing modern with ancient manners, we are pleased to compliment ourselves upon the point of gallantry; a certain obsequiousness, or deferential respect, which we are supposed to pay to females, as females.

I shall believe that this principle actuates our conduct, when I can forget, that in the nineteenth century of the era from which we date our civility,[1] we *are just beginning to leave off the very frequent practice of whipping females in public, in common with the coarsest male offenders.

I shall believe it to be influential, when I can shut my eyes to the fact that in England women are still occasionally—hanged.

I shall believe in it, when actresses are no longer subject to be hissed off a stage by gentlemen.

I shall believe in it, when Dorimant[2] hands a fish-wife across the kennel; or assists the apple-woman to pick up her wandering fruit, which some unlucky dray has just dissipated.

I shall believe in it, when the Dorimants in humbler life, who would be thought in their way notable adepts in this refinement, shall act upon it in places where they are not known, or think themselves not observed—when I shall see the traveller for some rich tradesman part with his admired box-coat, to spread it over the defenceless shoulders of the poor woman, who is passing to her parish on the roof of the same stage-coach with him, drenched in the rain—when I shall no longer see a woman standing up in the pit of a London theatre, till she is sick and faint with the exertion, with men about her, seated at their ease, and jeering at her distress; till one, that seems to have more manners or conscience than the rest, significantly declares "she should be welcome to his seat, if she were a little younger and handsomer". Place this

---

[1] *civility*, civilisation.

[2] *Dorimant*, a character in Etherege's *The Man of Mode*, a man of fashion.

dapper warehouseman, or that rider,[1] in a circle of their own female acquaintance, and you shall confess you have not seen a politer-bred man in Lothbury.

Lastly, I shall begin to believe that there is some such principle influencing our conduct, when more than one-half of the drudgery and coarse servitude of the world shall cease to be performed by women.

Until that day comes I shall never believe this boasted point to be anything more than a conventional fiction; a pageant got up between the sexes, in a certain rank, and at a certain time of life, in which both find their account equally.

I shall be even disposed to rank it among the salutary fictions of life, when in polite circles I shall see the same attentions paid to age as to youth, to homely features as to handsome, to coarse complexions as to clear—to the woman, as she is a woman, not as she is a beauty, a fortune, or a title.

I shall believe it to be something more than a name, when a well-dressed gentleman in a well-dressed company can advert to the topic of *female old age* without exciting, and intending to excite, a sneer:—when the phrases "antiquated virginity", and such a one has "overstood her market", pronounced in good company, shall raise immediate offence in man, or woman, that shall hear them spoken.*

*Joseph Paice, of Bread-street-hill, merchant, and one of the Directors of the South Sea Company—the same to whom Edwards, the Shakspeare commentator, has addressed a fine sonnet—was the only pattern of consistent gallantry I have ever met with. He took me under his shelter at an early age, and bestowed some pains upon me. I owe to his precepts and example whatever there is of the man of business (and that is not much) in my composition. It was not his fault that I did not profit more. Though bred a Presbyterian, and brought up a merchant, he was the finest gentleman of his time. He had not *one* system of attention to females in the drawing-room, and *another* in the shop, or at the stall. I do not mean that he made no distinction. But he never lost sight of sex, or overlooked it in the casualties of a disadvantageous situation. I have seen him stand bareheaded—smile if you please—to a poor servant-girl, while she has

[1] *rider*, commercial traveller.

been inquiring of him the way to some street—in such a posture of unforced civility, as neither to embarrass her in the acceptance, nor himself in the offer, of it. He was no dangler, in the common acceptation of the word, after women; but he reverenced and upheld, in every form in which it came before him, *womanhood*. I have seen him—nay, smile not—tenderly escorting a market-woman, whom he had encountered in a shower, exalting his umbrella over her poor basket of fruit, that it might receive no damage, with as much carefulness as if she had been a countess. To the reverend form of Female Eld[1] he would yield the wall (though it were to an ancient beggar-woman) with more ceremony than we can afford to show our grandams. He was the Preux Chevalier[2] of Age; the Sir Calidore,[3] or Sir Tristan,[4] to those who have no Calidores or Tristans to defend them. The roses, that had long faded thence, still bloomed for him in those withered and yellow cheeks.

He was never married, but in his youth he paid his addresses to the beautiful Susan Winstanley—old Winstanley's daughter of Clapton—who dying in the early days of their courtship, confirmed in him the resolution of perpetual bachelorship. It was during their short courtship, he told me, that he had been one day treating his mistress with a profusion of civil speeches—the common gallantries—to which kind of thing she had hitherto manifested no repugnance—but in this instance with no effect. He could not obtain from her a decent acknowledgment in return. She rather seemed to resent his compliments. He could not set it down to caprice, for the lady had always shown herself above that littleness. When he ventured on the following day, finding her a little better humoured, to expostulate with her on her coldness of yesterday, she confessed, with her usual frankness, that she had no sort of dislike to his attentions; that she could even endure some high-flown compliments; that a young woman placed in her situation had a right to expect all sort of civil things said to her; that she hoped she

---

[1] *Eld*, old age.
[2] *Preux Chevalier*, valiant knight.
[3] *Sir Calidore*, the knight who typifies courtesy in the *Faerie Queene*.
[4] *Sir Tristan*, a model of courtesy in Malory.

could digest a dose of adulation, short of insincerity, with as little injury to her humility as most young women; but that— a little before he had commenced his compliments—she had overheard him by accident, in rather rough language, rating a young woman, who had not brought home his cravats quite to the appointed time, and she thought to herself, "As I am Miss Susan Winstanley, and a young lady—a reputed beauty, and known to be a fortune—I can have my choice of the finest speeches from the mouth of this very fine gentleman who is courting me—but if I had been poor Mary Such-a-one (*naming the milliner*),—and had failed of bringing home the cravats to the appointed hour—though perhaps I had sat up half the night to forward them—what sort of compliments should I have received then? And my woman's pride came to my assistance; and I thought, that if it were only to do *me* honour, a female, like myself, might have received handsomer usage; and I was determined not to accept any fine speeches, to the compromise of that sex, the belonging to which was after all my strongest claim and title to them."*

I think the lady discovered both generosity, and a just way of thinking, in this rebuke which she gave her lover; and I have sometimes imagined, that the uncommon strain of courtesy, which through life regulated the actions and be- haviour of my friend towards all of womankind indis- criminately, owed its happy origin to this seasonable lesson from the lips of his lamented mistress.

I wish the whole female world would entertain the same notion of these things that Miss Winstanley showed. Then we should see something of the spirit of consistent gallantry; and no longer witness the anomaly of the same man—a pattern of true politeness to a wife—of cold contempt, or rudeness, to a sister—the idolater of his female mistress—the disparager and despiser of his no less female aunt, or un- fortunate—still female—maiden cousin. Just so much respect as a woman derogates from her own sex, in whatever con- dition placed—her handmaid or dependent—she deserves to have diminished from herself on that score; and probably will feel the diminution, when youth, and beauty, and ad- vantages, not inseparable from sex, shall lose of their attrac- tion. What a woman should demand of a man in courtship, or after it, is first—respect for her as she is a woman;—and next to that—to be respected by him above all other women. But let her stand upon her female character as upon a foundation; and let the attentions, incident to individual preference, be so many pretty additaments[1] and ornaments— as many, and as fanciful, as you please—to that main structure. Let her first lesson be—with sweet Susan Winstanley—to *reverence her sex.*

[1] *additaments*, additions.

3. THE PRAISE OF CHIMNEY-SWEEPERS

London Magazine (1822): Charles Lamb

I like to meet a sweep—understand me—not a grown sweeper—old chimney-sweepers are by no means attractive —but one of those tender novices, blooming through their first nigritude,[1] the maternal washings not quite effaced from the cheek—such as come forth with the dawn, or somewhat earlier, with their little professional notes[2] sounding like the *peep-peep* of a young sparrow; or liker to the matin lark should I pronounce them, in their aërial ascents[3] not seldom anticipating the sunrise?

I have a kindly yearning towards these dim specks—poor blots—innocent blacknesses—

I reverence these young Africans of our own growth— these almost clergy imps,[4] who sport their cloth without assumption; and from their little pulpits (the tops of chimneys), in the nipping air of a December morning, preach a lesson of patience to mankind.

When a child, what a mysterious pleasure it was to witness their operation! to see a chit no bigger than one's-self, enter, one knew not by what process, into what seemed the *fauces Averni*[5]—to pursue him in imagination, as he went sounding on through so many dark stifling caverns, horrid shades! to shudder with the idea that "now, surely he must be lost for ever!"—to revive at hearing his feeble shout of discovered day-light—and then (O fulness of delight!) running out of doors, to come just in time to see the sable phenomenon emerge in safety, the brandished weapon of his art victorious like some flag waved over a conquered citadel! I seem to remember having been told, that a bad sweep was once left in a stack with his brush, to indicate which way the wind blew. It was an awful spectacle, certainly; not much unlike

---

[1] *nigritude*, blackness, sootiness.
[2] *professional notes*, sweep! sweep!
[3] *aërial ascents*, chimney-climbing.
[4] *clergy imps*, i.e. in their black clothes.
[5] *fauces Averni*, jaws of hell. Vergil, *Æneid*.

the old stage direction in Macbeth, where the "Apparition of
a child crowned, with a tree in his hand, rises".

Reader, if thou meetest one of these small gentry in thy
early rambles, it is good to give him a penny,—it is better
to give him two-pence. If it be starving[1] weather, and to
the proper troubles of his hard occupation, a pair of kibed[2]
heels (no unusual accompaniment) be superadded, the demand on thy humanity will surely rise to a tester[3].

There is a composition, the ground-work of which I have
understood to be the sweet wood 'yclept[4] sassafras.[5] This
wood boiled down to a kind of tea, and tempered with an
infusion of milk and sugar, hath to some tastes a delicacy
beyond the China luxury. I know not how thy palate may
relish it; for myself, with every deference to the judicious
Mr Read, who hath time out of mind kept open a shop (the
only one he avers in London) for the vending of this "wholesome and pleasant beverage", on the south side of Fleet
Street, as thou approachest Bridge Street—*the only Salopian
house*—I have never yet adventured to dip my own particular
lip in a basin of his commended ingredients—a cautious pre-
monition to the olfactories[6] constantly whispering to me, that
my stomach must infallibly, with all due courtesy, decline
it. Yet I have seen palates, otherwise not uninstructed in
dietetical elegancies, sup it up with avidity.

I know not by what particular conformation of the organ
it happens, but I have always found that this composition is
surprisingly gratifying to the palate of a young chimney-
sweeper—whether the oily particles (sassafras is slightly
oleaginous) do attenuate and soften the fuliginous concretions,[7] which are sometimes found (in dissections[8]) to adhere
to the roof of the mouth in these unfledged practitioners; or
whether Nature, sensible that she had mingled too much of
bitter wood in the lot of these raw victims, caused to grow
out of the earth her sassafras for a sweet lenitive—but so it

[1] *starving*, freezing. [2] *kibed*, galled.
[3] *tester*, slang for sixpence. [4] *'yclept*, called.
[5] *sassafras*, a tree of the laurel family from the root of which an infusion
called *Salop* is prepared.
[6] *olfactories*, the sense of smell.
[7] *fuliginous concretions*, accumulations of soot.
[8] *in dissections*, i.e. in the dissecting-room.

is, that no possible taste or odour to the senses of a young chimney-sweeper can convey a delicate excitement comparable to this mixture. Being penniless, they will yet hang their black heads over the ascending steam, to gratify one sense if possible, seemingly no less pleased than those domestic animals—cats—when they purr over a new-found sprig of valerian. There is something more in these sympathies than philosophy can inculcate.

Now albeit Mr Read boasteth, not without reason, that his is the *only Salopian house*; yet be it known to thee, reader—if thou art one who keepest what are called good hours, thou art haply ignorant of the fact—he hath a race of industrious imitators, who from stalls, and under open sky, dispense the same savoury mess to humbler customers, at that dead time of the dawn, when (as extremes meet) the rake, reeling home from his midnight cups, and the hard-handed artizan leaving his bed to resume the premature labours of the day, jostle, not unfrequently to the manifest disconcerting of the former, for the honours of the pavement. It is the time when, in summer, between the expired and the not yet relumined kitchen-fires, the kennels[1] of our fair metropolis give forth their least satisfactory odours. The rake, who wisheth to dissipate his o'ernight vapours in more grateful coffee, curses the ungenial fume, as he passeth; but the artizan stops to taste, and blesses the fragrant breakfast.

This is *saloop*—the precocious[2] herb-woman's darling—the delight of the early gardener, who transports his smoking cabbages by break of day from Hammersmith to Covent Garden's famed piazzas—the delight, and oh! I fear, too often the envy, of the unpennied sweep. Him shouldst thou haply encounter,[3] with his dim visage pendent over the grateful steam, regale him with a sumptuous basin (it will cost thee but three-halfpennies) and a slice of delicate bread and butter (an added halfpenny)—so may thy culinary fires, eased of the o'ercharged secretions from thy worse-placed hospitalities,[4] curl up a lighter volume to the welkin—so may the

---

[1] *kennels*, gutters.   [2] *precocious*, early rising.
[3] *Him shouldst thou haply...*, perhaps an echo of *Paradise Lost*, I, 203.
[4] *eased of the o'ercharged...hospitalities*, cleansed of the accumulated soot deposited by cooking for the entertainment of your well-to-do friends.

descending soot never taint thy costly well-ingredienced
soups—nor the odious cry, quick-reaching from street to
street, of the *fired chimney*, invite the rattling engines from
ten adjacent parishes, to disturb for a casual scintillation[1]
thy peace and pocket!

I am by nature extremely susceptible of street affronts;
the jeers and taunts of the populace; the low-bred triumph
they display over the casual trip, or splashed stocking of a
gentleman. Yet can I endure the jocularity of a young sweep
with something more than forgiveness.—In the last winter
but one, pacing along Cheapside with my accustomed pre-
cipitation when I walk westward,[2] a treacherous slide brought
me upon my back in an instant. I scrambled up with pain
and shame enough—yet outwardly trying to face it down, as
if nothing had happened—when the roguish grin of one of
these young wits encountered me. There he stood, pointing
me out with his dusky finger to the mob, and to a poor
woman (I suppose his mother) in particular, till the tears for
the exquisiteness of the fun (so he thought it) worked themselves out at the corners of his poor red eyes, red from many
a previous weeping, and soot-inflamed, yet twinkling through
all with such a joy, snatched out of desolation, that Hogarth—
but Hogarth has got him already (how could he miss him?)
in the March to Finchley, grinning at the pye-man—there
he stood, as he stands in the picture, irremovable, as if the
jest was to last for ever—with such a maximum of glee,
and minimum of mischief, in his mirth—for the grin of a
genuine sweep hath absolutely no malice in it—that I could
have been content, if the honour of a gentleman might
endure it, to have remained his butt and his mockery till
midnight.

I am by theory obdurate to the seductiveness of what are
called a fine set of teeth. Every pair of rosy lips (the ladies
must pardon me) is a casket presumably holding such jewels;
but, methinks they should take leave to "air" them as frugally
as possible. The fine lady, or fine gentleman, who show me
their teeth, show me bones. Yet must I confess, that from
the mouth of a true sweep a display (even to ostentation) of

[1] *casual scintillation*, chance spark.
[2] *walk westward*, i.e. away from the day's work in the city.

those white and shiny ossifications,[1] strikes me as an agreeable
anomaly in manners, and an allowable piece of foppery. It is,
as when   A sable cloud
      Turns forth her silver lining on the night.[2]

It is like some remnant of gentry[3] not quite extinct; a badge
of better days; a hint of nobility: and, doubtless, under the
obscuring darkness and double night of their forlorn dis-
guisement, oftentimes lurketh good blood, and gentle conditions, derived from lost ancestry, and a lapsed pedigree.
The premature apprenticements of these tender victims give
but too much encouragement, I fear, to clandestine and
almost infantile abductions; the seeds of civility and true
courtesy, so often discernible in these young grafts (not
otherwise to be accounted for) plainly hint at some forced
adoptions; many noble Rachels[4] mourning for their children,
even in our days, countenance the fact; the tales of fairy
spiriting may shadow a lamentable verity, and the recovery
of the young Montagu[5] be but a solitary instance of good
fortune out of many irreparable and hopeless *defiliations*.[6]
    In one of the state-beds at Arundel Castle, a few years
since—under a ducal canopy—(that seat of the Howards is
an object of curiosity to visitors, chiefly for its beds, in which
the late duke was especially a connoisseur)—encircled with
curtains of delicatest crimson, with starry coronets inwoven—
folded between a pair of sheets whiter and softer than the lap
where Venus lulled Ascanius[7]—was discovered by chance,
after all methods of search had failed, at noon-day, fast asleep,
a lost chimney-sweeper. The little creature, having somehow
confounded his passage among the intricacies of those lordly
chimneys, by some unknown aperture had alighted upon this
magnificent chamber; and, tired with his tedious explorations,
was unable to resist the delicious invitement to repose, which
he there saw exhibited; so creeping between the sheets very

---

[1] *ossifications*, bone-structures.   [2] *A sable cloud, etc.*, Milton, *Comus*.
[3] *gentry*, gentility.   [4] *Rachels*, Jeremiah xxxi.
[5] *Montagu*. The son of Lady Mary Wortley Montagu ran away from
school and became a chimney-sweep. He was found and taken home.
[6] *defiliations*, depriving parents of a child.
[7] *Ascanius*, the son of Aeneas, who was himself the son of Venus.

quietly, laid his black head upon the pillow, and slept like a young Howard.

Such is the account given to the visitors at the Castle.— But I cannot help seeming to perceive a confirmation of what I had just hinted at in this story. A high instinct was at work in the case, or I am mistaken. Is it probable that a poor child of that description, with whatever weariness he might be visited, would have ventured, under such a penalty as he would be taught to expect, to uncover the sheets of a Duke's bed, and deliberately to lay himself down between them, when the rug, or the carpet, presented an obvious couch, still far above his pretensions—is this probable, I would ask, if the great power of nature, which I contend for, had not been manifested within him, prompting to the adventure? Doubtless this young nobleman (for such my mind misgives me that he must be) was allured by some memory, not amounting to full consciousness, of his condition in infancy, when he was used to be lapt[1] by his mother, or his nurse, in just such sheets as he there found, into which he was now but creeping back as into his proper *incunabula*,[2] and resting-place.—By no other theory, than by this sentiment of a pre-existent state (as I may call it), can I explain a deed so venturous, and, indeed, upon any other system, so indecorous, in this tender, but unseasonable, sleeper.

[1] *lapt*, wrapped, an Elizabethan usage.
[2] *incunabula*, swaddling-clothes.

4. OUR LADIES OF SORROW

From *Levana*[1] *and Our Ladies of Sorrow*: Thomas De Quincey

The eldest of the three is named *Mater Lachrymarum*, Our
Lady of Tears. She it is that night and day raves and moans,
calling for vanished faces. She stood in Rama,[2] where a voice
was heard of lamentation,—Rachel weeping for her children,
and refusing to be comforted. She it was that stood in
Bethlehem on the night when Herod's sword swept its
nurseries of Innocents, and the little feet were stiffened for
ever, which, heard at times as they tottered along floors over-
head, woke pulses of love in household hearts that were not
unmarked in heaven.

Her eyes are sweet and subtle, wild and sleepy, by turns;
oftentimes rising to the clouds, oftentimes challenging the
heavens. She wears a diadem round her head. And I knew
by childish memories that she could go abroad upon the
winds, when she heard the sobbing of litanies or the thunder-
ing of organs, and when she beheld the mustering of summer
clouds. This sister, the eldest, it is that carries keys more than
papal at her girdle, which open every cottage and every
palace. She, to my knowledge, sat all last summer by the
bedside of the blind beggar, him that so often and so gladly
I talked with, whose pious daughter, eight years old, with the
sunny countenance, resisted the temptations of play and
village mirth to travel all day long on dusty roads with her
afflicted father. For this did God send her a great reward.
In the spring-time of the year, and whilst yet her own Spring
was budding, he recalled her to himself. But her blind father
mourns for ever over *her*; still he dreams at midnight that the
little guiding hand is locked within his own; and still he
wakens to a darkness that is *now* within a second and a deeper

[1] Levana, a Roman goddess, "the tutelary power that controls the
education of the nursery". Levana educates by means of central forces
such as passion and temptation, and she reverences most of all the agencies
of grief. Her ministers are three, whom De Quincey names *The Sorrows*,
impersonations of the "mighty abstractions that incarnate themselves in
all individual suffering of man's heart".

[2] *Rama*, Jeremiah xxxi.

darkness. This *Mater Lachrymarum* has also been sitting all
this winter of 1844–5 within the bed-chamber of the Czar,
bringing before his eyes a daughter (not less pious) that
vanished to God not less suddenly, and left behind her a
darkness not less profound. By the power of the keys it is
that Our Lady of Tears glides a ghostly intruder into the
chambers of sleepless men, sleepless women, sleepless
children, from Ganges to Nile, from Nile to Mississippi.
And her, because she is the first-born of her house, and has
the widest empire, let us honour with the title of Madonna.

The second sister is called *Mater Suspiriorum*—Our Lady
of Sighs. She never scales the clouds, nor walks abroad upon
the winds. She wears no diadem. And her eyes, if they were
ever seen, would be neither sweet nor subtle; no man could
read their story; they would be found filled with perishing
dreams, and with wrecks of forgotten delirium. But she
raises not her eyes; her head, on which sits a dilapidated
turban, droops for ever, for ever fastens on the dust. She
weeps not. She groans not. But she sighs inaudibly at intervals. Her sister, Madonna, is oftentimes stormy and
frantic, raging in the highest against heaven, and demanding
back her darlings. But Our Lady of Sighs never clamours,
never defies, dreams not of rebellious aspirations. She is
humble to abjectness. Hers is the meekness that belongs to
the hopeless. Murmur she may, but it is in her sleep.
Whisper she may, but it is to herself in the twilight. Mutter
she does at times, but it is in solitary places that are desolate
as she is desolate, in ruined cities, and when the sun has gone
down to his rest. This sister is the visitor of the Pariah, of the
Jew, of the bondsman to the oar in the Mediterranean galleys;
and of the English criminal in Norfolk Island, blotted out
from the books of remembrance in sweet far-off England;
of the baffled penitent reverting his eyes for ever upon a
solitary grave, which to him seems the altar overthrown of
some past and bloody sacrifice, on which altar no oblations
can now be availing, whether towards pardon that he might
implore, or towards reparation that he might attempt. Every
slave that at noonday looks up to the tropical sun with timid
reproach, as he points with one hand to the earth, our general
mother, but for *him* a stepmother,—as he points with the

other hand to the Bible, our general teacher, but against *him*
sealed and sequestered;—every woman sitting in darkness,
without love to shelter her head, or hope to illumine her
solitude, because the heaven-born instincts kindling in her
nature germs of holy affections which God implanted in her
womanly bosom, having been stifled by social necessities,
now burn sullenly to waste, like sepulchral lamps amongst
the ancients; every nun defrauded of her unreturning May-
time by wicked kinsman, whom God will judge; every
captive in every dungeon; all that are betrayed and all that
are rejected outcasts by traditionary law, and children of
hereditary disgrace,—all these walk with Our Lady of Sighs.
She also carries a key; but she needs it little. For her kingdom is chiefly amongst the tents of Shem, and the houseless
vagrant of every clime. Yet in the very highest walks of man
she finds chapels of her own; and even in glorious England
there are some that, to the world, carry their heads as proudly
as the reindeer, who yet secretly have received her mark upon
their foreheads.

But the third sister, who is also the youngest—! Hush,
whisper whilst we talk of *her*! Her kingdom is not large, or
else no flesh should live; but within that kingdom all power
is hers. Her head, turreted like that of Cybele,[1] rises almost
beyond the reach of sight. She droops not; and her eyes
rising so high *might* be hidden by distance; but, being what
they are, they cannot be hidden; through the treble veil of
crape which she wears, the fierce light of a blazing misery,
that rests not for matins or for vespers, for noon of day or
noon of night, for ebbing or for flowing tide, may be read
from the very ground. She is the defier of God. She is also
the mother of lunacies, and the suggestress of suicides. Deep
lie the roots of her power; but narrow is the nation that she
rules. For she can approach only those in whom a profound
nature has been upheaved by central convulsions; in whom
the heart trembles, and the brain rocks under conspiracies of
tempest from without and tempest from within. Madonna

[1] *turreted like that of Cybele.* Cybele, the great nature goddess. The
Romans represented her as wearing the mural crown, a circle of gold, in-
dented like a battlement, bestowed on him who first mounted the wall of
a besieged place.

moves with uncertain steps, fast or slow, but still with tragic grace. Our Lady of Sighs creeps timidly and stealthily. But this youngest sister moves with incalculable motions, bounding, and with tiger's leaps. She carries no key; for, though coming rarely amongst men, she storms all doors at which she is permitted to enter at all. And her name is *Mater Tenebrarum*—Our Lady of Darkness.

These were the *Semnai Theai*, or Sublime Goddesses, these were the *Eumenides*, or Gracious Ladies (so called by antiquity in shuddering propitiation), of my Oxford dreams. Madonna spoke. She spoke by her mysterious hand. Touching my head, she said to Our Lady of Sighs; and what she spoke, translated out of the signs which (except in dreams) no man reads, was this:—

"Lo! here he is, whom in childhood I dedicated to my altars. This is he that once I made my darling. Him I led astray, him I beguiled, and from heaven I stole away his young heart to mine. Through me did he become idolatrous; and through me it was, by languishing desires, that he worshipped the worm, and prayed to the wormy grave. Holy was the grave to him; lovely was its darkness; saintly its corruption. Him, this young idolator, I have seasoned for thee, dear gentle Sister of Sighs! Do thou take him now to *thy* heart, and season him for our dreadful sister. And thou," —turning to the *Mater Tenebrarum*, she said,—"wicked sister, that temptest and hatest, do thou take him from *her*. See that thy sceptre lie heavy on his head. Suffer not woman and her tenderness to sit near him in his darkness. Banish the frailties of hope, wither the relenting of love, scorch the fountain of tears, curse him as only thou canst curse. So shall he be accomplished in the furnace, so shall he see the things that ought not to be seen, sights that are abominable, and secrets that are unutterable. So shall he read elder truths, sad truths, grand truths, fearful truths. So shall he rise again *before* he dies, and so shall our commission be accomplished which from God we had,—to plague his heart until we had unfolded the capacities of his spirit."

COMMENTARY

Romanticism was the rediscovery of the poetry of life. During a long period the true note of poetry had been rarely heard even in verse; the new movement reinspired both verse and prose. It was not until the early years of the nineteenth century that romanticism became self-conscious, but its first faint stirrings can be traced as far back as Goldsmith and Gray.

As the impulses behind the movement were poetic, and as the leading poets and prose writers were in close personal association, the prose of the period cannot be studied in isolation from poetry. At all times new tendencies must be more readily perceptible in poetry than in prose: the more plastic nature of the poet's material offers a wider choice of forms in which to experiment with new ideas; whereas prose, in the absence of pronounced structural features such as metre and rhyme, out of which formal patterns are made, is not so adaptable. The first example in the new manner of poetry was *The Lyrical Ballads* of Wordsworth and Coleridge, 1798, and in the following year appeared Campbell's *Pleasures of Hope*, which had all the traditional characteristics of the eighteenth century. Such palpable contrasts cannot be instanced in the history of prose; nor can we find there a parallel for such a rapid transformation as took place. The effect of *The Lyrical Ballads* was immediate: it expelled artificiality of diction from verse; but it was many years before prose threw off the solemn and decorous manner of the eighteenth century.

Romanticism was the spirit that led men to break away from the narrow limits of a commonsense view of life and to explore fresh sources of wonder and beauty. Its influence on form, as we have seen, was first apparent in poetry, but there was hardly a feature of the movement that did not in time react on both the form and substance of prose.

Of these features let us consider first the "Return to Nature", a phrase borrowed from Rousseau, and used in the wide sense of a return to a mode of life less dominated by social conventions. The interests of the Augustans had centred in urban life, but, under the influence of Latin pastoral poetry, they had paid lip-service to nature in the conventional idiom of the classics. The use of real landscape as a background to the human drama is rare in pre-romantic prose; it is foreshadowed in *Tom Jones* and *The Vicar of Wakefield*, but appreciation of scenic beauty for its own sake is first revealed in the letters of Gray (1716–1771). It was the poets of the Lake School that founded the new cult. Wordsworth's early love of external beauty deepened into a faith that there is in nature the active influence of a living force. His teaching once assimilated, no writer could view scenery with indifference, and few could regard it as a mere decorative background. Love of the country developed into fondness for particular localities, and the recognition that environment can mould character plays an important part in the work of writers as diverse as Scott, the Brontës, George Eliot and Thomas Hardy.

Wordsworth's pursuit of natural beauty led to contact with country folk, whom he learned to respect and love because they lived in tranquil harmony with their beautiful surroundings. In reading dignity into the simple annals of the poor he was not original; the doctrine had been made familiar by the theorists of the French Revolution. Where Wordsworth was unique was in reaching his convictions through emotional experience. His intense sympathies stimulated his imagination, and gave him the means of appealing to the hearts of others. He helped to make literature more democratic, and to arouse interest in classes of society which the eighteenth century had treated as outside the scope of congenial regard. Under such influences we shall find Hazlitt speaking in admiration of prize-fighters, and Borrow living with gipsies on terms of equality.

The second feature of romanticism was its emotional ecstasy: the lyrical spirit in the new poetry has its counterpart in the enthusiasm and unabashed egotism of the new prose. In the eighteenth century strong individuality had been discountenanced. Poetry had been too self-conscious for the frank expression of personal feeling, and even in that most intimate and confidential form of prose, the essay, the use of the first person was rare. "I" meant not Joseph Addison, but Mr Spectator, the mouthpiece of urbane opinion. When we say that the nineteenth century was lyrical, we mean not merely that more lyrics were written, but also that the language both of poetry and prose has absorbed colour from the feelings of the writer; he "mingles a lyric personality in the tale he tells, or the picture he paints, breaking their outlines with passion, or embroidering them with fancy".[1] In verse such lyrical exuberance is controlled by restrictions of form and space, but in prose the only restraint is taste; and it was because taste had changed that the egotism with which Lamb aired his quaint fancies and Hazlitt flaunted his fervid enthusiasms and antipathies no longer appeared irrelevant or vulgar.

The remaining features of romanticism may be regarded as various aspects of the quest for the sources of wonder in regions remote in respect of time or place. Already in the eighteenth century Percy and Chatterton had tried to draw aside the curtain of contempt which had veiled the so-called barbarous ages. Romantic imagination flung it right back, and discovered the past as a pageant of picturesque institutions and customs. As usual, it was the poets that led the fashion. *The Ancient Mariner* and *Christabel* are examples of romantic fantasies deriving credibility from appropriate atmosphere and archaic diction. In the tradition thus initiated Scott wrote *Waverley*. Its remarkable popularity inaugurated a new kind of fiction, to which the term "romance" may be applied, to distinguish it from the earlier realistic novel of manners; it also gave a new direction to the study of history. In the long line of romances that followed, Scott

[1] Herford, *The Age of Wordsworth.*

travelled far afield for his material, but he was at his best
amidst his native scenes in company with the character types
to which his youthful associations with the Scotch peasantry
and their legends gave him the clue. In his Scotch romances
his genius revealed the soul of a nation, and raised fiction
above the plane of mere entertainment.

Thus romance was the door through which nationalism
found its way into literature. The historians proper belong
to the middle of the century, but Macaulay, the greatest
of them, could not have achieved his phenomenal popularity,
had not Scott first humanised the study of history by showing
the part played by ordinary people in the shaping of events.

A notable stage in the steady growth of the reading public
is marked by the rise of the Review and the Magazine.
Neither was quite new; there had been reviews before, one
of which, the *Monthly*, had been served occasionally by good
writers, but more often by drudges hired to write puffs or
lampoons. Both owed something to essay periodicals like
the *Spectator* and *Rambler*, a type that had suffered from
being too exclusively literary and too dependent on the fertility
of a single mind. The new kind of review originated in the
collaboration of a group of one political persuasion, and had
for its object a serious survey of matters of general concern.
The first was the *Edinburgh*, founded in 1802, and edited by
Francis Jeffrey. Its amazing success produced rivals, chief
of which was the Tory *Quarterly*, first appearing in 1809
under the editorship of William Gifford. By the middle of
the century the reviews were recognised as the mouthpiece
of all that was authoritative. The magazines, more literary
and less serious in intention, offered hospitality to writing of
a more imaginative description. It was in the pages of the
London that the first essays of Lamb and De Quincey appeared.
The profession of letters owes much to the reviews. Their
circulation increased with amazing rapidity; by 1813 that
of the *Quarterly* had reached 13,000. The reviewers, though
as a rule men who devoted only part of their time to writing,

commanded high fees. Macaulay, for example, earned as much as £100 for an essay. The first to devote all his energies to books and to succeed as a man of letters without the help of journalistic hackwork was Carlyle.

William Hazlitt (1778–1830) was a young man of twenty when a meeting with Coleridge in 1798 filled him with enthusiasm for the new movement. He gradually gave up his ambition to be a painter, and adopted the profession of letters. As a journalist, essayist and critic he was one of the most vigorous and challenging writers of those stirring times. He worshipped strength and originality as much as he detested cant and sentiment. His combative nature and outspoken honesty made him more enemies than friends, and not even friendship could soften the fierceness of his convictions. The outstanding quality of his work is derived from his faculty of intense enjoyment—what he himself terms *gusto*. Life for him was not a spectacle to observe dispassionately, but a moving drama with a part for him to play. In his hands subjects that are topical or journalistic are endued with perennial interest by the infectiousness of his high excitement. An artist by temperament and training, he was quick to capture and record impressions, and so acute in his perceptions that he could set up familiar objects in a new light.

The extract selected is not a mere report of a prize fight made sensational by unduly emphasising the more brutal features. Though Hazlitt is by no means squeamish, it is not the physical prowess of the champions that he holds up for admiration, but their courage, resolution and endurance, those moral qualities that constitute the "high and heroic state of man", when spirit triumphs over the flesh. The account proceeds at a breathless pace, but the shaping hand of the artist is in control. The value of contrast is exploited to the full in the description of both the physical and moral qualities of the rivals. It emphasises the poetic justice of the victory of the unassuming Neate over the arrogant Gas-man, and it gives a rounding-off effect to the concluding words.

The style of Hazlitt is a clear reflection of the man himself. The length of his paragraphs and the hurry of his short, abrupt sentences suggest an impetuous and ardent temperament. He had no affectations; he despised literary jargon and was not afraid of a colloquialism. He was widely read, and had a memory that was full of echoes of fine phrases; but his quotation marks are a tribute to his intellectual honesty rather than his accuracy, for he never troubled to verify his borrowings.

Charles Lamb (1775–1834) became a writer less by deliberate choice than by force of circumstances, some knowledge of which is essential to an appreciation of his work. Having undertaken the charge of his sister Mary, who was subject to a dangerous recurrent madness, he had recourse to literary work to eke out his slender income as a clerk in the service of the East India Company. His qualifications were a sound classical education acquired at Christ's Hospital, a lively imagination, independent judgment and a fondness for browsing in old folios. His friendship with Coleridge, begun at school, was the means of introducing him to a literary circle which included Wordsworth, Hazlitt and Southey. In 1800 he was contributing to the *Morning Post*, but it was not until 1820, when he began to write essays for the newly established *London Magazine*, that he found his true bent. A life of Lamb, telling us all about himself, his friends and relations, and true in most essentials but the actual names, could be pieced together out of details to be found in the *Essays of Elia*. But Lamb's intention was not autobiographical. The essay in his hands is a work of art with an entity as distinct as that of a lyric poem. The subject is merely the means which enables the writer to present a picture of his mind as affected by the matter under discussion. Nor is the subject necessarily one on which he speaks authoritatively, for the charm of an essay is no more in proportion to the knowledge displayed than is that of good conversation. To read Elia is to be buttonholed by a man with a quaint and fascinating personality. Most egotists are bores; they view life in a mirror which magnifies their own image, and do not realise that what they see is a distortion. The only graces that can save egotism are modesty and a sense of humour. Lamb has no illusions about himself. He will invite the reader to join in the laugh at his own expense, and when he laughs at others it is without malice or bitterness. His exquisite wit is too tempered with kindliness and sympathy to make him a satirist, and he is more prone to pity than to condemn.

But it is idiosyncrasy that gives the *Essays of Elia* their inimitable *timbre*. Lamb was what earlier writers would have called an original. In an age given to the cult of rural piety he was, to use Wordsworth's phrase, "a scorner of the fields", not because he had Dr Johnson's insensibility, but because his affections centred in the old familiar places. He was born and bred a Londoner, and he loved London as a son loves his father. If the country appealed to him at all, it was only because of its associations with childhood holidays. But times change, and for people of strong attachments the old order as it passes leaves regrets as well as memories in its wake. His most characteristic work was produced in his maturity when it was easier to look backwards than forwards, and he had not the robustness of writers like Hazlitt, who live almost wholly in the present. Hence the undertone of tender melancholy which pervades all he wrote. The same attachment to what has been mellowed by time accounts for his literary tastes, his loving labours among the Elizabethan dramatists. With the seventeenth-century masters of prose he discovered a remarkable affinity, one which so coloured his outlook that he thought as they thought, and which so coloured his style that he insensibly adopted their rhythms and cadence. Given a subject like sassafras tea, he will discourse like Browne or Burton. The Jacobean turn and cadence are perceptible in such a sentence as *He was never married... perpetual bachelorship* (p. 182). It was from old writers that he acquired certain mannerisms of diction: his quaint archaisms, such as *unlucky dray, Female Eld, failed of, yield the wall*; and his partiality for latinisms, such as *civility, exalting his umbrella*. The latter are a feature of his wit, and the more whimsical his subject, the greater his fertility in the invention of polysyllables: *whether the oily particles (sassafras is slightly oleaginous) do attenuate and soften the fuliginous concretions.* His style, however, has great flexibility, and readily adapts itself to the theme: Elia in serious mood writes very differently from Elia, the jester. Compare the style of the two essays here quoted. The decline of gallantry is a subject that comes too near to the writer's most serious convictions to allow of amiable digressions. With Chimney-sweepers he is in his proper element. It is typical of his humour first to train a whole battery of resounding latinisms on the young imps, and then with freakish unexpectedness to turn the fire of mockery on his own grown-up dignity.

In his conception of what an essay should or could be Lamb showed originality. The eighteenth century had been incurably didactic, and the essay, in the hands of masters like Addison and Goldsmith, had assumed a conventional form appropriate to its didactic nature. Of the two essays here quoted *Modern Gallantry* comes nearest to tradition as regards structure. It might be analysed as follows:[1]

   1. A beginning on familiar ground—para. 1.

   2. Indication of theme (contradiction of 1)—para. 2.

   3. Its development by reference to experience—para. 2,*
      ...*hear them spoken* (pp. 180–1).

   4. Illustration by anecdote—*Joseph Paice,...title to them* (pp. 181–3).

   5. Deduction from illustration—*I think...lamented mistress* (p. 183).

   6. Summary of theme and statement of moral, with an emphatic end, *reverence her sex*.

---

[1] Suggested by an analysis of an essay of Goldsmith's in Herbert Read, *English Prose Style*, pp. 77–8.

This form, however, is not really typical of Lamb. He was not interested in politics; he had no formal philosophy or creed to preach; moreover, he wrote for the *London Magazine*, which, by demanding entertainment rather than instruction, assisted his development along lines congenial to his temperament. He set aside the conventional machinery of the essay, and was most at ease when he indulged in fantasies or followed the train of his impressions and memories. All he asked of the reader was "a fair construction as to an after-dinner conversation; allowing for the rashness and necessary incompleteness of first thoughts".

The *Confessions of an English Opium Eater* recounts the early career of *Thomas De Quincey* (1785–1859). He was the son of a wealthy merchant of Manchester, who died young. De Quincey, a sensitive and intellectually precocious boy, ran away from school, wandered for months in the mountains of Wales, was rescued in a state of destitution, and sent to Oxford. There he lived the life of a recluse, reading widely in a desultory fashion. By Coleridge he was introduced to Wordsworth, whom he met at Grasmere in the cottage which afterwards became his home for twenty years. There he applied himself to severe study, reading widely in German philosophy. It was at this time that the habit of taking opium to relieve suffering grew on him till he was completely enslaved. His marriage in 1816, and the sudden loss of his fortune pointed to the necessity of writing for a livelihood. He went to London, where his *Confessions* earned him immediate recognition. He wrote regularly for the magazines, contributing reviews, criticisms and essays grave and gay on any and every subject.

De Quincey's collected works filled fourteen volumes. Of that vast accumulation the only sort that concerns us here is the emotive prose represented by *Levana*. It is the prose counterpart of the poetic mysticism of Wordsworth and Coleridge, and has qualities of form and matter more conspicuously "romantic" than the work of Lamb and Hazlitt.

De Quincey invaded what had been regarded as exclusively the province of poetry, the region of dreams, intuitions and impalpable suggestion; he invented a new species of writing, which some call poetical prose, and others, prose-poetry. Neither term is entirely satisfactory if it implies that De Quincey uses a poet's licence with the principles of prose-composition, as Carlyle did, or that he confused the rhythms of prose with those of verse, as Dickens sometimes did. The element of poetry was no factitious addition; it was of the very texture of his writing. He was unusually susceptible to impressions that inspire mystery and awe; and his feeling for the melody and harmony of words inspired rhythms as majestic as his conceptions were sublime. *Levana* has such epic grandeur that no "miracle of expression" is out of place. "It is a permanent addition to the mythology of the human race."[1]

The style has all the features commonly recognised as the characteristics of poetical prose, most of which will be found in varying degree in almost all prose of a highly emotive nature.[2] They may be summed up as

1. Archaism in word and expression: *lamentation, girdle, sobbing of litanies, accomplished in the furnace.*

2. Romantic imagery, with which is associated the per-sonification of abstracts and the metaphorical use of verbs: *Herod's sword; pulses of love; walks abroad upon the winds; scorch the fountains of tears.*

3. Sustained rhythms, with their attendant train of poetic inversions and turns of phrase; periodic sentences (note the wonderful effect of suspense in the fourth paragraph): *the altar overthrown; Deep lie the roots of her power.*

Prose so conspicuously rhythmical invites a detailed analysis. With regard to the scansion that follows it must be

[1] Professor Masson.
[2] See Dobrée, *Modern Prose Style*, Oxford University Press.

understood that the foot-divisions are arbitrary, and that, within the limits of the principles set out on p. 6 each reader is entitled to his own interpretation of the foot-divisions:

The éldest | of the thrée | is námed | Máter | Làchry-márum |, Our Lády | of Teárs. | 1. Shé it is | that níght | and dáy | ráves | and móans, | cálling | for vánished | fáces. | 2. Shé stoód | in Ráma, | where a vóice | was heárd | of lámentàtion, | Ráchel | wéeping | fòr her chíldren, | and re-fúsing | to be cómforted. | 3. Shé it wàs | that stoód | in Béthlehem | on the níght | when Hérod's | swórd | swèpt | its núrseries | of Ínnocents, | and the líttle | féet | were stíffened | for éver, | whích, | heárd | at tímes | as they tóttered | along flóors | overheád, | wóke | púlses | of lóve | in hoúsehold heárts | that were not unmárked | in heáven |.

The key to the rhythm of this paragraph is the theme *She it is that...* which occurs with variations three times. The scansion of sentence 1 shows a tendency towards *gradation* of feet from short to long. This progressive lengthening is more marked in sentence 2; it occurs again in sentence 3 as far as *for ever*. Note how the rhythm dwells on the cruelty of *Hérod's* | *swórd* | *swèpt*, hurries on to a sudden pause of listening horror at *which*, and then resumes its swiftness of movement.

Interwoven with this prose-rhythm, there are beautiful cadences, heard as an undertone, the commonest being on the model of Máter Làchrymárum ($- \cup - \cup - \cup$).

Cf. { wéeping fòr her chíldren,
{ líttle féet were stíffened.

These are varied with a shorter cadence, ending in a stressed instead of a light syllable ($- \cup \cup -$):

Lády of Teárs,
flóors overheád,
púlses of lóve.

Chapter IX

The Romantic Movement (*cont.*)

1. JEANIE ASKS A FAVOUR

From *The Heart of Midlothian* (1818): Sir Walter Scott

"I was wanting to say to ye, Laird," said Jeanie, who felt the necessity of entering upon her business, "that I was gaun a lang journey, outby of my father's knowledge."

"Outby his knowledge, Jeanie!—Is that richt? Ye maun think o't again—it's no richt," said Dumbiedikes, with a countenance of great concern.

"If I were anes at Lunnon," said Jeanie, in exculpation, "I am amaist sure I could get means to speak to the queen about my sister's life."

"Lunnon—and the queen—and her sister's life!" said Dumbiedikes, whistling for very amazement—"the lassie's demented."

"I am no out o' my mind," said she, "and, sink or swim, I am determined to gang to Lunnon, if I suld beg my way frae door to door—and so I maun, unless ye wad lend me a small sum to pay my expenses—little thing will do it; and ye ken my father's a man of substance, and wad see nae man, far less you, Laird, come to loss by me."

Dumbiedikes, on comprehending the nature of this application, could scarce trust his ears—he made no answer whatever, but stood with his eyes riveted on the ground.

"I see ye are no for assisting me, Laird," said Jeanie; "sae fare ye weel—and gang and see my poor father as aften as ye can—he will be lonely eneugh now."

"Where is the silly bairn gaun?" said Dumbiedikes; and, laying hold of her hand, he led her into the house. "It's no that I didna think o't before," he said, "but it stack in my throat."

Thus speaking to himself, he led her into an old-fashioned parlour, shut the door behind them, and fastened it with a bolt. While Jeanie, surprised at this manœuvre, remained as near the door as possible, the Laird quitted her hand, and pressed upon a spring lock fixed in an oak panel in the wainscot, which instantly slipped aside. An iron strong-box was discovered in a recess of the wall; he opened this also, and, pulling out two or three drawers, showed that they were filled with leathern bags, full of gold and silver coin.

"This is my bank, Jeanie, lass," he said, looking first at her and then at the treasure, with an air of great complacency,—"nane o' your goldsmith's bills for me,—they bring folk to ruin."

Then suddenly changing his tone, he resolutely said,—"Jeanie, I will mak ye Lady Dumbiedikes afore the sun sets, and ye may ride to Lunnon in your ain coach, if ye like."

"Na, Laird," said Jeanie, "that can never be—my father's grief—my sister's situation—the discredit to you——"

"That's *my* business," said Dumbiedikes; "ye wad sae naething about that if ye werena a fule—and yet I like ye the better for't—ae wise body's eneugh in the married state. But if your heart's ower fu', tak what siller will serve ye, and let it be when ye come back again—as gude syne as sune."

"But, Laird," said Jeanie, who felt the necessity of being explicit with so extraordinary a lover, "I like another man better than you, and I canna marry ye."

"Another man better than me, Jeanie!" said Dumbiedikes —"how is that possible?—It's no possible, woman—ye hae ken'd me sae lang."

"Ay but, Laird," said Jeanie, with persevering simplicity, "I hae ken'd him langer."

"Langer!—It's no possible," exclaimed the poor Laird. "It canna be; ye were born on the land. O Jeanie woman, ye haena lookit—ye haena seen the half o' the gear." He drew out another drawer—"A' gowd, Jeanie, and there's bands for siller lent—And the rental book, Jeanie—clear three hunder sterling—deil a wadset,[1] heritable band, or burden—Ye haena lookit at them, woman—And then my mother's wardrobe, and my grandmother's forby—silk gowns wad stand on their ends, pearlin-lace as fine as spiders' webs, and rings and ear-rings to the boot of a' that—they are a' in the chamber of deas[2]— Oh, Jeanie, gang up the stair and look at them!"

[1] *wadset*, mortgage.   [2] *chamber of deas*, best chamber.

But Jeanie held fast her integrity, though beset with temptations, which perhaps the Laird of Dumbiedikes did not greatly err in supposing were those most affecting to her sex.

"It canna be, Laird—I have said it—and I canna break my word till him, if ye wad gie me the haill barony of Dalkeith, and Lugton into the bargain."

"Your word to *him*," said the Laird, somewhat pettishly; "but wha is he, Jeanie?—wha is he?—I haena heard his name yet—Come now, Jeanie, ye are but queering us—I am no trowing that there is sic a ane in the warld—ye are but making fashion—What is he?—wha is he?"

"Just Reuben Butler, that's schulemaster at Libberton," said Jeanie.

"Reuben Butler! Reuben Butler!" echoed the Laird of Dumbiedikes, pacing the apartment in high disdain,— "Reuben Butler, the dominie at Libberton—and a dominie depute too!—Reuben, the son of my cottar!—Very weel, Jeanie lass, wilfu' woman will hae her way—Reuben Butler! he hasna in his pouch the value o' the auld black coat he wears —but it disna signify." And, as he spoke, he shut successively and with vehemence, the drawers of his treasury. "A fair offer, Jeanie, is nae cause of feud—Ae man may bring a horse to the water, but twenty wunna gar him drink—And as for wasting my substance on other folk's joes[1]——"

There was something in the last hint that nettled Jeanie's honest pride.—"I was begging nane frae your honour," she said, "least of a' on sic a score as ye pit it on.—Gude morning to ye, sir; ye hae been kind to my father, and it isna in my heart to think otherwise than kindly of you."

So saying, she left the room, without listening to a faint "But Jeanie—Jeanie—stay, woman!" and traversing the court-yard with a quick step, she set out on her forward journey, her bosom glowing with that natural indignation and shame, which an honest mind feels at having subjected itself to ask a favour, which had been unexpectedly refused. When out of the Laird's ground, and once more upon the public road, her pace slackened, her anger cooled, and anxious anticipations of the consequence of this unexpected dis-

[1] *joes*, sweethearts.

appointment began to influence her with other feelings. Must she then actually beg her way to London? for such seemed the alternative; or must she turn back, and solicit her father for money; and by doing so lose time, which was precious, besides the risk of encountering his positive prohibition respecting her journey? Yet she saw no medium between these alternatives; and while she walked slowly on, was still meditating whether it were not better to return.

While she was thus in an uncertainty, she heard the clatter of a horse's hoofs, and a well-known voice calling her name. She looked round, and saw advancing towards her on a pony, whose bare back and halter assorted ill with the nightgown, slippers, and laced cocked-hat of the rider, a cavalier of no less importance than Dumbiedikes himself. In the energy of his pursuit, he had overcome even the Highland obstinacy of Rory Beau, and compelled that self-willed palfrey to canter the way his rider chose; which Rory, however, performed with all the symptoms of reluctance, turning his head, and accompanying every bound he made in advance with a sidelong motion, which indicated his extreme wish to turn round, —a manœuvre which nothing but the constant exercise of the Laird's heels and cudgel could possibly have counteracted.

When the Laird came up with Jeanie, the first words he uttered were,—"Jeanie, they say ane shouldna aye tak a woman at her first word?"

"Ay, but ye maun tak me at mine, Laird," said Jeanie, looking on the ground, and walking on without a pause.— "I hae but ae word to bestow on onybody, and that's aye a true ane."

"Then," said Dumbiedikes, "at least ye suldna ay tak a man at *his* first word. Ye maunna gang this wilfu' gate sillerless, come o't what like."—He put a purse into her hand. "I wad gie you Rory too, but he's as wilfu' as yourself, and he's ower weel used to a gate that maybe he and I hae gaen ower aften,[1] and he'll gang nae road else."

"But, Laird," said Jeanie, "though I ken my father will satisfy every penny of this siller, whatever there's o't, yet I wadna like to borrow it frae ane that maybe thinks of something mair than the paying o't back again."

[1] *a gate...I hae gaen ower aften,* i.e. the way to Jeanie's house.

"There's just twenty-five guineas o't," said Dumbiedikes, with a gentle sigh, "and whether your father pays or disna pay, I mak ye free till't without another word. Gang where ye like—do what ye like—and marry a' the Butlers in the country gin ye like—And sae, gude-morning to you, Jeanie."

2. THE MURDER OF THE BISHOP OF LIEGE

From *Quentin Durward* (1823): Sir Walter Scott

When the unhappy Prelate was brought before the footstool of the savage leader, although in former life only remarkable for his easy and good-natured temper, he showed in this extremity a sense of his dignity and noble blood, well becoming the high race from which he was descended. His look was composed and undismayed; his gesture, when the rude hands which dragged him forward were unloosed, was noble, and at the same time resigned, somewhat between the bearing of a feudal noble and of a Christian martyr; and so much was even De la Marck himself staggered by the firm demeanour of his prisoner, and recollection of the early benefits he had received from him, that he seemed irresolute, cast down his eyes, and it was not until he had emptied a large goblet of wine, that, resuming his haughty insolence of look and manner, he thus addressed his unfortunate captive:—"Louis of Bourbon," said the truculent soldier, drawing hard his breath, clenching his hands, setting his teeth, and using the other mechanical actions to rouse up and sustain his native ferocity of temper—"I sought your friendship, and you rejected mine. What would you now give that it had been otherwise?—Nikkel, be ready."

The butcher rose, seized his weapon, and stealing round behind De la Marck's chair, stood with it uplifted in his bare and sinewy arms.

"Look at that man, Louis of Bourbon," said De la Marck again—"What terms wilt thou now offer to escape this dangerous hour?"

The Bishop cast a melancholy but unshaken look upon the grisly satellite, who seemed prepared to execute the will of the tyrant, and then he said with firmness, "Hear me, William de la Marck; and good men all, if there be any here who deserve that name, hear the only terms I can offer to this ruffian.—William de la Marck, thou hast stirred up to sedition an imperial city—hast assaulted and taken the palace of a Prince of the Holy German Empire—slain his people—

plundered his goods—maltreated his person; for this thou art liable to the Ban of the Empire—hast deserved to be declared outlawed and fugitive, landless and rightless. Thou hast done more than all this. More than mere human laws hast thou broken—more than mere human vengeance hast thou deserved. Thou hast broken into the sanctuary of the Lord—laid violent hands upon a Father of the Church—defiled the house of God with blood and rapine, like a sacrilegious robber——"

"Hast thou yet done?" said De la Marck, fiercely interrupting him, and stamping with his foot.

"No," answered the Prelate, "for I have not yet told thee the terms which you demanded to hear from me."

"Go on," said De la Marck; "and let the terms please me better than the preface, or woe to thy grey head!" And flinging himself back in his seat, he grinded his teeth till the foam flew from his lips, as from the tusks of the savage animal whose name and spoils he wore.

"Such are thy crimes," resumed the Bishop, with calm determination; "now hear the terms, which, as a merciful Prince and a Christian Prelate, setting aside all personal offence, forgiving each peculiar injury, I condescend to offer. Fling down thy leading-staff—renounce thy command—unbind thy prisoners—restore thy spoil—distribute what else thou hast of goods, to relieve those whom thou hast made orphans and widows—array thyself in sackcloth and ashes—take a palmer's staff in thy hand, and go barefooted on pilgrimage to Rome, and we will ourselves be intercessors for thee with the Imperial Chamber at Ratisbon for thy life, with our Holy Father the Pope for thy miserable soul."

While Louis of Bourbon proposed these terms, in a tone as decided as if he still occupied his episcopal throne, and as if the usurper kneeled a suppliant at his feet, the tyrant slowly raised himself in his chair, the amazement with which he was at first filled giving way gradually to rage, until, as the Bishop ceased, he looked to Nikkel Blok, and raised his finger, without speaking a word. The ruffian struck, as if he had been doing his office in the common shambles, and the murdered Bishop sunk, without a groan, at the foot of his own episcopal throne. The Liegeois, who were not prepared for so horrible a catastrophe, and who had expected to hear the conference end in some terms of accommodation, started up unanimously, with cries of execration, mingled with shouts of vengeance.

But William de la Marck, raising his tremendous voice above the tumult, and shaking his clenched hand and extended arm, shouted aloud, "How now, ye porkers of Liege! ye wallowers in the mud of the Maes!—do ye dare to mate yourselves with the Wild Boar of Ardennes?—Up, ye Boar's brood!" (an expression by which he himself, and others, often designated his soldiers), "let these Flemish hogs see your tusks!"

Every one of his followers started up at the command, and mingled as they were among their late allies, prepared too for such a surprisal, each had, in an instant, his next neighbour by the collar, while his right hand brandished a broad dagger, that glimmered against lamplight and moonshine. Every arm was uplifted, but no one struck; for the victims were too much surprised for resistance, and it was probably the object of De la Marck only to impose terror on his civic confederates.

But the courage of Quentin Durward, prompt and alert in resolution beyond his years, and stimulated at the moment by all that could add energy to his natural shrewdness and resolution, gave a new turn to the scene. Imitating the action of the followers of De la Marck, he sprung on Carl Eberson, the son of their leader, and mastering him with ease, held his dirk at the boy's throat, while he exclaimed, "Is that your game? then here I play my part."

"Hold! hold!" exclaimed De la Marck, "it is a jest—a jest—Think you I would injure my good friends and allies of the city of Liege?—Soldiers, unloose your holds; sit down; take away the carrion" (giving the Bishop's corpse a thrust with his foot) "which hath caused this strife among friends, and let us drown unkindness in a fresh carouse."

3. THE OLIVE BRANCH

From *Pride and Prejudice* (1797): Jane Austen

"I hope, my dear," said Mr Bennet to his wife, as they were at breakfast the next morning, "that you have ordered a good dinner to-day, because I have reason to expect an addition to our family party."

"Who do you mean, my dear? I know of nobody that is coming, I am sure, unless Charlotte Lucas should happen to call in—and I hope *my* dinners are good enough for her. I do not believe she often sees such at home."

"The person of whom I speak is a gentleman, and a stranger."

Mrs Bennet's eyes sparkled.—"A gentleman and a stranger! It is Mr Bingley, I am sure. Why, Jane—you never dropt a word of this; you sly thing! Well, I am sure I shall be extremely glad to see Mr Bingley.—But—good Lord! how unlucky! there is not a bit of fish to be got to-day. Lydia, my love, ring the bell—I must speak to Hill this moment."

"It is *not* Mr Bingley," said her husband; "it is a person whom I never saw in the whole course of my life."

This roused a general astonishment; and he had the pleasure of being eagerly questioned by his wife and five daughters at once.

After amusing himself some time with their curiosity, he thus explained—

"About a month ago I received this letter; and about a fortnight ago I answered it, for I thought it a case of some delicacy, and requiring early attention. It is from my cousin, Mr Collins, who, when I am dead, may turn you all out of this house as soon as he pleases."

"Oh! my dear," cried his wife, "I cannot bear to hear that mentioned. Pray do not talk of that odious man. I do think it is the hardest thing in the world, that your estate should be entailed away from your own children; and I am sure, if I had been you, I should have tried long ago to do something or other about it."

Jane and Elizabeth attempted to explain to her the nature of an entail. They had often attempted it before, but it was a subject on which Mrs Bennet was beyond the reach of reason, and she continued to rail bitterly against the cruelty of settling an estate away from a family of five daughters, in favour of a man whom nobody cared anything about.

"It certainly is a most iniquitous affair," said Mr Bennet, "and nothing can clear Mr Collins from the guilt of inheriting Longbourn. But if you will listen to his letter, you may perhaps be a little softened by his manner of expressing himself."

"No, that I am sure I shall not; and I think it was very impertinent of him to write to you at all, and very hypocritical. I hate such false friends. Why could not he keep on quarrelling with you, as his father did before him?"

"Why, indeed; he does seem to have had some filial scruples on that head, as you will hear."

                    "Hunsford, near Westerham, Kent,
                              "15th October.
"Dear Sir,

"The disagreement subsisting between yourself and my late honoured father always gave me much uneasiness, and since I have had the misfortune to lose him, I have frequently wished to heal the breach; but for some time I was kept back by my own doubts, fearing lest it might seem disrespectful to his memory for me to be on good terms with any one with whom it had always pleased him to be at variance.—'There, Mrs Bennet.'—My mind, however, is now made up on the subject, for having received ordination at Easter, I have been so fortunate as to be distinguished by the patronage of the Right Honourable Lady Catherine de Bourgh, widow of Sir Lewis de Bourgh, whose bounty and beneficence has preferred me to the valuable rectory of this parish, where it shall be my earnest endeavour to demean myself with grateful respect towards her Ladyship, and be ever ready to perform those rites and ceremonies which are instituted by the Church of England. As a clergyman, moreover, I feel it my duty to promote and establish the blessing of peace in all families within the reach of my influence; and on these grounds I flatter myself that my present overtures of good-will are highly commendable, and that the circumstance of my being next in the entail of Longbourn estate will be kindly overlooked on your side, and not lead you to reject the offered olive-branch. I cannot be otherwise than concerned at being the means of injuring your amiable daughters, and beg leave to apologise for it, as well as to assure you of my readiness to make them every possible amends,—but of this hereafter. If you should have no objection to receive me into your house, I propose myself the satisfaction of waiting on you and your family, Monday, November 18th, by four o'clock, and shall probably trespass on your hospitality till the Saturday se'nnight following, which I can do without any inconvenience, as Lady Catherine is far from objecting to my occasional absence on a Sunday, provided that some other clergyman is engaged to do the duty of the day.—I remain, dear sir, with respectful compliments to your lady and daughters, your well-wisher and friend,

"WILLIAM COLLINS."

"At four o'clock, therefore, we may expect this peacemaking gentleman," said Mr Bennet, as he folded up the letter. "He seems to be a most conscientious and polite young man, upon my word, and I doubt not will prove a valuable acquaintance, especially if Lady Catherine should be so indulgent as to let him come to us again."

"There is some sense in what he says about the girls, however, and if he is disposed to make them any amends, I shall not be the person to discourage him."

"Though it is difficult", said Jane, "to guess in what way he can mean to make us the atonement he thinks our due, the wish is certainly to his credit."

Elizabeth was chiefly struck with his extraordinary deference for Lady Catherine, and his kind intention of christening, marrying, and burying his parishioners whenever it were required.

"He must be an oddity, I think," said she. "I cannot make him out.—There is something very pompous in his style.—And what can he mean by apologising for being next in the entail?—We cannot suppose he would help it if he could.—Can he be a sensible man, sir?"

"No, my dear; I think not. I have great hopes of finding him quite the reverse. There is a mixture of servility and self-importance in his letter, which promises well. I am impatient to see him."

"In point of composition", said Mary, "his letter does not seem defective. The idea of the olive-branch perhaps is not wholly new, yet I think it is well expressed."

To Catherine and Lydia, neither the letter nor its writer were in any degree interesting. It was next to impossible that their cousin should come in a scarlet coat, and it was now some weeks since they had received pleasure from the society of a man in any other colour. As for their mother, Mr Collins's letter had done away with much of her ill-will, and she was preparing to see him with a degree of composure which astonished her husband and daughters.

Mr Collins was punctual to his time, and was received with great politeness by the whole family. Mr Bennet indeed said little; but the ladies were ready enough to talk, and Mr Collins seemed neither in need of encouragement, nor inclined to be silent himself. He was a tall, heavy-looking young man of five-and-twenty. His air was grave and stately, and his manners were very formal. He had not been long seated before he complimented Mrs Bennet on having so fine a family of daughters; said he had heard much of their beauty, but that in this instance fame had fallen short of the truth; and added, that he did not doubt her seeing them all in due time well disposed of in marriage. This gallantry was not much to the taste of some of his hearers; but Mrs Bennet, who quarrelled with no compliments, answered most readily.

"You are very kind, I am sure; and I wish with all my heart it may prove so, for else they will be destitute enough. Things are settled so oddly."

"You allude, perhaps, to the entail of this estate."

"Ah! sir, I do indeed. It is a grievous affair to my poor girls, you must confess. Not that I mean to find fault with *you*, for such things I know are all chance in this world. There is no knowing how estates will go when once they come to be entailed "

"I am very sensible, madam, of the hardship to my fair cousins, and could say much on the subject, but that I am cautious of appearing forward and precipitate. But I can assure the young ladies that I come prepared to admire them. At present I will not say more; but, perhaps, when we are better acquainted——"

He was interrupted by a summons to dinner; and the girls smiled on each other. They were not the only objects of Mr Collins's admiration. The hall, the dining-room, and all its furniture, were examined and praised; and his commendation of everything would have touched Mrs Bennet's heart, but for the mortifying supposition of his viewing it all as his own future property. The dinner too in its turn was highly admired; and he begged to know to which of his fair cousins the excellency of its cooking was owing. But here he was set right by Mrs Bennet, who assured him with some asperity that they were very well able to keep a good cook, and that her daughters had nothing to do in the kitchen. He begged pardon for having displeased her. In a softened tone she declared herself not at all offended; but he continued to apologise for about a quarter of an hour.

4. PURITANS AND ROYALISTS

From Macaulay's *Essay on Milton*, first published in
The Edinburgh Review, 1825

The Puritans were men whose minds had derived a peculiar character from the daily contemplation of superior beings and eternal interests. Not content with acknowledging, in general terms, an overruling Providence, they habitually ascribed every event to the will of the Great Being, for whose power nothing was too vast, for whose inspection nothing was too minute. To know Him, to serve Him, to enjoy Him, was with them the great end of existence. They rejected with contempt the ceremonious homage which other sects substituted for the pure worship of the soul. Instead of catching occasional glimpses of the Deity through an obscuring veil, they aspired to gaze full on His intolerable brightness, and to commune with Him face to face. Hence originated their contempt for terrestrial distinctions. The difference between the greatest and the meanest of mankind seemed to vanish, when compared with the boundless interval which separated the whole race from Him on whom their own eyes were constantly fixed. They recognised no title to superiority but His favour; and, confident of that favour, they despised all the accomplishments and all the dignities of the world. If they were unacquainted with the works of philosophers and poets, they were deeply read in the oracles of God. If their names were not found in the registers of heralds, they were recorded in the Book of Life. If their steps were not accompanied by a splendid train of menials, legions of ministering angels had charge over them. Their palaces were houses not made with hands;[1] their diadems crowns of glory which should never fade away. On the rich and the eloquent, on nobles and priests, they looked down with contempt: for they esteemed themselves rich in a more precious treasure, and eloquent in a more sublime language, nobles by the right of an earlier creation, and priests by the imposition of a mightier hand. The very meanest of them was a being to whose fate a

---

[1] *houses not made with hands*, Acts vii. 48.

mysterious and terrible importance belonged, on whose
slightest action the spirits of light and darkness looked with
anxious interest, who had been destined,[1] before heaven and
earth were created, to enjoy a felicity which should continue
when heaven and earth should have passed away. Events
which short-sighted politicians ascribed to earthly causes had
been ordained on his account. For his sake empires had risen,
and flourished, and decayed. For his sake the Almighty had
proclaimed his will by the pen of the Evangelist, and the harp
of the prophet. He had been wrested by no common deliverer from the grasp of no common foe. He had been
ransomed by the sweat of no vulgar agony, by the blood of
no earthly sacrifice. It was for him that the sun had been
darkened, that the rocks had been rent, that the dead had
arisen, that all nature had shuddered at the sufferings of her
expiring God.

Thus the Puritan was made up of two different men, the
one all self-abasement, penitence, gratitude, passion; the
other proud, calm, inflexible, sagacious. He prostrated himself in the dust before his Maker: but he set his foot on the
neck of his king. In his devotional retirement he prayed with
convulsions, and groans, and tears. He was half-maddened
by glorious or terrible illusions. He heard the lyres of angels
or the tempting whispers of fiends. He caught a gleam of
the Beatific Vision,[2] or woke screaming from dreams of everlasting fire. Like Vane,[3] he thought himself intrusted with
the sceptre of the millennial year. Like Fleetwood,[4] he cried
in the bitterness of his soul that God had hid his face from
him. But when he took his seat in the council, or girt on his
sword for war, these tempestuous workings of the soul had
left no perceptible trace behind them. People who saw
nothing of the godly but their uncouth visages, and heard
nothing from them but their groans and their whining hymns,

[1] *who had been destined*, an allusion to the Calvinistic doctrine of Pre-
destination.

[2] *the Beatific Vision*, the sight of God himself revealed only to his
saints.

[3] *Vane*. Sir Harry Vane, one of the fifth-monarchy men, who believed
that the reign of Christ on earth would last a thousand years: hence
millennial year.

[4] *Fleetwood*, an able general, married Cromwell's daughter.

might laugh at them. But those had little reason to laugh who encountered them in the hall of debate or in the field of battle. These fanatics brought to civil and military affairs a coolness of judgment and an immutability of purpose which some writers have thought inconsistent with their religious zeal, but which were in fact the necessary effects of it. The intensity of their feelings on one subject made them tranquil on every other. One overpowering sentiment had subjected to itself pity and hatred, ambition and fear. Death had lost its terrors and pleasure its charms. They had their smiles and their tears, their raptures and their sorrows, but not for the things of this world. Enthusiasm had made them Stoics, had cleared their minds from every vulgar passion and prejudice, and raised them above the influence of danger and corruption. It sometimes might lead them to pursue unwise ends, but never to choose unwise means. They went through the world, like Sir Artegal's iron man Talus[1] with his flail, crushing and trampling down oppressors, mingling with human beings, but having neither part nor lot in human infirmities, insensible to fatigue, to pleasure, and to pain, not to be pierced by any weapon, not to be withstood by any barrier.

* * * * * * *

We now come to the Royalists. We shall attempt to speak of them, as we have spoken of their antagonists, with perfect candour. We shall not charge upon a whole party the profligacy and baseness of the horse-boys, gamblers and bravoes, whom the hope of licence and plunder attracted from all the dens of Whitefriars[2] to the standard of Charles, and who disgraced their associates by excesses which, under the stricter discipline of the Parliamentary armies, were never tolerated. We will select a more favourable specimen. Thinking as we do that the cause of the King was the cause of bigotry and tyranny, we yet cannot refrain from looking with complacency on the character of the honest old Cavaliers. We feel a

[1] *Talus*, Spenser's *Faerie Queene*, v, 1. Talus was the man of iron mould, who held a flail with which he threshed out falsehood.

[2] *dens of Whitefriars*, a district in London where there had formerly been a monastery of the Carmelites. At first a sanctuary for criminals, in the time of Charles I, it still afforded protection to debtors.

national pride in comparing them with the instruments which
the despots of other countries are compelled to employ, with
the mutes who throng their antechambers, and the Janissaries[1] who mount guard at their gates. Our royalist countrymen were not heartless, dangling courtiers, bowing at every
step, and simpering at every word. They were not mere
machines for destruction dressed up in uniforms, caned
into skill, intoxicated into valour, defending without love,
destroying without hatred. There was a freedom in their
subserviency, a nobleness in their very degradation. The
sentiment of individual independence was strong within them.
They were indeed misled, but by no base or selfish motive.
Compassion and romantic honour, the prejudices of childhood,
and the venerable names of history, threw over them a spell
potent as that of Duessa;[2] and, like the Red-Cross Knight,
they thought that they were doing battle for an injured beauty,
while they defended a false and loathsome sorceress. In truth
they scarcely entered at all into the merits of the political
question. It was not for a treacherous king or an intolerant
church that they fought, but for the old banner which had
waved in so many battles over the heads of their fathers, and
for the altars at which they had received the hands of their
brides. Though nothing could be more erroneous than their
political opinions, they possessed, in a far greater degree than
their adversaries, those qualities which are the grace of
private life. With many of the vices of the Round Table, they
had also many of its virtues, courtesy, generosity, veracity,
tenderness, and respect for women. They had far more both
of profound and of polite learning than the Puritans. Their
manners were more engaging, their tempers more amiable,
their tastes more elegant, and their households more cheerful.

[1] *Janissaries*, the body-guard of the Sultans of Turkey, recruited mainly
from the sons of Christians, and specially inured to hardship and cruelty.
[2] *Duessa, Faerie Queene*, I, 2.

5. MIRABEAU

From *The French Revolution* (1835–1837): Thomas Carlyle

Which of these Six Hundred individuals, in plain white
cravat, that have come up to regenerate France, might one
guess would become their *king*? For a king or leader they, as
all bodies of men, must have: be their work what it may,
there is one man there who, by character, faculty, position,
is fittest of all to do it; that man, as future not yet elected
king, walks there among the rest. He with the thick black
locks, will it be? With the *hure*, as himself calls it, or black
boar's-head, fit to be "shaken" as a senatorial portent? Through
whose shaggy beetle-brows, and rough-hewn, seamed, car-
buncled face, there look natural ugliness, smallpox, incon-
tinence, bankruptcy,—and burning fire of genius; like comet-
fire glaring fuliginous through murkiest confusions? It is
Gabriel Honoré Riquetti, de Mirabeau, the world-compeller;
man-ruling Deputy of Aix! According to the Baroness de
Staël, he steps proudly along, though looked at askance here;
and shakes his black *chevelure*, or lion's-mane; as if prophetic
of great deeds.

Yes, Reader, that is the Type-Frenchman of this epoch; as
Voltaire was of the last. He is French in his aspirations, acquisitions, in his virtues, in his vices; perhaps more French
than any other man;—and intrinsically such a mass of manhood too. Mark him well. The National Assembly were all
different without that one; nay, he might say with the old
Despot: "The National Assembly? I am that."

Of a southern climate, of wild southern blood: for the
Riquettis, or Arrighettis, had to fly from Florence and the
Guelfs, long centuries ago, and settled in Provence; where
from generation to generation they have ever approved themselves a peculiar kindred: irascible, indomitable, sharp-
cutting, true, like the steel they wore; of an intensity and
activity that sometimes verged towards madness, yet did not
reach it. One ancient Riquetti, in mad fulfilment of a mad
vow, chains two Mountains together; and the chain, with its
"iron star of five rays", is still to be seen. May not a modern
Riquetti *un*chain so much, and set it drifting,—which also
shall be seen?

Destiny has work for that swart burly-headed Mirabeau:
Destiny has watched over him, prepared him from afar. Did
not his Grandfather, stout *Col-d'Argent* (Silver-Stock, so they
named him), shattered and slashed by seven-and-twenty
wounds in one fell day, lie sunk together on the Bridge at
Casano;[1] while Prince Eugene's cavalry galloped and re-
galloped over him,—only the flying sergeant had thrown a
camp-kettle over that loved head; and Vendôme, dropping
his spy-glass, moaned out, "Mirabeau is *dead*, then!"
Nevertheless he was not dead, he awoke to breath, and
miraculous surgery;—for Gabriel was yet to be. With his
silver stock he kept his scarred head erect, through long years;
and wedded; and produced tough Marquis Victor,[2] the
Friend of Men. Whereby at last in the appointed year 1749,
this long-expected rough-hewn Gabriel Honoré did likewise see the light: roughest lion's whelp ever littered of that
rough breed. How the old lion (for our old Marquis too was
lion-like, most unconquerable, kingly-genial, most perverse)
gazed wondering on his offspring; and determined to train
him as no lion had yet been! It is in vain, O Marquis! This
cub, though thou slay him and flay him, will not learn to
draw in dogcart of Political Economy, and be a *Friend of Men*;
he will not be Thou, but must and will be Himself, another
than Thou. Divorce lawsuits, whole family save one in
prison and three-score *Lettres-de-Cachet*[3] for thy own sole
use, do but astonish the world.

Our luckless Gabriel, sinned against and sinning, has been
in the Isle of Rhé and heard the Atlantic from his tower; in
the Castle of If, and heard the Mediterranean at Marseilles.
He has been in the fortress of Joux; and forty-two months,
with hardly clothing to his back, in the Dungeon of Vin-
cennes;—all by *Lettre-de-Cachet*, from his lion father. He
has been in Pontarlier Jails (self-constituted prisoner); was
noticed fording estuaries of the sea (at low water), in flight
from the face of men. He has pleaded before Aix Parlements
(to get back to his wife); the public gathering on roofs, to
see since they could not hear: "the clatter-teeth (*claque-*

---

[1] *Casano*, a battle in the War of Spanish Succession, 1705. The Duke
of Vendôme successfully opposed the Austrians under Prince Eugene.

[2] *Marquis Victor* was the author of *Ami des Hommes* (1775).

[3] *Lettres-de-Cachet*, letters under the private seal of the king.

dents)!" snarls singular old Mirabeau; discerning in such admired forensic eloquence nothing but two clattering jaw-bones, and a head vacant, sonorous, of the drum species.

But as for Gabriel Honoré, in these strange wayfarings, what has he not seen and tried? From drill-sergeants, to prime ministers, to foreign and domestic booksellers, all manner of men he has seen. All manner of men he has gained; for at bottom it is a social, loving heart, that wild uncon-querable one:—more especially all manner of women. From the Archer's Daughter at Saintes to that young Sophie Madame Monnier,[1] whom he could not but "steal", and be beheaded for—in effigy! For indeed, hardly since the Arabian Prophet lay dead to Ali's admiration, was there seen such a Love-hero, with the strength of thirty men. In War, again, he has helped to conquer Corsica; fought duels, irregular brawls; horse-whipped calumnious barons. In Literature, he has written on *Despotism*, on *Lettres-de-Cachet*; Erotics Sapphic-Wertereau,[2] Obscenities, Pro-fanities; Books on the *Prussian Monarchy*, on *Cagliostro*, on *Calonne*, on *the Water Companies of Paris*:—each Book com-parable, we will say, to a bituminous alarum-fire; huge, smoky, sudden! The firepan, the kindling, the bitumen were his own; but the lumber, of rags, old wood and nameless combustible rubbish (for all is fuel to him), was gathered from hucksters, and ass-paniers, of every description under heaven. Whereby, indeed, hucksters enough have been heard to exclaim: Out upon it, the fire is *mine*!

Nay, consider it more generally, seldom had man such a talent for borrowing. The idea, the faculty of another man he can make his; the man himself he can make his. "All reflex and echo (*tout de reflet et de réverbère*)!" snarls old Mirabeau, who can see, but will not. Crabbed old Friend of Men! it is his sociality, his aggregative nature; and will now be the quality of qualities for him. In that forty years' "struggle against despotism", he has gained the glorious

---

[1] *Madame Monnier.* While a prisoner in the Fortress of Joux, Mirabeau won the love of the young wife of the Marquis de Monnier. He fled with her to Holland in 1776.

[2] *Erotics Sapphic-Wertereau*, love-poems, combining the qualities of the Greek poetess Sappho, and of Werther, the sentimental hero of Goethe's romance.

faculty of *self-help*, and yet not lost the glorious natural gift of *fellowship*, of being helped. Rare union: this man can live self-sufficing—yet lives also in the life of other men; can make men love him, work with him; a born king of men!

But consider further how, as the old Marquis still snarls, he has "made away with (*humé*, swallowed) all *Formulas*";— a fact which, if we meditate it, will in these days mean much. This is no man of system, then; he is only a man of instincts and insights. A man nevertheless who will glare fiercely on any object; and see through it, and conquer it: for he has intellect, he has will, force beyond other men. A man not with *logic-spectacles*; but with an *eye*! Unhappily without Decalogue,[1] moral Code or Theorem of any fixed sort; yet not without a strong living Soul in him, and Sincerity there: a Reality, not an Artificiality, not a Sham! And so he, having struggled "forty years against despotism", and "made away with all formulas", shall now become the spokesman of a Nation bent to do the same. For is it not precisely the struggle of France also to cast off despotism; to make away with *her* old formulas,—having found them naught, worn out, far from the reality? She will make away with *such* formulas; and even go *bare*, if need be, till she have found new ones.

Towards such work, in such manner, marches he, this singular Riquetti Mirabeau. In fiery rough figure, with black Samson-locks under the slouch-hat, he steps along there. A fiery fuliginous mass, which could not be choked and smothered, but would fill all France with smoke. And now it has got *air*; it will burn its whole substance, its whole smoke atmosphere too, and fill all France with flame. Strange lot! Forty years of that smouldering, with foul fire-damp and vapour enough; then victory over that;—and like a burning mountain he blazes heaven-high; and for twenty-three re-splendent months, pours out, in flame and molten fire-torrents, all that is in him, the Pharos[2] and Wonder sign of an amazed Europe;—and then lies hollow, cold for ever! Pass on, thou questionable Gabriel Honoré, the greatest of them all: in the whole National Deputies, in the whole Nation, there is none like and none second to thee.

[1] *Decalogue*, the ten commandments.
[2] *Pharos*, famous lighthouse in the Bay of Alexandria.

COMMENTARY

Sir Walter Scott (1771–1832) had from boyhood a genius for story-telling. It first found scope in verse tales like *Marmion*, the structure of which, consisting of a romantic story of love and fighting in a framework of history, anticipated that of his novels. The success of *Waverley*, 1814, proved that a new force had appeared in English fiction. *Old Mortality*, 1816, ran into 6000 copies in six weeks, and before the last of the thirty odd stories had appeared in 1831, the novel of national life had become a recognised type in fiction in most European countries.

In his early manhood Scott was an enthusiastic collector of the ballads and legends of the Scottish border. He thus indulged not only his tastes as an antiquarian and his passion for the romance of the past, but also his sympathy with simple people: the homestead appealed to him no less than the castle. The union of these distinct interests is a tribute to Scott's broad humanity and a source of strength to him as a writer. Before his time there had been a sharp division between the novel proper, or realistic sketch of manners, and the romance, or idealised story of adventure. Scott had in his hands material that enabled him to combine both kinds. Hence the structure peculiar to his novels, the twofold nature of their plot, in which the fortunes of the fictitious and rather conventional hero, moving amongst authentic historical figures, are interthreaded with the homely humours of less distinguished people realistically delineated. In a few of the novels, as, for example, *The Heart of Midlothian*, the latter interest predominates, and it is these particular novels which posterity is beginning to find most to its taste.

The Heart of Midlothian, 1818, belongs to the earlier class of novels in which the scene is laid in Scott's own country; *Quentin Durward*, 1823, to the later class, in which we are taken abroad in search of adventure. The story of Jeanie Deans, the peasant girl who goes on foot to London to plead with the queen for the life of her sister, proved that romantic adventures need lose nothing by being rendered in terms of homely life. Jeanie herself is admitted to be "the finest of all Scott's portraits of women". The portrait of Dumbiedikes is scarcely less noteworthy. Absurdly eccentric as he may appear in one isolated episode, the reading of the book shows him to be no mere caricature, but the natural product of his environment.

Scott's sympathetic rendering of provincial life was made possible by his familiarity with the dialect of the Lowlands. The use of dialect was not quite a novelty. Shakespeare had brought together a Welshman, an Irishman and a Scot, and caricatured each in his national idiom. Fielding and Smollett had used dialect in comic characters for humorous effect. Scott seems to have been the first to realise that refined and subtle characterisation can be achieved in dialect without loss of dignity. The vernacular of the Lowlands was worthy of the treatment it received at his hands: it was not a vulgar corruption of standard English, but a less literary variant, independently descended from Anglo-Saxon, and enriched by "popular" borrowings from French. Its value as a literary instrument of strength and delicacy had already been proved in the poetry of Burns, and it is owing to Scott's example that the use of dialect as an essential element of local colour has become general in fiction.

There can be little doubt that Scott achieved greater distinction of style in dialect than in the conventional medium. Whereas the former has the forcible directness and dry humour of the language of a people of few words, the latter is a somewhat loosely articulated version of eighteenth-century prose. With its copious vocabulary, in which the Latin element predominates, it has something of the formality of Gibbon, even to mannerisms such as "elegant variation". (The Bishop is *unhappy Prelate, unfortunate captive*; De la Marck, *the savage leader, the truculent soldier*.) The style of Gibbon had a statuesque quality suitable for history; the historical novel needs something more flexible. But Scott seldom varies his pace (note how the parenthesis after *Up, ye Boar's brood!* retards the movement)—his rhythm is monotonous, and his dialogue is no less formal than his narrative. Whilst expressing himself adequately on all occasions, he gives the impression that a more deliberate choice of epithets would have made for greater economy in words.

Scott's practice with regard to archaic diction in dialogue has been adopted by most writers of historical fiction. His language (to quote his own words) is a "composition between the true and the fictitious...the style of our grandfathers and great grandfathers, sufficiently antiquated to accord with the antiquated character of the narrative, yet copious enough to express all that is necessary to its interest". As a result of this convention the centuries that divide Richard I from James I make little difference to their respective modes of speech.

If distinction in art were a mere matter of dimensions, the miniature etching of *Jane Austen* would look very insignificant by the side of the vast canvas on which Scott flung his pageant of history; but *Pride and Prejudice* has as many admirers as *Waverley*. Written in 1797, it was not published until 1813, when the author was already nearing the end of her short and uneventful life, spent for the most part at the Rectory of Steventon in Hampshire. Within the narrow limits of her own social circle and experience she found ample material for her exquisite comedy of manners.

Except in a negative or reactionary sense, she was quite untouched by the Romantic movement. She burlesqued the Gothic romance, eschewed sensationalism, ridiculed the sentimentalists, and had no schemes of social amelioration beyond parish visiting. She has been aptly called "the fine flower of the eighteenth century"; in her work the tradition of "good sense" lives on. She was a realist who observed her characters with serene detachment, a satirist whose weapons were wit, humour and a delicate irony.

The plot of a Jane Austen novel is slight, but well conceived in plan and perfectly executed in detail. Though she never attempted the analysis of the passions, being content for her theme with the lighter conduct of men and women in social intercourse, she achieved an ideal rarely attained—the perfect interdependence of plot and characterisation: each step forward in the action derives its impetus from character. Her characterisation has no suspicion of caricature, nor does her refined comedy ever descend to farce. She shows us the spectacle of the follies committed by those who are deficient in good sense or good taste. Thus the pompous Collins is deluded by his conceit into the notion that one of his fair cousins will jump at the honour of becoming his wife; while Mrs Bennet, who has not the wit to conceal her own silliness, is persuaded by self-interest, snobbishness and vanity into viewing him as a desirable match.

The outstanding quality of Jane Austen's style is its crisp neatness and precision. The close scrutiny to which she appears to have submitted her every word results in marked economy and accuracy of expression. Her sentences, which are short without being abrupt, have a pleasing rhythm. She was an adept in the use of the unexpected turn so indispensable to light satire:

"... *Can he be a sensible man, sir?*"

"*No, my dear; I think not. I have great hopes of finding him quite the reverse....*"

A large proportion of her pages consists of conversation, which has the easy flow of the best dialogue. If to modern ears the mode of expression sounds rather prim and formal, it is not because the process of artistic refinement has been overdone, but because it is a genuine reproduction of the language of a period when, under the influence of reformers like Beau Nash, precision and restraint in speech were cultivated as part of the social graces of the well-bred. Within the limits of this exacting standard, however, Jane Austen found room for the discrimination of individuality;

there is almost as much variety in the speech of her characters as there is in their behaviour.

If all-round distinction is the measure of greatness, *Lord Macaulay* (1800–1859) must be regarded as one of the greatest men produced by the nineteenth century. With amazing versatility he shone as a politician, an orator and an administrator. Even as a man of letters he was unusually many sided, with this qualification that, whether he wrote as essayist, critic or poet, he always displayed a bias towards history; and it is as an historian that he will be best remembered. His ambition to write a history that would challenge the popularity of the latest novel was realised with the publication in 1848 of his *History of England*: 18,000 copies were sold within six months. Few works so popular have remained so authoritative. Its soundness derives from encyclopaedic knowledge, an abnormally retentive memory, and consummate skill in marshalling armies of facts. For its popularity three reasons may be assigned: firstly, its great narrative and pictorial power (Macaulay is much more animated than Gibbon); secondly, its novelty: he approached the study of the past in a more democratic spirit, tracing the course of events in the life and literature of the people, and giving prominence to the social as well as to the political aspects of history; thirdly, its unique style, a style which seems to have sprung fully armed from the head of its creator. The *Essay on Milton*, written at the age of twenty-five, contains all the characteristics which in his maturity he softened but never radically changed. On every page he wrote we find the same glittering devices. In his own words, they lie on the surface, for him that runs to read.

The style of Macaulay is built up on antithesis; it is therefore artificial, but not in the sense in which that of Lyly was artificial. Macaulay's antithetical manner is more fundamental; it is the reflex of personality, of a mind that preferred the concrete to the abstract, and in which life was mirrored

pictorially as a pageant in bright colours, as a succession of
dazzling personalities, each challenging contrast with the
other. Thus, in the Essay, Milton is set up against Dante; the
Puritan is in sharp contrast with the Royalist; whilst one
feature of the Puritan's composition, his humility before
God, is symmetrically opposed to another, his arrogance in
his dealings with men. To gratify this love of contrast,
Macaulay could not resist the temptation to deepen the
shadows and to heighten the lights, and it is this striving after
effect rather than wilful misrepresentation that accounts for
his frequent exaggeration.

This antithetical cast of mind is reflected in the composition,
and influences not only the general structure but the arrangement of the parts: it is seen in the opposition of paragraph
against paragraph, sentence against sentence, and so on,
down to the minutest detail of phrases and words.

Macaulay's typical sentence is exceptionally short; he
gains incisiveness by the omission of normal connectives,
but at the expense of a "snip-snap" effect which he attempts
to redeem from monotony by a long sentence, often in periodic
form, introduced with a mechanical regularity only slightly
less irritating. He achieves a rhythm that is more rhetorical
than musical by various forms of recurrence, such as the
triple grouping of words, phrases and sentences: *To know
Him, to serve Him, to enjoy Him*...; *For his sake empires had
risen, and flourished, and decayed*; and the three successive
sentences beginning, *If they were unacquainted*... p. 219.

If there is nothing subtle about Macaulay's art, it has at
least the merit of supreme clarity, which is nowhere more
apparent than in his skill in paragraphing. It is his almost
unvarying practice to open with a topic sentence containing
a definite statement, which in the remainder of the paragraph
he examines, illustrates or proves. The extract quoted is in
three paragraphs, each of which begins with a topic sentence
announcing to the reader the particular aspect of the discussion that is to follow.

Impatience of convention and the cult of individuality reach their extreme limits in Thomas Carlyle. His native genius was fashioned in the rugged mould of conditions so unusual that it could create nothing after the patterns of other men. He broke the age-long prestige of France in intellectual matters; he rough-hewed a strange new philosophy from Germany; and he presented it with such passionate conviction and in a style so arresting that it changed the whole trend of contemporary thought.

Thomas Carlyle (1795–1881) was born at Ecclefechan in Dumfriesshire. From his father, a stone-mason, he inherited natural gifts of a high order. He was sent at great sacrifice to Edinburgh, there to qualify as a minister of religion, but one of the most fundamentally religious of men was compelled by unorthodoxy to seek a calling outside the Church. For some years he was spiritually adrift; it was in the transcendental philosophy of Germany that he found an anchorage. Here was a philosophy which saw in the spirit the basis of all things, and in matter only an appearance; here he found a religion that transcended all creeds, that viewed the material world as the visible manifestation of God. The convert had now a mission: he was to be the exponent of German thought in England, the apostle of the new ethics. With his removal to Cheyne Row, Chelsea, and the publication of the *French Revolution* his reputation was established, and he remained, long after he had ceased to write, "the greatest single influence" on the nineteenth century.

This influence was exercised partly in what might be called tracts for the times, such as *Sartor Resartus*, and partly in histories like the *French Revolution*, in which, hardly less directly, he exhorted his generation. His conception of history was unique: knowledge of the past was not an end in itself. His familiarity with a particular period was as comprehensive as that of Macaulay, but he never ranged over a wide field for illustrative analogies. Macaulay's treatment was objective; his tone was complacent: civilisation under the banner of the British constitution was marching steadily along the glittering road of material progress towards the millennium. Carlyle had no veneration for government, either in its machinery (*Lettres-de-Cachet*), or its theories and systems (*dog-cart of Political Economy*); his typical hero has made away with all formulas. His method is subjective, that of an artist who selects what is significant. What he says in effect is: "Here is a record of successes and failures, a living warning that we to-day can ill afford not to heed." His favourite doctrine, with its roots in the stern morality of his northern ancestors, is: "what men sow that shall they reap". Experience teaches that failure is the consequence of levity, Sham, insincerity; success depends on Veracity, on holding fast to conviction (*he will not be Thou, but must and will be Himself*, p. 224). The greatest virtue is sense of duty; it is the duty of man to accomplish the work to which he is divinely appointed; effort is man's affinity with the creative energy of God. Hence the history of the world is the history of the great men that have worked in it, and great movements derive their motive force from persons, as did the French Revolution from Mirabeau. The greatness of a nation depends on its ability to recognise greatness in its natural leaders, and on its will to obey them.

Such are his chief doctrines, implicit in every chapter he wrote; but he laid no claim to an ordered system of philosophy; he taught as a poet, to whom glimpses of the mystery of things are revealed in flashes. So also with his style: it is that of a poet and therefore not to be judged by ordinary standards. It offended his contemporaries, and is harshly criticised even to this day, firstly, on the false assumption from a few superficial analogies that it was an attempt to graft German mannerisms on English stock; secondly, on the assumption, equally false, that a style so eccentric and powerful must exercise a disruptive influence on wholesome tradition. It is true that its external features leap to the eye: its excessive use of figures more proper to poetry (but excusable because they betoken an immediacy of experience that only poetry can express), such being Vision (the whole passage); Apostrophe (*It is in vain, O Marquis*, p. 224); Interrogation (*He with the thick black locks...confusions?* p. 223); Exclamation (*Strange lot!...cold for ever!* p. 226). We note at once the too liberal coinage of new words and compounds —*dim-brooding, safe-wrapt, kingly-genial, logic-spectacles, Samson-locks*; the use of plural abstracts—*murkiest confusions*, unorthodox capitals and italics. His sentences are short and jerky, irregular and loose in structure, and abrupt in rhythm. But though his style yields easily enough to superficial analysis, there could be no vainer task than to try to imitate it—how inimitable, for example, is his description of Mirabeau—*burning fire of genius; like comet-fire glaring fuliginous through murkiest confusions!*—the essence of such a style is the poet and prophet in the man himself, whose every word comes "direct and flaming from the heart". The only lesson to be learnt from Carlyle's style is to cultivate not eccentricity but sincerity.

Carlyle's message was disturbing and unwelcome. What then are the qualities that obliged men to listen to what they were not willing to hear? They are rich and various: first, there is his dynamic energy, his terrific earnestness, with its saving grace of genial humour and flashes of sardonic wit; secondly, his mastery of narrative, which, except when he pauses to moralise, moves with admirable verve and vigour; thirdly, a wonderful gift of description: he has an instinct for the most significant features of a situation and for the most effective grouping of men in relation to an event; lastly, there is his remarkable penetration into character: in a few felicitous phrases he gets nearer to the essential truth than do others in pages of analysis. There is no surer mark of genius.

Index to Commentary

For EU product safety concerns, contact us at Calle de José Abascal, 56–1°,
28003 Madrid, Spain or eugpsr@cambridge.org.

www.ingramcontent.com/pod-product-compliance
Ingram Content Group UK Ltd.
Pitfield, Milton Keynes, MK11 3LW, UK
UKHW012330130625
459647UK00009B/194